THE WORLD'S LARGEST INDUSTRIAL ENTERPRISES
1962–1983

The World's Largest Industrial Enterprises 1962–1983

John H. Dunning
and
Robert D. Pearce

St. Martin's Press   New York

Printed in Great Britain

First published in the United States of America in 1985

Library of Congress Cataloging in Publication Data

Dunning, John H.
    The world's largest industrial enterprises 1962–1983.
    Rev. ed. of: The world's largest industrial enterprises. 1981.
    Includes index.
    I. Big business. I. Pearce, R. D. (Robert D.)
II. Dunning, John H. World's largest industrial enterprises.
III. Title.
HD 2721.D87 1985   338.6'44   84-24810

ISBN 0-312-89278-0

Contents

Summary of the main findings of the study

PART I   INTRODUCTION

1   The study presents details of the world's largest industrial enterprises in 1983 and for the years 1962, 1967, 1972, 1977 and 1982. The data are drawn from those published annually by *Fortune* on the largest US and non-US industrial companies. These data are classified into 20 industrial sectors (which are grouped by level of research intensity) and by country (or region) of enterprise.

2   Two main samples of firms are derived from the data, viz. the *rationalised* sample which covers the largest industrial enterprises in any particular year – the number of firms in that sample varies from 483 firms in 1967 to 865 in 1977; and the *equalised* sample that consists of an equal number of the largest enterprises for each of the years, drawn from those in the rationalised sample. The equalised sample comprises 483 firms, that is, the number of firms contained in the 1967 sample.

PART II   THE DATA FOR 1983

3   The 806 firms which made up the 1983 rationalised sample had a sales turnover of $3167 billion. Of these 806 firms, 343 were US owned, with Japan occupying second place with 135 representatives. In total there were 251 European firms, of which those of EEC origin accounted for 192. The UK was the largest European contributor with 75 firms (77 including jointly-owned ventures), followed by Germany (51) and France (35). Of the remaining 77 firms, 25 originated from Canada and 37 from 'less developed countries' (LDCs). Seventy-one of the 806 enterprises were classified by *Fortune* as being 'government-owned firms' (GOFs).

4   The average size of the 343 US firms ($4.5 billion) is above the average for the whole sample ($3.9 billion), and contrasts notably with that for the UK ($3.2 billion) and Japan ($2.9 billion). Despite the relatively low average for UK firms, EEC enterprises overall have an above average size of $4.3 billion, which contrasts strongly with $2.5 billion for the 59 non-EEC European representatives.

5.   In 1983, 275 of the 806 firms were in the seven *highly research-intensive* (HRI) industries, 217 in five *medium research-intensive* (MRI) industries, and 196 in six *low research-intensive* (LRI) industries. The remaining enterprises were in two sectors ('petroleum' with 95 firms and 'other industries' with 23) which are not classified by research intensity. Average firm size varied considerably between industries, with 'petroleum and motor vehicles' by some margin the largest, and several other HRI industries also above the sample mean. The lower average firm sizes are to be found mainly in the MRI and LRI industries, where only 'tobacco' is above the sample mean.

1

6   The strongest areas of industrial specialisation for US firms were in several HRI industries (for example, 'aerospace', 'office equipment', 'pharmaceuticals'). Outside the HRI industries the US's comparative specialisation is strongest in 'paper and wood products'. Among HRI industries Europe's strongest specialisation is in 'industrial and agricultural chemicals' (where Germany has several leading firms). Europe, as a whole, has quite a strong tendency towards comparative specialisation in the MRI industries. Most European countries are relatively weak in the LRI industries, but the UK is a considerable exception, making these industries its major area of comparative specialisation (it is relatively unrepresented in most HRI industries). Japan shows a relatively stronger overall commitment to HRI industries than the US or Europe, this being most notable for 'electronics and electrical appliances' and 'motor vehicles'. Japan is, similarly, relatively strong in the MRI industries, so that its weakest area of specialisation is the LRI industries (though 'textiles, apparel and leather goods' is a significant exception).

7   The 806 firms in the 1983 rationalised sample had a total employment of 29.5 million. Of these enterprises we were able to obtain comparable 1982 employment figures for 745. Of these, 454 (61 per cent) had suffered declines in employment during the year and 271 (36 per cent) had increased their labour force. Japan produces the most relatively optimistic picture, with 61 firms increasing employment compared with 63 which reduced it. At the other extreme the bleakest picture is for Europe, where 156 firms cut their labour force and only 59 increased it.

8   In 1983 the average profitability (rate of return on sales) of US firms was considerably above that for Europe and Japan, though this may, to some degree, reflect accounting and reporting differences. The most profitable industries come from the HRI group ('office equipment' and 'pharmaceuticals') and the LRI group ('drink' and 'tobacco'). By contrast, all the MRI industries (except 'building materials') have very low profit rates, with 'metals' making aggregate losses. Between 1982 and 1983, profitability changes, at least by comparison with the employment changes reported above, revealed a moderately optimistic picture. For the 742 firms where the comparison was possible, 392 recorded higher rates of return on sales in 1983 than 1982 and 317 lower. For the USA, 187 firms had increases in profitability compared with 135 declines, while Europe recorded 113 increases compared with 93 declines. Japan, which we saw as more impressive than the US and Europe in terms of employment recovery, is less strong in terms of profitability, with 57 increases and 66 falls.

PART III   CHANGES IN THE SAMPLE COMPOSITION 1962–82

9   Of the largest 483 industrial enterprises in the world in 1962 and 1982, those of US origin fell from 292 to 213. The US's share of the sales of the 483 companies also decreased over the 20 years, from 58 per cent to 49 per cent. Though this decline seems to have persisted throughout the period it was most notable during the quinquennia 1967–72 and 1977–82. The number of European firms in the equalised sample fell from 142 in 1962 to 136 in 1967, but then recovered steadily to achieve a new high level of 147 in 1982. The sales share of European firms followed a similar pattern, at first falling from their 1962 share of 27 per cent but reaching 32 per cent by 1982. The contribution of Japanese firms to our sample of the world's largest enterprises has increased vastly during the two decades covered. In 1962 there were 29 Japanese enterprises in the 483, which accounted for 4 per cent of the total sample sales. By 1982 the number had risen to 79 and the share of sales to 12 per cent. Alongside Japan the other major source of new firms in the equalised sample is the 'other countries' group, whose representation increased from 20 in 1962 to 44 in 1982. This rise occurred mainly during the decade 1972–82, and was mainly due to the entry into the sample of firms from LDCs. 'Government-owned firms' (GOFs) have steadily increased their role in the sample. In 1962 there were 14 GOFs accounting for 2 per cent of sample sales, this rising to 23 firms and 4 per cent of sales by 1972. The next decade, however, saw a much more dramatic rise in the role of GOFs, so that by 1982 there were 50 of them in the equalised sample, accounting for 10 per cent of sales. Finally, it should be noted that the changes reported here may reflect

not only differential rates of growth of real economic activity but also differences in inflation rates and exchange rate fluctuation.

10   Changes in the industrial composition of the largest firms, particularly over the last decade, are distorted by the tremendous increase in oil prices. After generally maintaining its position in the sample between 1962 and 1972, 'petroleum' increased its number of firms from 40 in 1972 (36 in 1962) to 71 in 1982. Similarly the petroleum industry's share of equalised sample sales rose from 16 per cent in 1972 (the same as 1962) to 32 per cent in 1982. Once allowance is made for the rise in 'petroleum', several other industries are revealed as also increasing their share of sample activity over the 20 years. These include four of the seven HRI industries ('office equipment', 'electronics and electrical appliances', 'industrial and agricultural chemicals', 'pharmaceuticals'), and also two LRI industries ('publishing and printing', 'drink'). Five industries seem to have been in relative decline during the period, three from the MRI group ('rubber', 'shipbuilding', 'metals') and two from LRI ('textiles etc', 'food').

11   The USA showed a general tendency to increase its specialisation in the HRI industries over the period 1962–82, 'motor vehicles' being the only exception. By contrast, declines in specialisation were generalised in the MRI industries for the US though least extensive in 'industrial and farm equipment'. In the LRI industries some indication of increasing specialisation could be found for 'publishing and printing', and 'drink and tobacco', while the most notable decline was that of 'textiles, apparel and leather goods'. Like the USA, Europe increased its specialisation in HRI industries between 1962 and 1982. Among the individual countries, specialisation in HRI increased most notably in Germany, Italy and Sweden, and decreased for the UK. The two HRI industries where Europe seems to have most strongly increased its specialisation are 'chemicals' and 'motor vehicles'. Again, as was the case for the USA, the majority of the decline in specialisation in Europe, required to compensate for the increase in HRI industries, occurs in the MRI group. Generally this European decline in MRI industries persists at the national level, though least strongly for the UK. The one MRI industry where there is some increase in European specialisation is 'building materials', while the strongest declines are in 'industrial and farm equipment' and 'metals'. Overall, European specialisation in LRI industries changed little over the period, with increases in 'drink' and 'tobacco' and a strong fall in 'textiles etc.' being the more notable tendencies. The UK recorded an overall increase in specialisation in LRI industries (from an already substantial commitment to those industries in 1962), with notable rises in 'food', 'drink' and 'tobacco'. Japan's largest firms were more highly specialised in HRI industries in 1982 than they had been in 1962, rises in 'chemicals' and 'motor vehicles' offsetting a decline in 'electronics and electrical appliances'. The compensating decline in specialisation is spread between MRI and LRI industries, this being strongest for 'metals' and 'textiles'.

PART IV   EMPLOYMENT OF THE WORLD'S LARGEST ENTERPRISES

12   The 483 equalised sample firms employed 17.3 million workers in 1962, this rising steadily to 21.5 million in 1967 and 25.2 million in 1972, that is a 46 per cent rise over the decade. Predictably this rate of growth did not persist far beyond 1972 though equalised sample employment was again higher in 1977 at 26.5 million. Finally, a fall in employment did occur between 1977 and 1982, to 25.8 million, a level which is nevertheless 2 per cent higher than that at the start of the troubled decade.

13   Employment growth rates can be calculated for each successive five-year period, by taking all the firms from the rationalised sample for which employment data was available for both the first and last years of a quinquennium. When this is done, the overall rate of growth of employment was found to decline consistently over the two decades, from 23 per cent in 1962–67 to 14 per cent in 1967–72, 5 per cent in 1972–77 and finally a fall of 0.4 per cent in 1977–82.

PART V   CONCENTRATION, SIZE AND DIVERSIFICATION

14   For 1982, an attempt was made to assess the state of competition at the top of important industries by deriving 'leading firm concentration ratios'. These took the form of the sales of the three largest firms in an industry as a percentage of the sales of that industry's 20 largest firms. On this basis the most concentrated industries (with ratios of over 50 per cent) were 'tobacco' and 'office equipment', while the least concentrated (ratios below 30 per cent) were 'textiles etc.', 'paper and wood products', 'chemicals', 'electronics and electrical appliances' and 'industrial and farm equipment'.

15   Eleven industries had lower leading-firm concentration ratios in 1982 than they had in 1962. Though in five of these cases a tendency towards declining concentration had persisted throughout the two decades, in most of the others an increase in concentration towards the end of the period had partially offset earlier falls. Five industries had higher leading-firm concentration ratios in 1982 than in 1962.

16   The pattern often detected at the industry level, of an initial tendency towards lower concentration being reversed later, is also found in the more aggregated data. Thus, in 1962 the 25 largest firms accounted for 31 per cent of equalised sample sales, this fell to 28 per cent by 1972 but had risen again to 30 per cent by 1982. When this approach is applied to the US and non-US firms separately, the same type of pattern emerges, though in both cases the 1982 concentration had reached levels *above* that of 1962.

17   The US has the largest average firm size and its size superiority is most pronounced among the very large firms. However, this size superiority of the US has fallen markedly and persistently between 1962 and 1982.

18   Fourteen of the 20 industries had the same leading firm in 1982 as in 1977 and in five others the new leading firm had ranked second in 1977. On the other hand, 28 new firms had entered the top five in their respective industries since 1977, eight of these having achieved a position in the top three.

19   The firms in our sample reveal quite a strong tendency to be active in more than one industry, approximately 25 per cent of their sales being of products outside of their main industry. Similarly, the average firm was found to have activity in 2.8 industries other than its main one.

20   The majority of industries showed some tendency towards increasing industrial diversification between 1977 and 1982. The industries where the firms have opted to increase diversified activity most significantly are either those of medium or low research intensity or those which have proved most vulnerable to the recession of recent years (for example, 'motor vehicles', 'building materials', 'metals', 'textiles etc.' and 'publishing and printing'). There is also evidence of increased interpenetration among firms in the food-drink-tobacco nexus of industries.

PART VI   PROFITABILITY AND GROWTH 1962–82

21   Throughout the 20-year period covered by our study, US firms recorded consistently above-average profitability (rate of return on sales), though the rate was subject to persistent decline from 1967 onwards. European profitability has, by contrast, been below average throughout with declining rates of return persisting from 1962 to 1982. From 1962 to 1977 Japanese profitability levels were quite close to those for Europe, but in the most recent five years Japan resisted the further declines suffered by the USA and Europe.

22   Overall the HRI industries have the best profitability performance over the 20 years. However, in line with the predominant tendency, the profitability of these industries does

decline over time, this decline being most sustained and pronounced for European firms. The two HRI industries with the most troubled profitability records were 'industrial and agricultural chemicals' and 'motor vehicles'. The MRI industries proved to be, in aggregate, the most vulnerable group in terms of profitability, having not only a consistently below-average rate of return but also, from 1967 to 1982, the most sustained decline. Also all the industries in the group (except 'shipbuilding') proved subject to major profit collapse between 1977 and 1982. Though the LRI industries had overall profitability levels similar to those of MRI earlier in the period, they were generally successful in avoiding the serious declines which hit the other group from 1967 to 1982. Indeed, in 1982 the six LRI industries' average rate of return on sales was slightly above that for HRI industries and, for the first time, above the overall sample average.

23 Differences in inflation rates, both between time periods and between countries, and the exceptional performance of the 'petroleum' industry, make confident interpretation of relative sales growth performance difficult. Nevertheless, some broad impressions may be derived. Japan had the most notable above-average sales growth throughout the 20-year period, with rates very considerably above the norm in all periods except 1972–77. US firms' growth rates were persistently below average from 1967 to 1982, after equating the average from 1962 to 1967. After a relatively poor growth performance between 1962 and 1967, European firms then achieved a decade of above-average growth before falling back to a marginally below-average performance in the period 1977–82.

24 The growth of sales of the HRI industries was above average throughout the 1962–82 period, though decreasingly so. The only industry in this group to retain above-average growth through the whole period was 'pharmaceuticals', each of the others having just one quinquennium of below-average performance. The MRI group recorded below-average performance throughout the two decades, this being also true of 'metals' and 'rubber' among individual industries. The LRI industries' growth performance was less consistent than that of the other groups, with well below-average performance in the periods 1962–67 and 1972–77, marginally below average in the period 1967–72 and above average in the years 1977–82. Two LRI industries had below-average growth throughout the 20 years, 'textiles etc.' (very substantially so from 1972–82) and 'food' (though very marginally between 1977 and 1982). By contrast, 'tobacco', 'drink' and 'publishing and printing' were each above average for all except one quinquennium.

PART VII   INTERNATIONAL OPERATIONS

25 We estimate[1] that of the total sales of the 792 firms in the 1982 rationalised sample of $3204 billion, overseas production (that is, output of the firms' overseas subsidiaries) accounted for approximately $900 billion (that is, 28 per cent). Of this estimated $900 billion of overseas production, US-owned firms were responsible for $452 billion (50 per cent), European firms for $395 billion (44 per cent), and Japanese for only $23 billion (3 per cent). Firms in the 'petroleum' industry had overseas production of $360 billion, which was 40 per cent of the total, no other industry accounting for more than 10 per cent. The picture looks a little different when we express overseas production as a percentage of total production. This ratio is 39 per cent for Europe (with the UK, Sweden, Switzerland and the Netherlands recording particularly high values), 33 per cent for Canada, 30 per cent for the USA and 6 per cent for Japan. Industries where overseas production is an important proportion of total production include 'petroleum' (38 per cent), 'pharmaceuticals and consumer chemicals' (41 per cent), 'office equipment (including computers)' (33 per cent), 'rubber' (35 per cent), 'building materials' (32 per cent), 'food' (32 per cent), 'tobacco' (44 per cent). High levels of technological dynamism (as represented by R and D expenditure) seem to be a factor which is often related to overseas production, though whether this need, or should, be the case is a

1   This section of the summary is based on the estimated values reported in tables 7.5 and 7.6.

matter of some debate among economists. In other cases overseas production is prominent in market-oriented manufacturing industries, where it takes place as a complement to the firms' extended use of marketing expertise and established trademarks. Also the influence of backward integration into overseas production in resource-based industries is still of some importance, though probably less prevalent than it once was.

26   Our estimates suggest that the 792 rationalised sample firms in 1982 had parent-country exports of $450 billion (or approximately a fifth of their home-country production), of which Japan accounted for $95 billion (21 per cent compared with its 3 per cent of overseas production), the US for $90 billion (20 per cent compared with 50 per cent of overseas production) and Europe $200 billion (44 per cent). If parent-country exports are expressed as a percentage of parent-country production, Europe produces the highest ratio with 32 per cent (Germany, Netherlands, Sweden, Switzerland recording notably high values), followed by Japan and Canada (both 24 per cent) and the USA (8 per cent). At the industry level the highest ratios are recorded by three HRI industries ('aerospace', 'measurement, scientific and photographic equipment', 'motor vehicles', each slightly over 30 per cent). Several MRI industries also have high values (notably 'industrial and farm equipment' with 30 per cent), but lower values are prevalent in the LRI industries (where none exceeds 20 per cent).

27   If we express total overseas sales (that is, overseas production plus parent-country exports) as a percentage total production (the overseas sales ratio) then our estimates suggest that this ratio was 42 per cent in 1982 for the 792 rationalised sample firms. This tendency towards the internationalisation of markets was most prevalent for Europe, where the overall ratio was 58 per cent (including very high values for some of the smaller countries, for example Sweden, Switzerland and the Netherlands, as well as over 50 per cent for several major economies, for example Germany, France and the UK), followed by the USA (35 per cent) and Japan (29 per cent). High overseas sales ratios are most prevalent for the HRI industries, where only 'aerospace' (36 per cent) does not record a value of between 40 per cent and 50 per cent. Two MRI industries ('industrial and farm equipment' and 'rubber') are also in the 40 per cent to 50 per cent range, along with 'tobacco' (from LRI) and 'petroleum'. No industry has a value below 25 per cent and only three ('shipbuilding', 'paper and wood products', and 'publishing and printing') below 30 per cent.

28   As already suggested, there are quite distinctive differences between firms of different countries in terms of the way they choose to service the overseas markets that they are able to win; some having a strong preference for overseas production, while others are more oriented to exporting from the parent country. To formalise analysis of this distinction we derive a fourth ratio, the overseas market sourcing ratio, which expresses overseas production as a percentage of total overseas sales. This shows that in 1982 the world's largest enterprises were distinctly more inclined to meet foreign markets by overseas production than by exports. Thus overseas production was almost exactly double exports, that is, the overseas market sourcing ratio was 67 per cent. The overall average for Europe was also 67 per cent, this covering very high values for the UK and Switzerland (that is, overseas production oriented) and a pronouncedly low value for Germany (that is, export oriented). The USA was very strongly oriented to overseas production with a sourcing ratio of 84 per cent, while Japan was the extreme opposite with a ratio of only 19 per cent. At the industry level, orientation to overseas production is most generalised among the LRI industries, where four have ratios of over 80 per cent and the other two of over 50 per cent. Of the five MRI industries only one has a value over 80 per cent and three less than 50 per cent. On balance the HRI industries tend to be oriented to overseas production, only two having values of the sourcing ratio less than 50 per cent, and two with values of over 75 per cent. 'Petroleum' is very strongly oriented to overseas production.

29   For a substantial sample of firms we were able to compare 1977 and 1982 values of the ratios. Overall this indicates an increase in the internationalisation of the activity of the largest firms during that period, this owing much more to rises in overseas production than to expanded exports. Rather more tentatively we can also make comparisons with 1972 values of

the ratios. This suggests that the tendency towards increased internationalisation of activity had been stronger between 1972 and 1977 than in the second period, and that during those years it had owed rather more to export growth.

30   Information on the direction of change in overseas production ratio between 1977 and 1982 was available for 389 firms. Of these, 49 per cent were found to have a higher ratio in 1982 and 23 per cent lower. The US showed a slightly below-average tendency towards expanded overseas production, and Europe slightly above. Most notable though is the case of Japan, with 18 out of 28 firms covered (64 per cent) having higher ratios in 1982, and only two lower.

31   For 248 of the 389 firms just discussed similar information was also available for changes between 1972 and 1977. This suggests that the tendency towards rising overseas production ratios had slowed during the decade. Thus in the period 1972–77, 157 of the 248 firms had rises in overseas production ratio, this number falling to 116 in years 1977–82. Similarly, 64 firms had falls in the ratio in the period 1977–82 compared with only 29 in the earlier period. This slowing in the movement towards overseas production was most pronounced for US firms.

32   A survey of firms in 1979 had enquired as to their expectations concerning the change in their overseas production ratio from 1977–82. Comparing their replies to the revealed outcome suggests strongly that the slowing in the tendency toward increased overseas production, which we noted above, was not fully expected or desired by the firms, but rather the result of adverse circumstances preventing fulfilment of their plans. Further a similar survey in 1983, concerning plans for overseas production between 1982 and 1987, suggests that the world's leading industrial enterprises still aim to expand international production, perhaps in some cases completing plans thwarted between 1977 and 1982.

PART VIII   RESEARCH AND DEVELOPMENT EXPENDITURES

33   We were able to obtain information on the research and development (R and D) expenditure of 427 of the firms in the 1982 rationalised sample, and to express this in the form of R and D expenditure as a percentage of sales. Industry averages of this ratio conform very much to intuitive expectations. Thus those industries where persistent innovation of essentially new products is a major element in competition report the higher ratios. On the other hand, those where both products and processes are accepted as being standardised and unlikely to be open to radical change, so that advertising and other marketing activity represents the basic form of competition, have the lower R and D ratios. There also seems to be no general tendency for the USA, Japan or Europe to be persistently the most R and D oriented area, each of them having the highest R and D ratio in at least two industries.

34   For 122 firms we were able to obtain information on the proportion of their R and D expenditure carried out in overseas subsidiaries. For these firms, then, we were thus able to derive the R and D expenditure as a percentage of sales ratio separately for home-country and overseas operations. The results show clearly that the belief that R and D efforts are relatively concentrated in the multinational (or transnational) enterprises' (MNEs) home countries is substantially confirmed. Nevertheless, quite significant R and D activity overseas is to be found in a number of HRI and LRI industries.

Part I   Introduction

(a)   STRUCTURE AND AIMS OF THE STUDY

The purpose of this study is to draw a statistical portrait of the largest industrial enterprises in the non-Communist world over the period 1962–1983; to interpret the data; and to evaluate and compare the performance of these concerns. Since the majority of these companies can now be considered as multinational (or transnational) enterprises[1] (MNEs), the study also reviews, in some detail, the nature and extent of the overseas operations of these enterprises in 1982; the changes which have occurred since 1972, and how the enterprises themselves view the prospects for these activities up to 1987. We also discuss the ways in which the foreign production of enterprises relates to other means of sourcing foreign markets, for example by exports. Other aspects of the world's largest enterprises subjected to scrutiny in the study include their research intensity, the size, distribution and concentration of the firms and the extent and nature of their industrial diversification.

(b)   THE DATA

The basic data for the study have been derived from those published annually by *Fortune*[2] on the largest US and non-US industrial companies.[3] Part II uses the data for 1983, published after completion of the rest of the study, and analyses the structure by industry and country of the world's largest 806 manufacturing enterprises (outside Communist countries) in that year. Data on profitability and employment are also presented.

Parts III to VI use data for the years 1962, 1967, 1972, 1977 and 1982 to provide a comparative analysis of the changing structure by industry and country of ownership of the world's largest manufacturing enterprises in those years. Their changing levels of employment, growth of sales, and profitability are also analysed, along with some aspects of concentration and diversification within these largest enterprises. The use of these particular years, and of five-year periods, is arbitrary, but we do not believe that the use of other years or of shorter periods would reveal patterns or trends significantly different from those which emerge from this study. It is clear, though, that differences in the performance of firms of different nationalities in any one year may reflect the economic conditions, market structure and accounting practices of the countries in which they operate, which may inhibit meaningful efficiency comparisons.

In Part VII, we analyse the ways in which enterprises service their foreign markets, based on 1982 *Fortune* data. The main sources of information for this part of the study are data

---

1   that is, firms with producing activity in more than one country.
2   See especially *Fortune*, July and August 1963; June and September 1968; May and September 1973; 8 May and 13 August 1978; 2 May and 22 August 1983; 30 April and 20 August 1984.
3   Enterprises covered by the *Fortune* data 'must derive more than 50% of their sales from manufacturing and/or mining' activities.

8

provided by the enterprises to the authors, and derived from company accounts and various directories. Details of these are set out in Part VII.

The basic *Fortune* data on sales, assets, profits and employment have, for some non-US firms, been adjusted to overcome or, at least, reduce, a number of problems. For example, in the years 1962, 1967 and 1972 *Fortune* did not, in the case of a few non-US firms, report sales, assets, profits and employment at the same level of consolidation. Clearly, this makes for serious difficulties in, most notably, the rate of return calculations. However, from 1977 onwards *Fortune* scrupulously reported all data for each of the firms at the same level of consolidation, but to achieve this it has been necessary to report some of the data at different levels of consolidation from earlier years. This too poses difficulties for our analysis.

In adjusting the *Fortune* data for some non-US enterprises we have sought to achieve three objectives:

(i)   For any enterprise, for a particular year, all data should be internally consistent, that is, embrace the same level of consolidation. We have done our best to ensure this, though some of the figures are our own estimates; that is, *Fortune* figures at the inappropriate level of consolidation are replaced by our estimates of the figures at the desired level of consolidation.

(ii)   Figures should be at the same level of consolidation for all years covered by the comparative analysis, that is, 1962, 1967, 1972, 1977 and 1982. We believe we have eliminated any major discrepancies of this type. Nevertheless, some minor differences remained intractable. Thus, the basic level of consolidation utilised by the *Fortune* data is defined as including 'consolidated subsidiaries more than 50 per cent owned, either fully or on a prorated basis' but, in some or all years, some firms, especially those of continental European origin, also embrace 'certain subsidiaries owned 50 per cent or less, either fully or on a prorated basis', or include only 'wholly owned subsidiaries'. We do not believe that remaining discrepancies in the level of reporting between years lead to any systematic distortion of results.

(iii)   Whenever possible, the data should achieve internal consistency at the usual level of consolidation for *Fortune* data, as defined above. This was not always possible; some of the enterprises reported consistently at other levels of consolidation. Notably, we have had to use the data for some enterprises at the 'parent company only' level. In 1983, for example, firms whose data we could not adjust from the 'parent company only' level accounted for just under 2 per cent of the sales in our 806-firm sample of that year's largest enterprises.

In making the kinds of adjustment just discussed we have used company accounts and various directories. We have also observed *Fortune* data for intervening years, which often gives an indication of the relationship between the levels of consolidation used at different times.

A further adjustment which we found it desirable to make follows upon the inclusion in the 1982 and 1983 *Fortune* data of the giant Italian state-owned conglomerate IRI. Before 1982 IRI had been represented in the data by any of its constituent enterprises large enough to merit inclusion independently in the *Fortune* listing of leading non-US enterprises. However, the sudden arrival in our sample of an enterprise of this magnitude would be reflected in disproportionate changes in the national, area and industry sub-totals to which it is allocated. We therefore decided to omit IRI in 1982 and 1983 but, for consistency with earlier years, to replace it by estimated figures for its three member firms which had separately achieved positions in the 1981 *Fortune* listing (i.e. Italsider; Dalmine; Alfa Romeo). For similar reasons we omit Iranian National Oil from the 1977 data, this being the only year covered by our study for which the firm's results were available.

(c)   ORGANISATION OF THE DATA

(i)   *Country of origin*

The allocation of each enterprise to a country of origin provides few problems. Even though many of the firms covered are MNEs, with producing affiliates in several countries, all but a very few have an easily identifiable parent country. Notable exceptions are those enterprises where ownership and managerial control are binational. Of these, Shell (Netherlands/UK) and Unilever (UK/Netherlands) existed throughout our period, while Dunlop-Pirelli (UK/Italy) existed for 1972 and 1977 and Agfa-Gevaert (Germany/Belgium) for 1967 and 1972.[1]

A point to note with regard to the geographical presentation of the data is that, in the tables concerned with the comparison of results over the 1962–82 period, we treat the EEC as having been 'the nine'[2] in *all* years. Though this is not, of course, the case, there would be no value, from the point of view of data presentation, in using subtotals whose national composition changed between years.

(ii) Industrial classification

In our study we use a classification of 20 industry groups, details of which are given in Appendix 1. Firms are classified to that industry which accounts for the greatest proportion of their sales. The sources used to make this allocation are listed in the section of Part VI which discusses the industrial diversification of the sample firms. Where our sources enabled us to detect changes in a firm's main industry during the 20-year period covered, these were taken into account, though full retrospective information on this was not available for all firms.

Eighteen of our 20 industries are also classified as being of *high research intensity* (HRI), *medium research intensity* (MRI), or *low research intensity* (LRI). The basis for the research intensity classification is expenditure on Research and Development (R and D) expressed as a percentage of sales. The calculations were made using data on the R and D expenditure of 427 of our sample enterprises in 1982, derived from sources listed in Part VIII. It was decided to make the calculation on the basis of the *unweighted* industry average of the measure. Thus, the R and D as a percentage of sales measure was worked out *separately* for each firm in an industry and these separate values then averaged to obtain the final industry value. It was hoped that this unweighted average would better reflect the general nature of research intensity throughout an industry, rather than being strongly influenced by the performance of the largest firms.[3] As can be seen from the tables presented in subsequent parts, we classify seven industries as HRI, the R and D as a percentage of sales for these varying from 2.8 per cent up to 6.8 per cent. Five industries are classified as MRI, with values of the index from 1.1 per cent up to 2.4 per cent; while the values for the six industries classified as LRI ranged from 0.4 per cent to 0.8 per cent. Finally, two industries are not classified in this way; 'petroleum', because of its unique circumstances and performance in the past decade, and 'other manufacturing' because of its disparate nature.

(d) THE NATURE OF THE SAMPLES

We derive two types of sample from the *Fortune* data, which we term the *rationalised* sample and *equalised* sample.

(i) The rationalised sample

The rationalised sample is derived by excluding from the *Fortune* data any US enterprises smaller than the smallest non-US enterprise covered. This then gives a sample which covers the X largest industrial enterprises in the world for that year. For example, for the year 1962, *Fortune* published information on 200 non-US firms and 500 US firms. However, since 203 of the US firms were smaller than the 200th non-US firm we have excluded these from our analysis; this, then reduces the sample in that year to 497. Also excluded are any US firms

---

1   Before being taken over by Bayer.
2   Germany, France, Italy, Belgium, the Netherlands, Luxembourg, the UK, Ireland and Denmark.
3   In Part VIII we revert to the more normal use of weighted averages in assessing R and D performance. This then reflects a summary of *actual* R and D done in an industry, allowing for above or below-average performance by the largest firms.

10

which are subsidiaries of MNEs in the non-US sample and any non-US firms which are subsidiaries of US MNEs.

The rationalised samples cover 497 firms in 1962, 483 in 1967, 636 in 1972, 865 in 1977 and 792 in 1982; the increasing numbers reflect *Fortune's* steadily enlarged coverage of non-US firms. The value of these data is that they give an immediate and clear picture of the composition of industry and nationality of ownership of the world's largest industrial companies in each of the years covered.

(ii)   The equalised sample

The obvious deficiency of the sample just described is that any attempt to draw conclusions about changing patterns over the period 1962 to 1982 may be clouded by distortions due to differences in sample size. To overcome this we derive an equalised sample which consists of an equal number of the largest enterprises for each of the years, drawn from those contained in the rationalised sample. This means that the equalised sample includes the number of enterprises in the smallest rationalised sample, of the years covered by the study. This year was 1967 and the number of enterprises was 483. Though it drastically reduces the size of the sample, this procedure does allow us to comment on the changing pattern of the world's largest industrial companies without the danger of systematic bias due to different sample size.

PART II The data for 1983

In this part we report on the *Fortune* data for 1983, which became available after completion of the main sections of the study. We discuss the structure of a rationalised sample (of 806 firms) for that year, and also the employment and profitability of the firms in that sample.

(a) THE PICTURE IN 1983 (tables 2.1 to 2.6)

In this section various aspects of the composition of our rationalised sample of the 806 largest industrial enterprises in 1983 are reviewed. Table 2.1 gives the breakdown by industry and country of the 806 firms, while Table 2.2 presents their 1983 sales. Tables 2.3 and 2.4 help us in our discussion of the extent to which countries are shown to have differing types of specialisation in terms of the industrial composition of their activity. Thus, Table 2.3 reveals the percentage breakdown of each *country*'s sales between industries, while, by contrast, Table 2.4 presents the percentage breakdown of the total activity in each *industry* between areas and countries. Finally, Tables 2.5 and 2.6 provide additional evidence on the size distribution of firms. In Tables 2.5 (a) and 2.5 (b) the numbers of firms from each country and industry which fall within particular size groups (for example, over $25 billion; between $10 billion and $25 billion etc.) are shown. Taking a slightly different perspective, Tables 2.6 (a) and 2.6 (b) show the number of firms from each country or industry which fall within a particular ranking of firms, for example, 25 largest, 26th to 50th etc.

(i) The geographical origin of enterprises

The 806 firms in the 1983 rationalised sample had a sales turnover (after authors' adjustments as outlined in Part I) of $3167 billion. Of these 806 firms, 343 (43 per cent) were US owned. Japan was in a clear second position with 135 firms (17 per cent of the total). There were 251 European firms (31 per cent of the total), of which EEC member countries accounted for 192 (24 per cent). The UK remained the largest European contributor with 75 firms (77 including jointly-owned ventures), followed by Germany (51) and France (35). The remaining EEC countries provided a further 29 firms (excluding those jointly owned with the UK). Non-EEC European countries contributed 59 firms to the 1983 rationalised sample. Of these, Sweden was responsible for 19, Switzerland for 12 and Spain for 10. Of all the European enterprises in the sample, those of UK, German and French origin accounted for 64 per cent in 1983.

Of the remaining 77 firms, 25 originated from Canada, eight from South Africa and seven from Australia. The less developed or developing countries (LDCs)[1] accounted for the other 37 firms, though, of these, only South Korea (10), Brasil (five) and India and Taiwan (three each) were represented by more than two firms. Altogether 16 'Third World' countries (excluding the LDCs of Europe) had at least one firm in the rationalised sample in 1983.

---

1 Excluding those of Europe.

As we would expect, the distribution by sales turnover of these 806 enterprises approximates quite closely to their distribution by numbers. However, there are some variations worthy of comment. Notably US firms account for 49 per cent of the value of sales (Table 2.4) compared with 43 per cent of the number of enterprises. Thus, the average sales of US firms was $4.5 billion compared to $3.9 billion for the whole sample (or $3.5 billion for the 463 non-US firms). This is clearly reflected in the size distribution data of tables 2.5 (a) and 2.6 (a). Most notably, US firms are dominant at the very top of the size pyramid, with 12 of the 15 firms with 1983 turnover in excess of $25 billion and 14 of the 25 largest enterprises in that year. Interestingly, US dominance is immediately much less once we get below this extreme size group, with only eight of the next 25 firms (that is, those ranked 26th to 50th) and only 17 of the 46 (37 per cent) with sales over $10 billion but less than $25 billion. Nevertheless, in a broader perspective, US firms are of above-average prominence towards the top of the sample, with 145 of the 300 largest firms (48 per cent) compared with 198 of the remaining 506 (39 per cent). Similarly, the US accounts for 128 (48 per cent) of the 266 firms with sales over $3 billion in 1983 compared with 215 out of 540 (40 per cent) with sales of less than $3 billion.

Japan represents the opposite extreme to the US, with a below-average firm size of $2.9 billion, so that its 17 per cent share of the numbers of firms reduces to 13 per cent of the value of sales. This results both from a lack of extreme giant firms and a further slightly below-average representation in the upper parts of the size distribution. Thus, there are no Japanese firms in the over-$25 billion sales group and Japan only has two representatives in the largest 25 firms. Further, there are 40 Japanese firms in the largest 300 (13 per cent) compared with 95 (19 per cent) in the remaining 506.

The average size of European firms in 1983 ($3.9 billion) was almost identical with that of the whole sample, so that Europe accounted for 31 per cent of sales and numbers. In terms of size distribution, European firms tend to cancel out an above-average representation at the top (34 of the largest 100) with a similarly above-average share of the smaller firms — that is, 103 of the smallest 306 (34 per cent).

This overall picture for Europe does, however, disguise major differences between countries. Thus, EEC enterprises, which accounted for 77 per cent of European firms, accounted for 85 per cent of their turnover. Again this owes quite a lot to the position among the largest firms, where the EEC accounts for 19 of the 21 European enterprises with sales of over $10 billion and for 30 of the 34 European representatives in the 100 largest firms. Reflecting this, most EEC countries have average firm sizes above the European average — for example, Germany $4.1 billion, France $4.2 billion, Italy $5.2 billion, the Netherlands $4.0 billion and Belgium $4.4 billion. The notable exception is the UK, with an average firm size of $3.2 billion compared with the EEC average of $4.3 billion.[1] Thus the UK, which accounts for 39 per cent of all EEC firms in the sample, only has 29 per cent of those with sales over $3 billion and 44 per cent of those under $3 billion turnover. The 59 non-EEC European firms have an average firm size of $2.5 billion. We have suggested above (in our discussion of the EEC firms) that non-EEC firms are sparsely represented among the really large enterprises, and, indeed, their above-average representation among the smaller firms is a crucial influence on their low average size. Thus non-EEC European firms accounted for 7 per cent of the 806 enterprises in 1983, but for 10 per cent of the smallest 306 compared with 6 per cent of the largest 500.

The 77 'other country' firms, which average $3.2 billion sales, account for 8 per cent of all sales and 10 per cent of all firms. The average size of the 40 firms from Canada, Australia and South Africa is only $2.2 billion, so that the average for the 37 'Third World' enterprises in this group is $4.2 billion — a figure which, as much as anything else, reflects the size of the national petroleum companies of these countries.

(ii) Industrial composition

In 1983, 275 (34 per cent) of the 806 rationalised sample enterprises were in *high research*

1   This does exclude the two large Anglo-Dutch enterprises.

intensive (HRI) industries, 217 (27 per cent) in *medium research intensive* (MRI) industries, and 196 (24 per cent) in the *low research intensive* (LRI) group. Of the remainder 95 (12 per cent of the rationalised sample) were in petroleum.

In the HRI group three industries were represented by more than 50 enterprises — that is, 'industrial and agricultural chemicals' with 66 (or 8 per cent of the rationalised sample), 'electronics and electrical appliances' with 62 (8 per cent) and 'motor vehicles' with 53 (7 per cent). 'Pharmaceuticals and consumer chemicals' was also quite prominent with 39 firms (5 per cent), while the other three industries in the group totalled 55 enterprises.

The distribution of firms within the MRI group of industries was less even, with 'metals' dominating; the 108 firms in this industry accounting for half of those in the sector and 13 per cent of the rationalised sample. This made 'metals' the largest industry in our sample in terms of firm numbers. One other industry in the MRI group exceeded 50 firms, that is, 'industrial and farm equipment' with 57 or 7 per cent of the rationalised sample. The remaining three industries in the group totalled 52 firms.

'Food' was the most prominent industry in the LRI group, its 78 firms (that is, 10 per cent of the sample) making it the only industry in the sector with over 50 representatives. 'Paper and wood products' comes a clear second in the group, with 42 firms (5 per cent). None of the remaining four industries in the LRI group exceeds 25 firms, their total of 76 being 10 per cent of the rationalised sample.

Data on the industrial distribution of sales (Table 2.3) reveal a number of significant differences when compared with numbers. The most notable of these concerns the 'petroleum' industry, which comprised 12 per cent of the 806 firms but 29 per cent of their sales. This results in an average firm size in the industry of $9.5 billion compared with the sample average of $3.9 billion. This is clearly reflected in the size distribution data of tables 2.5 (b) and 2.6 (b). Thus, 'petroleum' firms take 17 of the top 25 places in the sample and 11 of the 15 enterprises with sales of over $25 billion. Further, 'petroleum' firms account for 33 of the largest 100 compared with 12 per cent of the full 806. By contrast, 'petroleum' firms only took 27 of the bottom 406 places on the ranking, that is, 7 per cent. Similarly, the industry's firms accounted for 41 of the 144 firms with sales of over $5 billion (that is, 29 per cent) and for only 54 of the 662 with sales below $5 billion (that is, 8 per cent).

The HRI industries accounted for 38 per cent of sales compared with their 34 per cent of numbers, to give an above-average firm size of $4.4 billion. The strongest contribution to this was made by 'motor vehicles' firms, with an average firm size of $6.8 billion. Like 'petroleum', the large average size of 'motor vehicles' firms reflects strong representation near the top of the size distribution. Thus, 'motor vehicles' firms accounted for 12 of the 61 firms over $10 billion sales (20 per cent) and for only 41 of the 745 with sales below $10 billion (6 per cent). Similarly, while they account for 7 per cent of those in the full rationalised sample, they had 11 in the top 50 (22 per cent). 'Office equipment (including computers)' also has an above-average firm size, $4.7 billion, this reflecting one giant enterprise (over $25 billion and in the top 15) and a relatively substantial representation in the size group around and just above average ($3 billion to $10 billion), rather than the type of concentrated representation in the largest firms noted for 'petroleum' and 'motor vehicles'. Another HRI industry with above-average size firms ($4.6 billion) is 'electronics and electrical appliances'. After 'petroleum' and 'motor vehicles' this industry is the strongest in terms of very large firms (six in the top 50 and seven with sales of over $10 billion). This is backed up by continuing strong representation in the size groups just below the top (in a way not matched by 'motor vehicles') with 18 firms ranked between 51 and 200 (12 per cent) compared with 38 below 200 (that is, 6 per cent of these 606 smallest firms). The last HRI with an average firm size ($4.4 billion) above that for the overall sample is 'aerospace'. This owes much to strong representation in the middle range of firms and very few at the lower end of the distribution. Thus, despite only having two firms with over $10 billion sales, and only one in the top 50, 'aerospace' has 17 firms in the top 400 compared with six in the bottom 406.

The below-average firm size in the 'industrial and agricultural chemicals' industry ($3.5 billion) reflects a consistent representation of firms in the smaller size groups, and the lack of firms right at the top of the ranking. In fact, the industry is healthily represented just below the top with 11 firms ranked between 26 and 100 and 15 firms with sales over $5 billion (which makes it comparable with 'electronics' and 'motor vehicles' in that respect). The two

14

remaining HRI industries both have an average firm size well below that for the sample, that is, 'pharmaceuticals and consumer chemicals' with $2.6 billion and 'measurement, scientific and photographic equipment' with $2.2 billion. These are basically industries where relatively small firms (in the context of our sample) predominate, with 'pharmaceuticals and consumer chemicals' having 37 of its 39 firms below $5 billion and 'measurement, scientific and photographic equipment' nine of its 10 below $3 billion.

The average size of firms in the MRI industries, at $2.2 billion, is just half that of those in the HRI industries; while the 217 MRI firms were 27 per cent of the rationalised sample by numbers, their sales accounted for 16 per cent of those of sample firms. These industries have relatively few large firms with only one ('metals') representative in the top 50, and only two (both 'metals') of over $10 billion (out of 61 of this size in the sample). The general nature of the distribution of firms in these industries is indicated by the fact that these five industries have 33 firms in the largest 200 (that is, 17 per cent), 112 of the firms ranked 201 to 600 (28 per cent) and 72 of these ranked below 600 (that is, 35 per cent).

Among the MRI industries the highest average firm sizes are recorded by 'shipbuilding, railroad and transportation equipment' and 'rubber' (both $2.9 billion), both of these lacking really large firms but also avoiding disproportionate representation in the lowest size groups. The low average for 'metals' ($2.5 billion) is perhaps more due to lack of very large firms than overemphasis on small ones; thus the industry has only 5 per cent of the largest 100 firms, 15 per cent of those ranked 101 to 400 and 14 per cent of those below 400. The remaining two MRI industries do seem to be cases of concentration among the smaller firms. 'Industrial and farm equipment' (average size $1.9 billion) accounts for 20 of the 393 firms with sales over $2 billion (that is, 5 per cent) and for 37 of those below $2 billion (9 per cent). Similarly, 'building materials' (average size $1.7 billion) has only five firms over $2 billion and 24 below that size.

The LRI industry firms represent 24 per cent of the sample by numbers and 16 per cent of sample sales to give an average firm size for the group of $2.5 billion. By far the highest average firm size in this group is that of the 'tobacco' industry at $4.6 billion (the only industry, except 'petroleum', outside the HRI sector to exceed the sample average). The 11 firms in the 'tobacco' industry are fairly well dispersed through the size distribution, and the high average size reflects both the fact that three of the firms are in the largest 100 and also that only three are ranked below 600. The 'food' industry accounts for 10 per cent of the sample firms and 8 per cent of their sales, to give an average size of $3.0 billion, which is below the sample average but second highest in the LRI group and higher than any MRI industry. As was the case for 'tobacco', the firms in the 'food' industry are well dispersed through the size distribution, with the strongest representation around and just below average size. Thus, 'food' only has 10 of the 144 firms with sales over $5 billion (that is, 7 per cent) and 36 out of the 413 with sales below $2 billion (9 per cent), but 32 of the 249 with sales between $2 billion and $5 billion (that is, 13 per cent). The average size for the 'drink' industry ($2.6 billion) emerges from the fact that the four relatively large firms (over $5 billion) are countered by 11 (of the industry's 19 representatives) having sales of less than $2 billion. Each of the three remaining LRI industries has over 60 per cent of its firms with sales of below $2 billion, while only one ('paper and wood products') has a firm of over $5 billion sales. Thus, all have a very low average sales size — that is, 'paper and wood products' $1.9 billion, 'textiles, apparel and leather goods' $1.7 billion, 'publishing and printing' $1.6 billion.

(iii) Comparative specialisation

We next consider whether there are any significant differences between the industrial distribution of the largest firms according to their home countries. In doing so we shall make use of the concept of 'revealed comparative advantage' (RCA). We define a country's RCA — or more particularly that of the firms of a particular country — in a particular industry as its share of total sample sales in that industry, divided by that country's total share of all sample sales. Where the resulting ratio is more than 1 a country may be said to have a positive RCA in that industry; where it is less than 1 the country has a negative RCA, or is disadvantaged, in that industry. For example, it can be seen in Table 2.4 that US-owned firms account for 82.6 per cent of total sample sales in 'aerospace', but for only 49.2 per cent of total sample sales overall – that is, the USA has an RCA of 1.7 in 'aerospace', so that 'aerospace' is revealed as an industry in which the US is relatively strong. For our discussion it should be noted that the differing sizes of area samples may distort the comparisons, though we believe that the results are a reasonable reflection of the industrial specialisation of different areas in 1983 (at least as reflected by their largest enterprises).

In 1983, US companies accounted for 51.1 per cent of the sales in HRI industries, compared with 49.2 per cent of the sales of the whole sample. This almost neutral aggregate RCA, however, hides substantial differences between the HRI industries. Thus for three of the largest industries in the group, 'electronics and electrical appliances', 'industrial and agricultural chemicals', and 'motor vehicles', US firms accounted for a below-average share of sample sales, that is, they have an RCA of below 1. The US does, however, have strong RCAs in 'aerospace' and also in three of the most dynamically innovation-oriented of industries – 'office equipment (including computers)', 'pharmaceuticals and consumer chemicals', and 'measurement, scientific and photographic equipment'.

In aggregate, US firms have a very low RCA (0.66) in the MRI industries. This low aggregate value owes most to the very low levels of specialisation in 'shipbuilding, railroad and transportation equipment', 'metals' and 'building materials', though the RCA is also negative for 'industrial and farm equipment' and only marginally positive for 'rubber'.

As was the case for HRI industries, the US RCA in the LRI group is very slightly positive (52.7 per cent of the sample sales in LRI industries compared with 49.2 per cent of overall sample sales). By contrast with the HRI sector, though, this overall neutral result is reflected by similar results for four of the six industries. Thus, 'publishing and printing', 'food' and 'tobacco' all have RCAs between 1 and 1.1, while that for 'drink' is almost precisely 1. The two exceptions are a notably low RCA in 'textiles, apparel and leather goods' (0.84) and a high value in 'paper and wood products' (1.33). Finally, the USA had a modest positive specialisation in 'petroleum', with a RCA of 1.12.

European firms accounted for 29.9 per cent of sales in the HRI industries (compared with 30.7 per cent of the total sample) to give, as was the case for the USA, a virtually neutral overall RCA for this group. This neutral result was also repeated for both the EEC and 'other Europe' subsectors. Among the major countries (that is, those contributing over 1 per cent of sample sales) differences do emerge, however, with Germany, France, Italy, the Netherlands and Sweden having RCAs of over 1.1 in the HRI group, with the UK's very low value (0.63) being the major offsetting case. Europe has RCAs of over 1 for each of the three HRI industries where the USA value was less than 1. These are modest in the cases of 'electronics and electrical appliiances' (where Dutch, Swedish and, to a lesser degree, German, French and Swiss firms reveal the strong specialisation) and 'motor vehicles' (where Germany, France, Italy and Sweden all have RCAs well above 1), but more comprehensive in the case of 'industrial and agricultural chemicals' (where Germany, the Netherlands and Switzerland have RCAs of at least 2). In the four HRI industries where Europe has a revealed comparative disadvantage, the RCA is in the region of 0.6 for 'aerospace' (where France does possess a strong level of specialisation) and 'pharmaceuticals and consumer chemicals' (despite a Swiss RCA of over 4), but less than 0.2 for 'office equipment' (despite a value slightly over 1 for Italy) and 'measurement, scientific and photographic equipment'.

The UK's share of sample sales is lower for each of the HRI industries (it is not represented in any of them) than its share of total sample sales (that is, RCAs less than 1), something which is not true for any other major European country. The more relatively healthy RCAs for the UK in HRI industries (that is, over 0.85) are in 'electronics and electrical appliances', 'industrial and agricultural chemicals' and 'pharmaceuticals and consumer chemicals'.

European firms accounted for 38.5 per cent of sample sales in the MRI industries (compared with 30.7 per cent of the total sample), making this the one group of industries with a European RCA of over 1 (that is, 1.25). This was true for both EEC and 'other Europe' subgroups, though more strikingly so for the latter. Of the major European countries the strongest RCAs (over 1.4) in the MRI industries were in Germany, France, Sweden and Switzerland, with only Italy and the Netherlands having values of less than 1. Both 'metals' and 'building materials' had RCAs of 1.4 for Europe as a whole; though in the latter case this reflects, predominantly, very high values for France and the UK. For 'metals', however, this strong European RCA was quite generalised in the EEC, with values in excess of 1 for Germany

16

(substantially), France, Italy and (marginally) the UK, while Sweden and Switzerland had a comparative disadvantage in the industry. The European RCA of 1.1 in 'industrial and farm equipment' results from a high value for 'other European' countries (due to the strength of Sweden and Switzerland in this industry) counteracting a value below 1 for the EEC (where Germany and the UK alone have a comparative advantage). Europe is neutral (RCA of 1) with regard to specialisation in 'rubber', and very much at a comparative disadvantage in 'ship-building, railroad and transportation equipment', despite Sweden's relative strength in that industry.

As with the HRI industries, Europe as a whole has a neutral RCA in the LRI industries. This, however, is due almost exclusively to the substantial UK commitment to these industries, only Switzerland among the major countries also having a RCA of over 1. UK firms, which account for 7.8 per cent of the total sample sales, account for 15.8 per cent of LRI industry sales (that is, a RCA of 2.0). Of the six LRI industries the only one in which the UK does not have a RCA of at least 1 is 'publishing and printing', while the value exceeds 4 in 'drink' and 'tobacco', and is over 1.6 in both 'textiles, apparel and leather goods' and 'food'. As already suggested, the strong UK commitment to most LRI industries tends to contrast strongly with most other European countries. Thus in 'textiles, apparel and leather goods' and 'tobacco' no other major European country (that is, with over 1 per cent of sample sales) has an RCA of over 0.6, while in 'drink' the Netherlands (with an RCA just over 2) is the only other major country represented, and in 'food', Switzerland is the only other country to have an RCA in excess of 1 (omitting the Dutch share in Unilever). The outcome of these factors results in 'tobacco', 'drink' and 'food' having RCAs of over 1, and 'textiles, apparel and leather goods' less than 1, for Europe as a whole. The two remaining LRI industries have the lowest RCAs in the group, though Sweden has a strong specialisation in both 'paper and wood products' and 'publishing and printing', and Germany in the latter industry. Finally, Europe's RCA for 'petroleum' is 0.9 (27.5 per cent of 'petroleum' sales compared with 30.7 per cent of sample sales), with only Italy of the major countries having an RCA of over 1 (though this might also be true of the UK and the Netherlands if account were taken of their shares in Shell).

Japan (unlike the USA and Europe) has a clear comparative specialisation in the HRI industries. Thus Japan accounts for 17.4 per cent of HRI industry sales compared with 12.5 per cent of total sales, or an RCA of 1.4. This is by no means the general case, and this particular result would appear dependent on the strong commitment to 'electronics and electrical appliances' and 'motor vehicles', though 'measurement, scientific and photographic equipment' and (more marginally) 'industrial and agricultural chemicals' also had RCAs in excess of 1. Overall, Japan has a similar specialisation in the MRI industries (RCA again 1.4), though here there is remarkably little difference between the five industries, their individual RCAs varying from 1.1 for 'shipbuilding, railroad and transportation equipment' up to 1.4 for 'industrial and farm equipment' and 'metals'. It is, then, the LRI industries where Japan has the lowest degree of specialisation with an overall RCA of 0.8, despite a value of 2.5 in 'textiles, apparel and leather goods'. The only other LRI industry in which Japan has a, very slight, comparative advantage is 'publishing and printing', whilst 'paper and wood products' and 'food' have values close to the sector average of 0.8. Japan has a relatively low commitment to 'petroleum', with 5.3 per cent of the industry's sales to give an RCA of 0.4.

At present the 'other countries' group has a relatively tenuous commitment to the HRI industries, though South Korea's RCA of 1.7 in 'electronics and electrical appliances' is worthy of note. Though these countries' RCA of 1.6 in the MRI industries owes a lot to South Korea's strength in 'shipbuilding, railroad and transportation equipment', the RCA is over 1 in 'metals' also (over 1 for Canada), while Canada has a strong comparative advantage in 'building materials'. These countries have, also, a slightly below-average commitment to the LRI industries, the notable exceptions being the relative specialisation of Canada in 'paper and wood products', 'publishing and printing' and 'drink', and of South Korea in 'textiles, apparel and leather goods'. The inclusion in the sample of the national oil companies of a large number of LDCs underlies the specialisation of the 'other countries' group in the 'petroleum' industry.

(iv) Government ownership

In 1983, 71 (or 8.8 per cent) of the 806 companies in our rationalised sample were categorised by *Fortune* as 'government-owned firms' (GOFs). These had total sales of $299 billion or 9.4 per cent of the sales of the total sample. As a reflection of this the GOFs have an average firm size slightly above the sample average, that is, $4.2 million compared with $3.9 billion. This is also clearly mirrored in the position of the GOFs in the rankings of sample firms. Thus, compared with their 9 per cent of the overall sample, GOFs occupy 13 of the top 100 places, 12 of the next 100, 17 (that is, 9 per cent) of the firms ranked 201 to 500 and only 19 (that is, 6 per cent) of the lowest 306 places.

There were 50 European-based GOFs in the rationalised sample in 1983, these having total sales of $204 billion or 21.1 per cent of the 251 European firms in the 806. Of these, 32 originate from the EEC. France accounted for 17 of the European GOFs (compared with 35 in the 806, so that 48.6 per cent of French firms were government owned), the UK for five (compared with 75 overall, or 6.7 per cent), Italy also for five (compared with 12 overall, or 41.7 per cent) and Germany for three (out of 51, or 5.9 per cent). On the basis of turnover, GOFs accounted for 59.0 per cent of the total sales of the French sample firms, for 54.8 per cent of the Italian, for 9.2 per cent of the UK and 4.2 per cent of the German.

From the rest of Europe, there were 18 GOFs in the 1983 rationalised sample, including seven from Spain, three from Sweden and two each from Austria, Finland and Norway. These 18 GOFs represented 30.5 per cent of total 'other Europe' firms in the sample, and accounted for 28.8 per cent of their sales.

Of the 21 GOFs from the 'other countries' group, Canada and South Africa accounted for one each, the remainder being spread over 13 LDCs with only Brasil (five), India and Chile (with two each) accounting for more than one. Thus, 19 of the 37 (non-European) LDC-based firms in the sample are government owned. GOFs accounted for 38.8 per cent of all sales of 'other country' firms, but for 57.5 per cent of those from the LDCs of the group.

The most strongly represented industries among GOFs were 'petroleum', with 24, and 'metals' with 21 (that is, between them 63 per cent of all GOFs in the sample). Three HRI industries are quite prominent among the GOFs — 'industrial and agricultural chemicals' and 'aerospace', with five each, and 'motor vehicles' with four. Five industries have two GOFs ('electronics and electrical appliances', 'industrial and farm equipment', 'shipbuilding, railroad and transportation equipment', 'tobacco' and 'other manufacturing industries'), and 'office equipment' and 'building materials' one each. The sales of government-owned 'metals' firms represented 20.1 per cent of total sample sales in that industry, while government-owned 'petroleum' firms accounted for 16.5 per cent of that industry's sample total. GOFs also accounted for a notable share of sample sales in 'building materials' (15.8 per cent), 'shipbuilding, railroad and transportation equipment' (11.8 per cent), 'aerospace' (9.6 per cent) and 'industrial and agricultural chemicals' (8.6 per cent).

(b)   EMPLOYMENT OF SAMPLE FIRMS (Table 2.7)

The 806 firms in the 1983 rationalised sample had a total employment of 29.5 million. Of this, the 343 US firms accounted for 12.9 million (44 per cent) and the 135 Japanese for 2.4 million (8 per cent). Overall the employment of the 152 European firms was 11.5 million (39 per cent), the UK firms having the largest labour force of 3.6 million (12 per cent), followed by Germany 2.7 million (9 per cent) and France 1.8 million (6 per cent).

The seven HRI industries had a total labour force of 14.0 million (48 per cent of sample total) in 1983. This sector includes the two industries with the largest labour forces, that is, 'electronics and electrical appliances' with 4.3 million (15 per cent) and 'motor vehicles' with 3.7 million (13 per cent), as well as the smallest, 'measurement, scientific and photographic equipment', with 0.3 million. The total employment of the five MRI industries was 6.3 million (21 per cent), this being dominated by 'metals' with 3.3 million (11 per cent) and, to a lesser degree, 'industrial and farm equipment' with 1.4 million (5 per cent). The six LRI industries had a total employment of 5.5 million (19 per cent), though only 'food' exceeded 1 million (with 2.4 million or 8 per cent of total employment). The employment of the 'petroleum' firms was 2.6 million. Finally the 71 GOFs in the sample had total employment of 3.3 million (11 per cent of sample total).

Of the 806 firms covered in Table 2.7, we were able to obtain comparable 1982 employment figures for 747. Of these 454 (61 per cent) had suffered declines in employment levels during the year, compared with 271 (36 per cent) which had increased their labour force.

Of the countries represented by reasonably large numbers of firms, the healthiest employment performance is that of Japan, where 61 firms increased their labour force compared with 63 which reduced it. Differences in employment changes were notable between industries for Japanese firms. Thus, among the industries represented by over 10 firms, a very positive picture emerges for 'metals' (11 firms with employment up and three with employment down), 'electronics and electrical appliances' (11 up, two down) and 'motor vehicles' (12 up, six down), and a negative position for 'food' (one up, 11 down) and 'industrial and agricultural chemicals' (four up, 13 down).

Of the US-owned firms, 196 reduced employment levels between 1982 and 1983 and 128 increased them. Differences between industries were rather less marked than for Japanese firms, except for the dramatic revivals in fortunes for the 'motor vehicles' firms (12 up, two down) and 'aerospace' (10 up, two down). Industries close to parity included 'publishing and printing' (six up, five down); 'paper and wood products' (eight up, nine down); 'pharmaceuticals and consumer chemicals' (10 up, 11 down) and 'office equipment (seven up, nine down). Still in a particularly bleak employment position in the USA were 'industrial and agricultural chemicals' (seven up, 17 down), 'petroleum' (nine up, 28 down), 'metals' (seven up, 26 down; a notable contrast with this industry in Japan), and 'industrial and farm equipment' (eight up, 19 down).

The bleakest picture, however, is that for Europe where 156 firms recorded reduced labour forces between 1982 and 1983, while only 59 recorded increases. This is a substantially generalised pattern, with Germany (eight up, 38 down), France (eight up, 21 down), the UK (19 up, 47 down), Sweden (four up, 13 down) and Switzerland (two up, 10 down) all suffering badly. Among the more substantially represented industries the most disappointing performances for European firms include 'industrial and agricultural chemicals' (four up, 12 down), 'petroleum' (six up, 14 down), 'metals' (nine up, 27 down), 'electronics and electrical appliances' (four up, 10 down) and 'motor vehicles' (four up, 12 down; by contrast with the relative recovery in the USA and Japan) and 'industrial and farm equipment' (four up, 16 down). Only relatively better were 'pharmaceuticals and consumer chemicals' (five up, five down) and 'food' (eight up, 11 down).

Of the 'other countries' firms, 23 increased employment and 39 reduced it. The most adversely affected firms were those from Canada (six up, 17 down) and Australia and South Africa (both one up, five down). The most interesting industry result for these countries is that for 'petroleum', where nine firms increased their labour forces compared with eight which reduced them, while for all other 'petroleum' firms (that is, those from the USA, Europe and Japan) only 17 increased their employment level compared with 49 which lowered it.

Overall, six industries recorded more cases of employment increase than decline ('pharmaceuticals and consumer chemicals', 'electronics and electrical appliances', 'shipbuilding, railroad and transportation equipment', 'motor vehicles' and 'aerospace'), while two ('measurement, scientific and photographic equipment' and 'office equipment') achieved parity. The worst affected industries, where firms with employment cuts were more than twice those with employment increases, were 'industrial and agricultural chemicals', 'petroleum', 'rubber', 'metals' and 'industrial and farm equipment'.

(c)   PROFITABILITY IN 1983 (tables 2.8 and 2.9)

In Table 2.8 we set out data on the rate of return on sales for the 789 firms from the 1983 sample of 806 enterprises which provided profit figures, classified by country and industry.[1] We should caution the reader very strongly that these figures will reflect, not only real

---

1   In Table 2.9 we present similar data for rate of return on assets. To simplify exposition, our discussion concentrated on the rate of return on sales measure. Though differences in detail can be found between the two sets of results, the broad picture is substantially comparable.

differences in the profitability of these firms, but also national differences in accounting practices and reporting requirements. The results, especially intercountry results, should therefore be treated with some reservation and seen only as broad indicators of the comparative performance of enterprises.

In 1983, the USA seems to have had a considerably better rate of return on sales performance than that recorded by most other developed countries. Among HRI industries (the most profitable group) 'office equipment' and 'pharmaceuticals and consumer chemicals' were the outstanding performers, while even the least impressive, 'aerospace' and 'industrial and agricultural chemicals', produced results only marginally below the average for all US firms. The picture is similar for the LRI industries. The relatively healthy overall average for the group reflects both particularly strong performances in 'tobacco'; 'publishing and printing' and 'drink' and the fact that the weaker results, from 'food' and 'paper and wood products', were only moderately below the average for all US enterprises. By contrast, weak performances were generalised in the MRI sector. This was most notable, of course, for the two loss-making industries ('metals' and 'industrial and farm equipment'), but also reflects the fact that each of the three others in the group also ranked among the eight least profitable US industries.

The broad picture suggests that the profitability level of European firms in 1983 was considerably below that of US firms, with only Switzerland (of the countries represented by a reasonably large number of firms) having a higher rate of return on sales, most other countries a rate less than half that of the USA, and France and Italy recording aggregate losses.

For European enterprises in the HRI group, 'pharmaceuticals and consumer chemicals' produced a very strong result, but in each of the other six industries the rate of return on sales was less than half that for the comparable US firms. Aggregate losses were reported for 'aerospace' and 'motor vehicles' (where only Germany and Sweden, among the major European motor-producing countries, made overall profits). In addition to 'pharmaceuticals and consumer chemicals', 'office equipment' and 'electronics and electrical appliances' (where UK firms produced strong results) were the only HRI industries with a rate of return on sales performance above the average for all European firms. As was the case for the USA, the MRI industries are the most troubled in Europe in terms of profitability. Three of the five record overall losses: 'metals' (where overall losses are recorded by eight of the 13 European countries with entries in the industry), 'rubber' and 'shipbuilding, railroad and transportation equipment'. The notable exception among the MRI industries is 'building materials', whose relatively high profitability level mainly reflects a strong performance by UK firms. For Europe it is the LRI industries which are most profitable in the aggregate, with four of the six producing rate of return on sales results well above the area average (most notably in the case of 'drink'), and only 'paper and wood products' below average.

Japan's overall rate-of-return figure is modestly above that for Europe, but only half that for the USA. The HRI group are the clear profitability leaders, only 'industrial and agricultural chemicals' (of the six industries with representative firms) having a rate of return below the Japanese average. By contrast with the USA and Europe, the profitability of the MRI industries betters that of the LRI group. 'Metals' and 'industrial and farm equipment' are important industries in the group where Japanese firms perform notably better than their US and European counterparts. 'Building materials', which provided the healthiest results in the MRI sector for both the USA and Europe, also shares leadership of the group (along with 'industrial and farm equipment') for Japan. Of the five LRI industries in which Japan has representative firms, three ('textiles, apparel and leather goods'; 'paper and wood products'; and 'food') rank among the four with the lowest rate of return on sales. By contrast, 'publishing and printing' and 'drink' both rank in the top five.

The 'petroleum' industry has an overall rate of return figure very close to the rationalised sample average. This, however, reflects a diversity of experience, with the industry well above average profitability in Europe, slightly below average in the USA and rather more substantially below average in Japan. Among the 'other countries' group, 'petroleum' records aggregate losses, though this reflects a small number of cases of severe loss-making rather than a generalised tendency.

The widespread loss-making among GOFs, taken in conjunction with the extremely high profitability of some government-owned 'petroleum' firms (as well as the extreme losses of a

20

few national firms in this industry), suggests that any aggregate rate-of-return figures for GOFs have little value. Nevertheless, a few points can be made on their profitability. Of the 68 GOFs for which profit data is available, 31 (that is, 46 per cent) made losses in 1983. This compares with 93 of 721 privately-owned firms (that is, 13 per cent). It should, of course, be made clear that no strong conclusion can be drawn from this because many cases could be pointed out where firms have become government owned *because* they had become loss-makers rather than having become loss-makers *because* they are government owned. Again, in some cases, GOFs may have operated at minimal margins as a direct result of government policy seeking to subsidise other industries buying inputs from them. This could be the case in 'metals' where 14 of the 19 GOFs for which data was available made losses (that is, 74 per cent) compared with 33 out of 87 privately-owned firms (that is, 38 per cent). In 'petroleum' five out of 24 GOFs made losses (21 per cent) compared with six out of 68 privately-owned enterprises (9 per cent). In 'motor vehicles', all three GOFs for which data was available made losses, compared with eight out of 48 (17 per cent) of privately-owned enterprises. We should, perhaps, conclude by recording one industry where loss-making was at a much above-average level, that is, 'industrial and farm equipment' with 14 out of 57 firms recording losses (25 per cent), but where government ownership was relatively below average (two firms) and where the GOFs were among the firms in the black in 1983. 'Rubber' is also a case where loss-making is of above-average prominence in a substantially privately-run industry.

Comparison of the 1983 rate of return on sales figures from Table 2.8 with those for 1982 in tables 6.1 to 6.3, provides some clues that the world's largest enterprises might, in profit terms at least, have been starting to move away from the lower recessionary levels during that year. Though the USA and Japan both show overall improvements in rate of return on sales, the most substantial signs of recovery are found for Europe. Also several of the industries which were clearly most severely hit by the recessionary conditions in 1982 had revealed definite signs of improvement by 1983. 'Motor vehicles' is the most dramatic case of restored profitability, but 'rubber' had returned marginally to the black, and the extent of losses in 'metals' seemed to have been somewhat alleviated. The relatively healthy worldwide performance of 'building materials' in 1983, which we commented on earlier, seems to represent a notable improvement on 1982.[1]

As an alternative perspective on profitability changes between 1982 and 1983 we may note that, for the 742 firms where the comparison was possible, 392 recorded higher rates of return on sales in 1983 than in 1982 and 317 lower. For the USA 187 firms had increases in profitability compared with 135 with declines. Industries for which this tendency was particularly strong in the USA were 'pharmaceuticals and consumer chemicals' (17 firms with the rate of return on sales up and only four with the rate down), 'motor vehicles' (10 up, three down), 'aerospace' (eight up, three down), 'metals' (21 up, 12 down), 'publishing and printing' (10 up, two down), 'paper and wood products' (13 up, seven down), and 'building materials' (nine up, two down). Important industries where falls in profitability at the firm level still predominated in the USA between 1982 and 1983 were 'food' (14 up, 17 down), 'petroleum' (16 up, 19 down) and 'industrial and farm equipment' (11 up, 15 down).

For Europe, 113 firms reported an increased rate of return on sales between 1982 and 1983, and 93 recorded declines. Quite substantial differences can be seen at the national level, however. Germany (26 up, 16 down), the Netherlands (seven up, two down) and Switzerland (six up, three down) show up most strongly, while the UK (31 up, 37 down), Spain (two up, seven down) and Sweden (five up, 11 down) are less impressive. At the industry level in Europe the tendency towards modest profit recovery seems fairly generalised, the one exceptional case being 'industrial and agricultural chemicals' (13 up, four down).

Japan, which we saw as more impressive than the USA and Europe in terms of employment recovery, is less strong in terms of profitability, with 57 increases and 66 falls in rate of return on sales. The most impressive profitability recovery in Japan was for 'petroleum' firms (eight

<hr>

1 Of course the coverage of the 1983 and 1982 rationalised samples does differ, and this will clearly influence the aggregate results. However, for reasons discussed in Part VI, we believe this is not likely to systematically affect the results in a way that would invalidate the very broad conclusions drawn above.

up, one down), while the weakest situations were in 'metals' (three up, 11 down) and 'motor vehicles' (six up, 10 down).

The 'other countries' firms recorded 35 increases in profitability and 23 falls, Canada being in a strong position (16 up, eight down). Both 'metals' (nine up, three down) and 'petroleum' (10 up, six down) firms from these countries show up quite well.

Table 2.1

Composition of the largest 806 industrial firms, 1983, by industry and country: number of firms

	USA	Europe (total)	EEC (total)	Germany	France	Italy	Netherlands	Belgium	UK	UK Netherlands	Other Europe (total)	Austria	Finland	Norway	Sweden
High research intensity															
Aerospace	14	9	9	2	4	1			2						
Office equipment (incl. computers)	16	4	4	1	1	1			1						
Electronics and electrical appliances	26	19	16	4	4	1	1		6		3				2
Measurement, scientific and photographic equipment	7	1	1	1											
Industrial and agricultural chemicals	26	20	15	5	4	1	2	1	2		5	1		1	1
Pharmaceuticals and consumer chemicals	23	10	8	3	1				4		2				1
Motor vehicles (incl. components)	15	19	14	6	3	2			3		5	1			2
Total	127	82	67	22	17	6	3	1	18		15	2		1	5
Medium research intensity															
Industrial and farm equipment	27	20	12	5	1				6		8		1		5
Shipbuilding, railroad and transportation equipment	2	3	1						1		2				1
Rubber	5	4	3	1	1				1		1		1		
Building materials	11	10	9		2				7		1				
Metal manufacturing and products	33	40	33[3]	12	5	3	2	2	8		7	1	1	1	2
Total	78	77	58	18	9	3	2	2	23		19	1	3	1	8
Low research intensity															
Textiles, apparel and leather goods	10	6	5[5]	1	1				3		1				
Paper and wood products	21	11	5	1					3		6		3		3
Publishing and printing	12	5	4	2	1				1		1				1
Food	37	22	19		4		2		12	1	3				
Drink	6	9	9[6]	1	1		1		7						
Tobacco	3	6	5						3		1				
Total	89	59	47	5	7		3		29	1	12		3		5
Petroleum	39	26	14[7]	2	2	3		1	4	1	12[8]	1	1	1	1
Other manufacturing	10	7	6	4			1		1		1				
TOTAL	343	251	192	51	35	12	9	4	75	2	59	4	7	3	19

23

Table 2.1 (cont.)

	Switzerland	Spain	Turkey	Japan	Other Countries (total)	Australia	Canada	South Africa	Brazil	Chile	India	Mexico	South Korea	Taiwan	TOTAL
High research intensity															
Aerospace				2											23
Office equipment (incl. computers)		1		14									1		22
Electronics and electrical appliances	1				3[1]										62
Measurement, scientific and photographic equipment				2			1								10
Industrial and agricultural chemicals	1	1		17				1							66
Pharmaceuticals and consumer chemicals	2			6	3		1							1	39
Motor vehicles (incl. components)			1	19											53
Total	4	2	1	60	6		2	1					1	1	275
Medium research intensity															
Industrial and farm equipment	2			9	1		1								57
Shipbuilding, railroad and transportation equipment				2	2										9
Rubber	1			4	1	1							2		14
Building materials	1	1		5	3[2]	1	1			1					29
Metal manufacturing and products	1			14	21[4]	1	5	3	4		1	1	2	1	108
Total	5	1		34	28	3	7	3	4	1	1	1	4	1	217
Low research intensity															
Textiles, apparel and leather goods			1	7	1		4						1		24
Paper and wood products				6	4		2								42
Publishing and printing				2	3		2								22
Food	2			14	5	1	3	2							78
Drink		1		1	3	1	1								19
Tobacco					2	1									11
Total	2	1	1	30	18	3	12	2					1		196
Petroleum	1	6	1	9	21[9]	1	3	1	1	1	2	1	4	1	95
Other manufacturing				2	4[10]		1	1							23
TOTAL	12	10	3	135	77	7	25	8	5	2	3	2	10	3	806

1 Includes one firm from Israel.
2 Includes one firm from New Zealand.
3 Includes one firm from Luxembourg.
4 Includes one firm each from Zaire and Zambia.
5 Includes one firm from Ireland.
6 Includes one firm from Denmark.
7 Includes one firm from Greece.
8 Includes one firm from Portugal.
9 Includes one firm each from Argentina, Columbia, Kuwait, Pakistan, Peru, Philippines and Venezuela.
10 Includes one firm from Netherlands Antilles.

Source: *Fortune*, 30 April and 20 August 1984, organised as described in Part I.

Industry	USA	Europe (total)	EEC (total)	Germany	France	Italy	Netherlands	Belgium	UK	UK Netherlands	Other Europe (total)	Austria	Finland	Norway	Sweden
High Research Intensity															
Aerospace	83,024	17,464	17,464	3,230	7,608	1,123			5,503						
Office equipment (incl. computers)	92,437	6,368	6,368	1,062	1,527	2,458			1,321						
Electronics and electrial appliances	109,141	88,680	76,058	22,700	16,382	1,184	16,177		19,615		12,622				7,548
Measurement, scientific and photographic equipment	17,495	914	914	914											
Industrial and agricultural chemicals	85,063	109,150	95,114	45,490	11,109	7,014	12,210	3,886	15,405		14,036	868		4,077	765
Pharmaceuticals and consumer chemicals	73,480	20,003	13,312	4,454	1,805				7,053		6,691	843			
Motor vehicles (incl. components)	155,466	117,246	96,834	43,545	26,912	16,256			10,121		20,412				15,670
Total	616,106	359,825	306,064	121,395	65,343	28,035	28,387	3,886	59,018		53,761	1,711		4,077	23,983
Medium Research Intensity															
Industrial and farm equipment	50,254	37,182	23,640	11,355	2,162				10,123		13,542		884		9,816
Shipbuilding, railroad and transportation equipment	2,706	4,030	1,825						1,825		2,205				1,231
Rubber	21,018	12,875	9,145	1,325	5,390				2,430		3,730		974		
Building materials	15,656	20,582	19,276		9,969				9,307		1,306				
Metal manufacturing and products	70,539	116,091	100,231[3]	46,311	16,147	7,316	2,981	5,079	21,458	20,291	15,860	6,632	1,248	852	2,678
Total	160,173	190,760	154,117	58,991	33,668	7,316	2,981	5,079	45,143	20,291	36,643	6,632	3,106	852	13,725
Low Research Intensity															
Textiles, apparel and leather goods	16,470	9,650	7,316	1,026	957				5,333		2,334				3,135
Paper and wood products	52,160	14,351	8,297[5]	1,023					6,306		6,054		2,919		
Publishing and printing	18,472	6,803	5,773	3,442	1,224				1,107		1,030				1,030
Food	123,584	76,820	60,147		7,292		2,159		30,405		16,673				1,196
Drink	24,109	18,419	18,419[6]		822		1,250		16,365						
Tobacco	25,859	21,847	20,093	891					18,380		1,754				
Total	260,654	147,890	120,045	6,382	10,295		3,409		77,896		27,845		2,919		5,361
Petroleum	498,744	249,509	220,382[7]	10,152	36,538	26,974		8,717	56,527	80,551	29,127[8]	2,626	4,264	3,602	1,123
Other manufacturing	20,982	23,043	21,136	11,473			1,421		8,242		1,907				
TOTAL	1,556,659	971,027	821,744	208,393	145,844	62,325	36,198	17,682	246,826	100,842	149,283	10,969	10,289	8,531	44,192

25

Table 2.2 (cont.)

	Switzerland	Spain	Turkey	Japan	Other Countries (total)	Australia	Canada	South Africa	Brasil	Chile	India	Mexico	South Korea	Taiwan	TOTAL
High Research Intensity															
Aerospace															100,488
Office equipment (incl. computers)	5,074			5,395			2,680								104,200
Electronics and electrical appliances				75,892	12,747[1]								7,167		286,460
Measurement, scientific and photographic equipment				3,684	6,927										22,093
Industrial and agricultural chemicals	7,018	1,308		30,680			3,111	1,455						2,361	231,820
Pharmaceuticals and consumer chemicals	6,691			7,812											101,295
Motor vehicles (incl. components)		971	2,928	86,069											358,781
Total	18,783	2,279	2,928	209,532	19,674		5,791	1,455					7,167	2,361	1,205,137
Medium Research Intensity															
Industrial and farm equipment	2,842			18,703	1,207		1,207								107,346
Shipbuilding, railroad and transportation equipment				3,576	15,613								15,613		25,925
Rubber	3,730			6,033	1,264	1,264									41,190
Building materials	1,306			7,575	4,346[2]	1,114	1,482								48,159
Metal manufacturing and products	3,438	1,012		48,837	37,295[4]	4,289	10,643	4,370	4,341	1,774	2,927	1,003	4,284	845	272,762
Total	11,316	1,012		84,724	59,725	6,667	13,332	4,370	4,341	1,774	2,927	1,003	19,897	845	495,382
Low Research Intensity															
Textiles, apparel and leather goods			2,334	12,487	2,107								2,107		40,714
Paper and wood products				8,529	5,610	1,410	5,610								80,650
Publishing and printing				4,822	5,502		4,092								35,598
Food	15,477			22,530	14,508	2,460	3,980	8,068							237,442
Drink				2,017	4,649		4,649								49,194
Tobacco		1,754			2,863	1,151	1,712								50,569
Total	15,477	1,754	2,334	50,385	35,239	5,021	20,043	8,068					2,107		494,168
Petroleum	1,907	11,479	3,838	48,174	109,333[9]	1,784	8,416	1,349	16,258	1,388	11,503	16,140	19,042	5,313	905,760
Other manufacturing				2,995	19,238[10]		10,351	1,590							66,258
TOTAL	47,483	16,524	9,100	395,810	243,209	13,472	57,933	16,832	20,599	3,162	14,430	17,143	48,213	8,519	3,166,705

1 Includes sales of one firm from Israel ($2,900 mln).
2 Includes sales of one firm from New Zealand ($1,750 mln).
3 Includes sales of one firm from Luxembourg ($939 mln).
4 Includes sales of one firm each from Zaire ($787 mln) and Zambia ($2,032 mln).
5 Includes sales of one firm from Ireland ($968 mln).
6 Includes sales of one firm from Denmark ($804 mln).
7 Includes sales of one firm from Greece ($923 mln).
8 Includes sales of one firm from Portugal ($2,195 mln).
9 Includes sales of one firm each from Argentina ($6,782 mln); Colombia ($1,851 mln); Kuwait ($10,744 mln); Pakistan ($866 mln); Peru ($1,262 mln); Philippines ($2,407 mln); Venezuela ($6,012 mln).
10 Includes sales of one firm from Netherlands Antilles ($5,513 mln).

Source: *Fortune* 30 April 1984 and 20 August 1984, organised as described in Part I.

Table 2.3

Percentage industrial distribution of sales of 806 largest industrial firms, 1983, by area and country

	USA	Europe (total)	EEC (total)	Germany	France	Italy	Nether-lands	Belgium	UK	UK Nether-lands	Other Europe (total)	Austria	Finland	Norway	Sweden
High Research Intensity															
Aerospace	5.3	1.8	2.1	1.5	5.2	1.8			2.2						
Office equipment (incl. computers)	5.9	0.7	0.8	0.5	1.0	3.9			0.5						
Electronics and electrical appliances	7.0	9.1	9.3	10.9	11.2	1.9	44.7		7.9		8.5				17.1
Measurement, scientific and photographic equipment	1.1	0.1	0.1	0.4											
Industrial and agricultural chemicals	5.5	11.2	11.6	21.8	7.6	11.3	33.7	22.0	6.2		9.4	7.9		47.8	1.7
Pharmaceuticals and consumer chemicals	4.7	2.1	1.6	2.1	1.2	26.1			2.9		4.5				
Motor vehicles (incl. components)	10.0	12.1	11.8	20.9	18.5				4.1		13.7	7.7			35.5
Total	39.6	37.1	37.2	58.3	44.8	45.0	78.4	22.0	23.9		36.0	15.6		47.8	54.3
Medium Research Intensity															
Industrial and farm equipment	3.2	3.8	2.9	5.4	1.5				4.1		9.1		8.6		22.2
Shipbuilding, railroad and transportation equipment	0.2	0.4	0.2						0.7		1.5		9.5		2.8
Rubber	1.4	1.3	1.1	0.6	3.7				1.0		2.5				
Building materials	1.0	2.1	2.3		6.8				3.8		0.9				
Metal manufacturing and products	4.5	12.0	12.2	22.2	11.1	11.7	8.2	28.7	8.7		10.6	60.5	12.1	10.0	6.1
Total	10.3	19.6	18.8	28.3	23.1	11.7	8.2	28.7	18.3		24.5	60.5	30.2	10.0	31.1
Low Research Intensity															
Textiles, apparel and leather goods	1.1	1.0	0.9	0.5	0.7				2.2		1.6				
Paper and wood products	3.4	1.5	1.0	0.5					2.6		4.1		28.4		7.1
Publishing and printing	1.2	0.7	0.7	1.7	0.8				0.4		0.7				2.3
Food	7.9	7.9	7.3		5.0		6.0		12.3	20.1	11.2				2.7
Drink	1.5	1.9	2.2				3.5		6.6						
Tobacco	1.7	2.2	2.4	0.4	0.6				7.4		1.2				
Total	16.7	15.2	14.6	3.1	7.1		9.5		31.6	20.1	18.7		28.4		12.1
Petroleum	32.0	25.7	26.8	4.9	25.1	43.3	3.9	49.3	22.9	79.9	19.5	23.9	41.4	42.2	2.5
Other manufacturing	1.3	2.4	2.6	5.5					3.3		1.3				
TOTAL	100.0	100.0	100.0	100.0	100.0	100.0	100.0	100.0	100.0	100.0	100.0	100.0	100.0	100.0	100.0

27

Table 2.3 (cont.)

	Switzerland	Spain	Turkey	Japan	Other Countries (total)	Australia	Canada	South Africa	Brazil	Chile	India	Mexico	South Korea	Taiwan	TOTAL
High Research Intensity															
Aerospace				1.4											3.2
Office equipment (incl. computers)													14.9		3.3
Electronics and electrical appliances	10.7			19.2	5.2		4.6								9.0
Measurement, scientific and photographic equipment				0.9											0.7
Industrial and agricultural chemicals	14.8	7.9		7.8			5.4	8.6							7.3
Pharmaceuticals and consumer chemicals	14.1	5.9		2.0	2.8										3.2
Motor vehicles (incl. components)			32.2	21.7										27.7	11.3
Total	39.6	13.8	32.2	52.9	8.1		10.0	8.6					14.9	27.7	38.1
Medium Research Intensity															
Industrial and farm equipment	6.0			4.7	0.5		2.1								3.4
Shipbuilding, railroad and transportation equipment				0.9	6.4								32.4		0.8
Rubber	7.9			1.5	0.5	9.4	2.6								1.3
Building materials	2.8			1.9	1.8	8.3									1.5
Metal manufacturing and products	7.2	6.1		12.3	15.3	31.8	18.4	26.0	21.1	56.1	20.3	5.9	8.9	9.9	8.6
Total	23.8	6.1		21.4	24.6	49.5	23.0	26.0	21.1	56.1	20.3	5.9	41.3	9.9	15.6
Low Research Intensity															
Textiles, apparel and leather goods			25.6	3.2	0.9		9.7						4.4		1.3
Paper and wood products				2.2	2.3		7.1								2.5
Publishing and printing				1.2	2.3	10.5	6.9								1.1
Food	32.6			5.7	6.0	18.3	8.0	47.9							7.5
Drink				0.5	1.9		3.0								1.6
Tobacco		10.6			1.2	8.5									1.6
Total	32.6	10.6	25.6	12.7	14.5	37.3	34.6	47.9					4.4		15.6
Petroleum			42.2	12.2	45.0	13.2	14.5	8.0	78.9	43.9	79.7	94.1	39.5	62.4	28.6
Other manufacturing	4.0	69.5		0.8	7.9		17.9	9.4							2.1
TOTAL	100.0	100.0	100.0	100.0	100.0	100.0	100.0	100.0	100.0	100.0	100.0	100.0	100.0	100.0	100.0

Source: Table 2.2.

28

Table 2.4

Percentage geographical distribution of sales of 806 largest industrial firms, 1983, by industry

	USA	Europe (total)	EEC (total)	Germany	France	Italy	Nether-lands	Belgium	UK	UK Nether-lands	Other Europe (total)	Austria	Finland	Norway	Sweden
High Research Intensity															
Aerospace	82.6	17.4	17.4	3.2	7.6	1.1			5.5						
Office equipment (incl. computers)	88.7	6.1	6.1	1.0	1.5	2.4			1.3						
Electronics and electrical appliances	38.1	31.0	26.6	7.9	5.7	0.4	5.6		6.8		4.4				2.6
Measurement, scientific and photographic equipment	79.2	4.1	4.1	4.1											
Industrial and agricultural chemicals	36.7	47.1	41.0	19.6	4.8	3.0	5.3	1.7	6.6		6.1				0.3
Pharmaceuticals and consumer chemicals	72.5	19.7	13.1	4.4	1.8				7.0		6.6	0.4		1.8	4.4
Motor vehicles (incl. components)	43.3	32.7	27.0	12.1	7.5	4.5			2.8		5.7	0.2			
Total	51.1	29.9	25.4	10.1	5.4	2.3	2.4	0.3	4.9		4.5	0.1		0.3	2.0
Medium Research Intensity															
Industrial and farm equipment	46.8	34.6	22.0	10.6	2.0				9.4		12.6		0.8		9.1
Shipbuilding, railroad and transportation equipment	10.4	15.5	7.0						7.0		8.5		3.8		4.7
Rubber	51.0	31.3	22.2	3.2	13.1				5.9		9.1				
Building materials	32.5	42.7	40.0		20.7				19.3		2.7				
Metal manufacturing and products	25.9	42.6	36.7	17.0	5.9	2.7	1.1	1.9	7.9		5.8	2.4	0.5	0.3	1.0
Total	32.3	38.5	31.1	11.9	6.8	1.5	0.6	1.0	9.1		7.4	1.3	0.6	0.2	2.8
Low Research Intensity															
Textiles, apparel and leather goods	40.5	23.7	18.0	2.5	2.4				13.1		5.7				3.9
Paper and wood products	64.7	17.8	10.3	1.3					7.8		7.5		3.6		2.9
Publishing and printing	51.9	19.1	16.2	9.7	3.4				3.1		2.9				0.5
Food	52.0	32.4	25.3		3.1		0.9		12.8	8.5	7.0				
Drink	49.0	37.4	37.4				2.5		33.3						
Tobacco	51.1	43.2	39.7	1.8	1.6				36.3		3.5				
Total	52.7	29.9	24.3	1.3	2.1		0.7		15.8	4.1	5.6		0.6		1.1
Petroleum	55.1	27.5	24.3	1.1	4.0	3.0		1.0	6.2	8.9	3.2	0.3	0.5	0.4	0.1
Other manufacturing	31.7	34.8	31.9	17.3			2.1		12.4		2.9				
TOTAL	49.2	30.7	25.9	6.6	4.6	2.0	1.1	0.6	7.8	3.2	4.7	0.3	0.3	0.3	1.4

Table 2.4 (cont.)

	Switzer-land	Spain	Turkey	Japan	Other Countries (total)	Australia	Canada	South Africa	Brazil	Chile	India	Mexico	South Korea	Taiwan	TOTAL
High Research Intensity															
Aerospace															100.0
Office equipment (incl. computers)				5.2											100.0
Electronics and electrical appliances	1.8			26.5	4.4		0.9						2.5	1.0	100.0
Measurement, scientific and photographic equipment				16.7											100.0
Industrial and agricultural chemicals	3.0	0.6		13.2	3.0		1.3	0.6							100.0
Pharmaceuticals and consumer chemicals	6.6	0.3		7.7											100.0
Motor vehicles (incl. components)			0.8	24.0											100.0
Total	1.6	0.2	0.2	17.4	1.6		0.5	0.1					0.6	0.2	100.0
Medium Research Intensity															
Industrial and farm equipment	2.6			17.4	1.1		1.1								100.0
Shipbuilding, railroad and transportation equipment				13.8	60.2								60.2		100.0
Rubber	9.1			14.6	3.1	3.1	3.1								100.0
Building materials	2.7			15.7	9.0	2.3									100.0
Metal manufacturing and products	1.3	0.4		17.9	13.7	1.6	3.9	1.6	1.6	0.7	1.1	0.4	1.6	0.3	100.0
Total	2.3	0.2		17.1	12.1	1.3	2.7	0.9	0.9	0.4	0.6	0.2	4.0	0.2	100.0
Low Research Intensity															
Textiles, apparel and leather goods			5.7	30.7	5.2		7.0						5.2		100.0
Paper and wood products				10.6	7.0		11.5								100.0
Publishing and printing	6.5			13.5	15.5		1.7								100.0
Food				9.5	6.1	4.0	9.5	3.4							100.0
Drink				4.1	9.5	1.0	3.4								100.0
Tobacco		3.5			5.7	2.3									100.0
Total	3.1	0.4	0.5	10.2	7.1	1.0	4.1	1.6					0.4		100.0
Petroleum	2.9	1.3	0.4	5.3	12.1	2.7	0.9	0.1	1.8	0.2	1.3	1.8	2.1	0.6	100.0
Other manufacturing			0.3	4.5	29.0		15.6	2.4							100.0
TOTAL	1.5	0.5	0.3	12.5	7.7	0.4	1.8	0.5	0.7	0.1	0.5	0.5	1.5	0.3	100.0

Source: Table 2.2

Table 2.5 (a)
Distribution of firms by size group and country, 1983 (number of firms)

Size Group $ billion (Sales)

	Over 25 bln	10 bln to 25 bln	5 bln to 10 bln	3 bln to 5 bln	2 bln to 3 bln	1 bln to 2 bln	less than 1 bln
USA	12	17	36	63	49	106	60
Europe (Total)	3	18	24	36	39	90	41
EEC (Total)	3	16	21	23	32	69	28[1]
Germany		7	5	7	7	17	8
France		4	5	5	3	14	4
Italy	1	1	1	1	2	5	1
Netherlands		1	2		1	3	2
Belgium			1	2		1	
UK	1	2	7	8	19	29	9
UK-Netherlands	1	1					
Other Europe (total)		2	3	13	7[2]	21	13
Austria		1			1		2
Finland				1		3	3
Norway				2			1
Sweden		1		3	2	11	2
Switzerland		1	2	4	1	3	1
Spain				2		4	4
Turkey				1	2		
Japan		7	12	17	21	58	20
Other countries (total)		4[3]	11[4]	6	18[5]	31[6]	7[7]
Australia				1	1	5	
Canada		1		4	6	12	2
South Africa			1		1	6	
Brazil		1				2	2
Chile						2	
India			1		2		
Mexico		1				1	
South Korea			5	1	4		
Taiwan			1		1		1
TOTAL	15	46	83	122	127	285	128

1   Includes one firm each from Luxembourg, Denmark, Ireland and Greece.
2   Includes one firm from Portugal.
3   Includes one firm from Kuwait.
4   Includes one firm each from Argentina, Venezuela and Netherlands Antilles.
5   Includes one firm each from Israel, Philippines, and Zambia.
6   Includes one firm each from Colombia, New Zealand and Peru.
7   Includes one firm each from Pakistan and Zaire.

Source: *Fortune* 30 April 1984 and 20 August 1984, organised as described in Part I.

Table 2.5 (b)
Distribution of firms by size group and industry, 1983
Size Group $ billion (Sales)

	Over 25 bln	10 bln to 25 bln	5 bln to 10 bln	3 bln to 5 bln	2 bln to 3 bln	1 bln to 2 bln	Less than 1 bln
High Research Intensity							
Aerospace		2	6	4	5	4	2
Office equipment (incl. computers)	1		3	7	1	6	4
Electronics and electrical appliances	1	6	10	10	10	20	5
Measurement, scientific and photographic equipment		1			1	5	3
Industrial and agricultural chemicals		6	9	8	9	24	10
Pharmaceuticals and consumer chemicals		1	1	12	3	18	4
Motor vehicles (incl. components)	2	10	4	4	9	14	10
Total	4	26	33	45	38	91	38
Medium Research Intensity							
Industrial and farm equipment			1	10	9	23	14
Shipbuilding, railroad and transportation equipment			2		1	4	2
Rubber			2	4	3	3	2
Building materials			1		4	18	6
Metal manufacturing and products		2	9	20	18	39	20
Total		2	15	34	35	87	44
Low Research Intensity							
Textiles, apparel and leather goods				1	8	10	5
Paper and wood products			1	6	6	22	7
Publishing and printing				1	5	11	5
Food		2	8	16	16	29	7
Drink			4	1	3	6	5
Tobacco		2	1	2	1	3	2
Total		4	14	27	39	81	31
Petroleum	11	13	17	14	13	16	11
Other manufacturing		1	4	2	2	10	4
TOTAL	15	46	83	122	127	285	128

Source: *Fortune* 30 April 1984 and 20 August 1984, organised as described in Part I.

Table 2.6 (a)
Ranking of firms[1] 1983, by country (numbers of firms)

Firms Ranked

	1 to 25	26 to 50	51 to 100	101 to 200	201 to 300	301 to 400	401 to 500	501 to 600	601 to 700	701 to 806
USA	14	8	24	48	51	35	45	29	42	47
Europe (total)	7	12	15	29	28	31	26	36	32	35
EEC (total)	7	10	13	22	19	25	24	26	21[2]	25[3]
Germany		6	4	8	2	6	4	4	9	8
France	2	1	3	5	3	3	8	5	2	3
Italy	1	1	1		2	1	1		4	1
Netherlands	1		1	1		1		3		2
Belgium			1	1	1	1				
UK	1	2	3	7	11	13	11	14	5	8
UK-Netherlands	2									
Other Europe (total)		2	2	7	9	6[4]	2	10	11	10
Austria			1			1				2
Finland				1				1	3	2
Norway				1	1					1
Sweden		1		2	2	1		6	5	2
Switzerland		1	1	1	4	2	1	1		1
Spain				1	1		1	2	3	2
Turkey				1	1	1				
Japan	2	5	3	16	14	19	18	22	18	18
Other Countries (total)	2		8[5]	7[6]	7[7]	15[8]	11[9]	13[10]	8	6[11]
Australia				1		1	1	2	2	
Canada			1	1	4	5	5	5	3	1
South Africa			1			1	1	4	1	
Brazil	1						1		1	2
Chile							1	1		
India			1		1	1				
Mexico	1								1	
South Korea			3	2	1	4				
Taiwan				1		1				1
TOTAL	25	25	50	100	100	100	100	100	100	106

1   Firms ranked by sales.
2   Including one firm from Ireland.
3   Including one firm each from Luxembourg, Denmark and Greece.
4   Including one firm from Portugal.
5   Including one firm each from Argentina and Kuwait.
6   Including one firm each from Netherlands Antilles and Venezuela.
7   Including one firm from Israel.
8   Including one firm each from Philippines and Zambia.
9   Including one firm each from Colombia and New Zealand.
10   Including one firm from Peru.
11   Including one firm each from Pakistan and Zaire.

Source: *Fortune* 30 April 1984 and 20 August 1984 organised as described in Part I

Table 2.6 (b)
Ranking of firms[1], 1983 by industry (number of firms)

	1 to 25	26 to 50	51 to 100	101 to 200	201 to 300	301 to 400	401 to 500	501 to 600	601 to 700	701 to 806
High Research Intensity										
Aerospace		1	4	4	4	4	1	2	1	2
Office equipment (incl. computers)	1		1	7	2	1	4	1	2	3
Electronics and electrical appliances	3	3	6	12	7	6	6	10	5	4
Measurement, scientific and photo- graphic equipment			1		1		1	1	3	3
Industrial and agricultural chemicals		4	7	7	7	8	13	6	6	8
Pharmaceuticals and consumer chemicals		1		4	11	3	8	4	5	3
Motor vehicles (incl. components)	3	8	2	4	9	3	7	5	4	8
Total	7	17	21	38	41	25	40	29	26	31
Medium Research Intensity										
Industrial and farm equipment				4	10	7	5	7	13	11
Shipbuilding, railroad and transportation equipment			1	1		1	2	2	1	1
Rubber			1	2	3	3		2	1	2
Building materials			1		2	2	6	7	6	5
Metal manufacturing and products		1	4	18	13	15	14	11	15	17
Total		1	7	25	28	28	27	29	36	36
Low Research Intensity										
Textiles, apparel and leather goods					4	6	1	4	6	3
Paper and wood products				4	5	4	8	5	10	6
Publishing and printing				1		5	4	4	3	5
Food	1	1	4	12	11	13	7	13	9	7
Drink			2	2	1	3		3	4	4
Tobacco		2	1	2		1	2		1	2
Total	1	3	7	21	21	32	22	29	33	27
Petroleum	17	4	12	14	8	13	6	8	4	9
Other manufacturing			3	2	2	2	5	5	1	3
TOTAL	25	25	50	100	100	100	100	100	100	106

1 Firms ranked by sales.

Source: *Fortune* 30 April 1984 and 20 August 1984, organised as described in Part I.

Table 2.7

Employment of the largest 806 industrial firms,[1] 1983, by industry and country

	USA	Europe (total)	EEC (total)	Germany	France	Italy	Netherlands
High Research Intensity							
Aerospace	939,271	263,432	263,432	49,129	79,323	14,700	
Office equipment (incl. computers)	1,130,117	113,823	113,823	17,521	25,929	47,800	
Electronics and electrical appliances	1,671,386	1,740,355	1,490,155	432,214	280,539	26,984	343,000
Measurement, scientific and photographic equipment	247,757	23,109	23,109	23,109			
Industrial and agricultural chemicals	776,555	1,148,706	1,023,241	495,988	159,069	72,813	94,185
Pharmaceuticals and consumer chemicals	745,306	280,368	196,407	54,772	25,522		
Motor vehicles (incl. components)	1,450,194	1,727,397	1,542,920	594,199	440,600	288,175	
Total	6,960,586	5,297,190	4,653,087	1,666,932	1,010,982	450,472	437,185
Medium Research Intensity							
Industrial and farm equipment	614,181	623,774	396,104	153,024	45,000		
Shipbuilding, railroad and transportation equipment	56,100	98,610	62,583				
Rubber	272,794	267,688	199,688	26,688	120,000		
Building materials	190,064	308,536	290,836		158,167		
Metal manufacturing and products	644,903	1,447,629	1,246,023[4]	522,414	222,240	102,308	42,534
Total	1,778,042	2,746,237	2,195,234	702,126	545,407	102,308	42,534
Low Research Intensity							
Textiles, apparel and leather goods	318,475	204,798	178,798	21,580	17,332		
Paper and wood products	440,821	217,330	126,704[6]	10,407	11,600		
Publishing and printing	179,929	96,922	81,548	42,381			
Food	1,113,187	950,841	791,004		60,311		9,822
Drink	261,220	406,977	406,977[7]	9,419	8,313		21,254
Tobacco	238,228	332,795	324,099				
Total	2,551,860	2,209,663	1,909,130	83,787	97,556		31,076
Petroleum	1,290,143	718,540	654,598[8]	55,188	124,424	135,844	17,100
Other manufacturing	274,981	505,831	474,605	189,505			
TOTAL	12,855,612	11,477,461	9,886,654	2,697,538	1,778,369	688,624	527,895

35

Table 2.7 (cont.)

	Belgium	UK	UK-Netherlands	Other Europe (total)	Austria	Finland	Norway	Sweden
High Research Intensity								
Aerospace		120,280						159,600
Office equipment (incl. computers)		22,573						7,226
Electronics and electrical appliances		407,418		250,200				
Measurement, scientific and photographic equipment								
Industrial and agricultural chemicals	44,186	157,000		125,465	8,230		18,838	
Pharmaceuticals and consumer chemicals		116,113		83,961				
Motor vehicles (incl. components)		219,946		184,477	15,515			115,344
Total	44,186	1,043,330		644,103	23,745		18,838	282,170
Medium Research Intensity								
Industrial and farm equipment		198,080		227,670		15,099		158,047
Shipbuilding, railroad and transportation equipment		62,583		36,027		17,605		18,422
Rubber		53,000		68,000				
Building materials		132,669		17,700				
Metal manufacturing and products	44,297	296,214		201,606	72,288	23,651	9,943	38,922
Total	44,297	742,546		551,003	72,288	56,355	9,943	215,391
Low Research Intensity								
Textiles, apparel and leather goods		139,886		26,000				42,996
Paper and wood products		104,178		90,626				15,374
Publishing and printing		27,567		15,374				8,212
Food		453,871		159,837		47,630		
Drink		372,456	267,000					
Tobacco		306,367		8,696				
Total		1,404,325	267,000	300,533		47,630		66,582
Petroleum	21,000	161,042	156,000	63,942[9]	7,621	7,176	3,534	5,711
Other manufacturing		268,000		31,226				
TOTAL	109,483	3,619,243	423,000	1,590,807	103,654	111,161	32,315	569,854

36

Table 2.7 (cont.)

	Switzerland	Spain	Turkey	Japan	Other Countries (total)	Australia	Canada	South Africa	Brazil	Chile	India	Mexico	South Korea	Taiwan	TOTAL
High Research Intensity															
Aerospace															1,202,703
Office equipment (incl. computers)				71,630											1,315,570
Electronics and electrical appliances	90,600			696,502	175,773[2]		39,318						102,255		4,284,016
Measurement, scientific and photographic equipment				37,115										38,823	307,981
Industrial and agricultural chemicals	79,173	11,998		138,147	83,928		18,605	26,500							2,147,336
Pharmaceutical and consumer chemicals	83,961			55,361											1,081,035
Motor vehicles (incl. components)		25,170	28,448	515,299											3,692,890
Total	253,734	37,168	28,448	1,514,054	259,701		57,923	26,500					102,255	38,823	14,031,531
Medium Research Intensity															
Industrial and farm equipment	54,524	22,356		145,701	27,609		27,609								1,411,265
Shipbuilding, railroad and transportation equipment				35,012	161,000								161,000		350,722
Rubber	68,000			56,769	18,500	18,500									615,751
Building materials	17,700			52,539	50,960[3]	13,000	15,175								602,099
Metal manufacturing and products	34,446			316,371	909,359[5]	54,000	151,685	130,071	76,791	25,660	205,626	31,721	57,658	15,000	3,318,262
Total	174,670	22,356		606,392	1,167,428	85,500	194,469	130,071	76,791	25,660	205,626	31,721	218,658	15,000	6,298,099
Low Research Intensity															
Textiles, apparel and leather goods			26,000	91,476	20,441		59,153						20,441		635,190
Paper and wood products				40,027	59,153	20,300	48,100								757,331
Publishing and printing				24,556	68,400		24,000								369,807
Food	151,625			94,340	224,664	14,703	35,500	185,961							2,383,032
Drink				10,861	35,500	11,000	50,000								714,558
Tobacco		8,696			61,000										632,023
Total	151,625	8,696	26,000	261,260	469,158	46,003	216,753	185,961					20,441		5,491,941
Petroleum		17,389	15,417	34,644	574,437[10]		21,901	30,770	56,835	3,537	60,947	157,000	102,200	19,521	2,617,764
Other manufacturing	31,226			20,259	240,792[11]	31,665	121,127	19,000							1,041,863
TOTAL	611,255	85,609	69,865	2,436,609	2,711,516	163,168	612,173	392,302	133,626	29,197	266,573	188,721	443,554	73,344	29,481,198

1 As ranked by sales.
2 Including employment of one firm from Israel [34,200].
3 Including employment of one firm from New Zealand [22,785].
4 Including employment of one firm from Luxembourg [16,016].
5 Including employment of one firm each from Zaire [36,986] and Zambia [124,161].
6 Including employment of one firm from Ireland [12,119].
7 Including employment of one firm from Denmark [13,267].
8 Including employment of one firm from Greece [1,100].
9 Including employment of one firm from Portugal [7,094].
10 Including employment of one firm each from Argentina [32,773]; Colombia [7,916]; Kuwait [14,240]; Pakistan [1,927]; Peru [8,809]; Philippines [11,586] and Venezuela [44,475].
11 Including employment of one firm from Netherlands Antilles [69,000].

Source:— *Fortune* 30 April 1984 and 20 August 1984, organised as described in Part I. Includes authors' estimates for some firms.

Table 2.8
Rate of return on sales of the largest industrial firms,[1] 1983 by industry and country

	USA	Europe (total)	EEC (total)	Germany	France	Italy	Netherlands	Belgium	UK	UK-Netherlands	Other Europe (total)	Austria	Finland	Norway	Sweden
High Research Intensity															
Aerospace	3.7	−0.8	−0.8	1.2	0.0	7.9			−3.1						
Office equipment (incl. computers)	8.9	3.3	3.3	3.4	−5.4	4.1			4.5						
Electronics and electrical appliances	4.6	2.2	2.2	1.6	−0.3				5.6		2.0				1.4
Measurement, scientific and photographic equipment	5.8	1.1	1.1	1.1											
Industrial and agricultural chemicals	3.9	1.6	1.5	1.4	0.7	−3.0	1.7	2.2	4.1		2.6	0.6		1.6	2.6
Pharmaceuticals and consumer chemicals	8.9	12.2	5.4	1.9	4.4				7.9		25.6				0.5
Motor vehicles (incl. components)	4.3	−0.3	−0.2	1.3	−2.0				−2.3		−0.6	−1.9			
Total	5.5	1.7	1.3	1.4	−0.8	0.3	1.5	2.2	3.3		4.1	−0.6		1.6	0.8
Medium Research Intensity															
Industrial and farm equipment	−0.4	0.9	0.9	0.2	−3.0				2.5		1.0		0.8		1.6
Shipbuilding, railroad and transportation equipment	3.1	−3.3	−11.7						−11.7		3.7		2.1		5.0
Rubber	2.7	−5.7	−5.7	1.2	−5.3				−10.4						
Building materials	3.6	2.5	2.6	0.3	0.9				4.4		1.8				
Metal manufacturing and products	−1.9	−3.6	−3.9	0.3	−10.0	−18.3	0.1	−12.5	−5.1		−1.4	0.0	1.4	2.7	−1.1
Total	−0.2	−2.1	−2.5	0.3	−5.6	−18.3	0.1	−12.5	−2.0		0.1	0.0	1.4	2.7	1.4
Low Research Intensity															
Textiles, apparel and leather goods	4.3	1.4	1.2		0.7				1.3		1.9		−0.4		2.6
Paper and wood products	3.6	0.5	0.0	0.5					−0.5		1.1				2.7
Publishing and printing	7.6	2.2	2.1	0.4	3.5				5.7		2.7				0.4
Food	3.1	2.6	2.2		1.9		2.4		1.8	2.9	3.9				
Drink	6.0	6.1	6.1	0.1			5.6		6.3						
Tobacco	8.4	3.3	3.5		−1.7				3.9		0.6				
Total	4.4	2.8	2.8	0.4	1.7		3.5		3.1	2.9	2.9		−0.4		2.1
Petroleum	3.8	2.6	2.7	−0.7	1.6	3.4	3.1	3.2	3.5	5.2	1.9	0.0	0.3	5.2	1.3
Other manufacturing	−2.1	−0.6	−0.4	0.4					−2.3		−2.1				
TOTAL	4.1	1.4	1.2	0.9	−1.1	−3.5	1.7	−1.5	2.1	4.7	2.4	−0.1	0.4	3.2	1.2

Table 2.8 (cont.)

	Switzer-land	Spain	Turkey	Japan	Other Countries (total)	Australia	Canada	South Africa	Brazil	Chile	India	Mexico	South Korea	Taiwan	TOTAL
High Research Intensity															
Aerospace				4.3											2.9
Office equipment (incl. computers)				3.1											8.3
Electronics and electrical appliances	2.8			3.9	2.8		8.1						1.1		3.4
Measurement, scientific and photographic equipment		−8.0		1.2				7.9							5.3
Industrial and agricultural chemicals	5.3			3.9	4.0		1.2							5.3	2.5
Pharmaceuticals and consumer chemicals	25.6			2.4											9.1
Motor vehicles (incl. components)		−25.7	2.0												2.5
Total	11.9	−15.5	2.0	2.6	3.2		4.4	7.9					1.1	5.3	3.9
Medium Research Intensity															
Industrial and farm equipment	−1.0			2.3	−9.1		−9.1						1.4		0.4
Shipbuilding, railroad and transportation equipment				1.9	1.4										0.9
Rubber				1.0	2.5	2.5									0.4
Building materials	1.8	−19.1		2.3	2.8	0.4	5.7								2.9
Metal manufacturing and products	−1.1			1.2	2.8	5.1	−0.7	11.1	8.1	12.5	−0.4	0.0	1.8	−0.6	−1.4
Total	−0.6	−19.1		1.6	2.2	3.8	−0.8	11.1	8.1	12.5	−0.4	0.0	1.5	−0.6	−0.3
Low Research Intensity															
Textiles, apparel and leather goods			1.9	0.8	0.1		2.0						0.1		2.3
Paper and wood products				0.6	2.0	3.0	5.1								2.6
Publishing and printing				3.3	4.6	3.3	1.8								5.5
Food	4.2			0.7	2.7		7.0	3.0							2.7
Drink		0.6		3.8	7.0		7.7								6.0
Tobacco					5.7	2.7									6.0
Total	4.2	0.6	1.9	1.1	3.5	3.0	4.2	3.0					0.1		3.5
Petroleum	−2.1	0.5	7.8	1.3	−1.8	0.7	−9.2	15.5	3.0	6.0	1.7	0.0	0.8	8.1	2.7
Other manufacturing				0.5	8.8		1.1	30.4							1.7
TOTAL	6.4	−2.9	4.4	2.0	1.2	3.1	0.6	9.1	4.1	9.6	1.3	0.0	1.1	6.5	2.8

1   Data covers all firms from the 806 covered in Table 2.1 for which income data were available.

Source: *Fortune* 30 April 1984 and 20 August 1984, organised as described in Part I.

Table 2.9

Rate of return on assets of the largest industrial firms,[1] 1983, by industry and country

	USA	Europe (total)	EEC (total)	Germany	France	Italy	Netherlands	Belgium	UK	UK-Netherlands	Other Europe (total)	Austria	Finland	Norway	Sweden
High Research Intensity															
Aerospace	5.4	-0.6	-0.6	1.2	0.0				-3.7						
Office equipment (incl. computers)	8.9	3.3	3.3	3.7	-5.9				7.0						
Electronics and electrical appliances	5.6	2.3	2.4	1.7	-0.3	6.3	1.5		7.7		1.7				1.6
Measurement, scientific and photographic equipment	5.7	1.3	1.3	1.3											
Industrial and agricultural chemicals	4.0	2.1	2.0	2.1	0.7	-3.3	3.0	2.8	4.4		2.5	1.1		2.1	3.5
Pharmaceuticals and consumer chemicals	10.4	12.9	6.9	2.3	6.1				10.0		20.4				
Motor vehicles (incl. components)	7.3	-0.5	-0.4	2.1	-2.8				-3.1		-1.0	-2.1			0.8
Total	6.9	2.1	1.6	2.0	-0.8	-0.2	1.9	2.8	4.1		4.4	-0.9		2.1	1.2
Medium Research Intensity															
Industrial and farm equipment	-0.4	0.9	0.9	0.2	-1.3				3.0		1.0		1.0		1.6
Shipbuilding, railroad and transportation equipment	5.9	-3.4	-22.7						-22.7						
Rubber	3.9	-5.8	-5.8	2.3	-4.3				-15.5		2.8		1.4		4.1
Building materials	4.4	2.6	2.9		1.0				4.5		0.8				
Metal manufacturing and products	-2.0	-3.7	-4.2	0.4	-9.7		0.1	-16.8	-4.4		-1.4	0.0	1.4	3.3	-1.1
Total	-0.2	-2.0	-2.5	0.4	-5.1		0.1	-16.8	-2.0		0.1	0.0	1.3	3.3	1.3
Low Research Intensity															
Textiles, apparel and leather goods	6.9	2.1	2.0		1.1				2.2		2.1				2.4
Paper and wood products	3.6	0.5	0.0	0.8					-0.8		0.9				3.4
Publishing and printing	9.3	3.7	3.7	1.0	6.7				6.0		3.4		-0.3		1.3
Food	5.7	4.8	4.4		3.0		5.6		4.0	5.2	6.2				
Drink	8.7	6.1	6.1				5.5		6.2						
Tobacco	9.1	4.1	4.2	0.1	-1.6				4.7		1.9				
Total	6.2	4.2	4.3	0.7	2.6		5.5		4.5	5.2	3.7		-0.3		2.5
Petroleum	4.7	3.4	3.5	-1.8	2.0			4.9	4.5	5.9	3.1	0.0	0.5	4.4	1.8
Other manufacturing	-2.6	-0.5	-0.5	0.5		-4.6	11.8		-2.3						
TOTAL	5.1	1.7	1.5	1.3	-1.2	-3.2	2.2	-2.2	2.7	5.8	2.8	-0.2	0.4	3.4	1.4

Table 2.9 (cont.)

	Switzer-land	Spain	Turkey	Japan	Other Countries (total)	Australia	Canada	South Africa	Brazil	Chile	India	Mexico	South Korea	Taiwan	TOTAL
High Research Intensity															
Aerospace				4.2											3.8
Office equipment (incl. computers)	1.9			3.1	3.5		9.4	9.3					1.5		8.3
Electronics and electrical appliances				3.6											3.7
Measurement, scientific and photographic equipment				1.1			0.6							4.9	5.2
Industrial and agricultural chemicals	4.1	8.7		3.9	2.8										2.7
Pharmaceuticals and consumer chemicals	20.4			2.9											10.4
Motor vehicles (incl. components)		-13.4	5.5												3.7
Total	8.9	-11.6	5.5	2.8	3.1		3.0	9.3					1.5	4.9	4.6
Medium Research Intensity															
Industrial and farm equipment	-0.8			1.8	-7.4		-7.4						1.8		0.4
Shipbuilding, railroad and transportation equipment				1.1	1.8										1.0
Rubber				1.2	4.7	4.7	4.5								0.5
Building materials	0.8			1.9	2.1	0.7									2.9
Metal manufacturing and products	-0.9	-9.3		0.9	1.5	3.2	-0.4	8.4	2.5	7.0	-0.2	0.0	1.4	-0.2	-1.1
Total	-0.4	-9.3		1.2	1.5	3.1	0.5	8.4	2.5	7.0	-0.2	0.0	1.7	-0.2	-0.2
Low Research Intensity															
Textiles, apparel and leather goods			2.1	0.8	0.1		2.0						0.1		3.0
Paper and wood products				0.6	2.0		7.6								2.6
Publishing and printing				4.6	6.7		5.9								7.5
Food	6.4			1.5	4.1	4.1	3.4	4.0							4.9
Drink					3.4	3.4	10.6								6.3
Tobacco		1.9		3.4	8.4	4.5									7.1
Total	6.4	1.9	2.1	1.4	3.9	3.8	4.2	4.0					0.1		4.9
Petroleum		1.0	9.4	2.1	-1.6		-4.2	13.9	3.5		2.7	0.0	1.4	10.8	3.2
Other manufacturing				0.7	5.8	0.7	0.8	9.6							1.7
TOTAL	6.2	-4.6	6.4	2.1	0.9	3.0	0.4	7.8	3.0	7.0	1.3	0.0	1.5	6.0	3.3

1 Data covers all firms from the 806 covered in Table 2.1 for which asset and income data were available.

Source:– *Fortune* 30 April and 20 August 1984, organised as described in Part I.

41

PART III Changes in the sample composition 1962–82

In this part, we look at the ways in which the composition of the world's largest industrial enterprises has evolved over the period 1962–82. We describe the changes in the shares of enterprises of different nationalities, and in those of particular industries; we also examine the extent to which there have been shifts in the industrial specialisation of different areas and countries. We should, at this point, emphasise that the growth of the $ value of the sales of individual firms will be influenced by differential rates of inflation between countries and by exchange-rate changes. In particular, this will tend to affect the composition of samples at the margin. Further reference to this factor will be made in parts IV and VI.

Tables 3.1 and 3.2 provide information on the geographical and industrial composition of the rationalised samples from 1962 to 1982. This information is provided here since it is the firms from these rationalised samples that are used for the analysis of parts VI, VII and VIII; it is also of some interest in the context of the discussion of this part. However, our main analysis utilises the equalised samples, that is, the 483 largest firms in each year, since the steadily increasing size of the rationalised sample is likely to distort the results.[1]

(a) THE GEOGRAPHICAL ORIGIN OF ENTERPRISES (Table 3.3)

Of the largest 483 industrial enterprises in the world in 1962 and 1982, those of US origin fell from 292 (60.5 per cent) to 213 (44.1 per cent). The US share of the sales of these 483 companies also decreased over the 20 years, from 67.6 per cent to 49.2 per cent. Though this decline seems to have persisted throughout the period, it was most notable during the quinquennia 1967–72 and, particularly in terms of numbers of firms, between 1977 and 1982.

The number of European firms in the equalised sample fell from 142 in 1962 to 136 in 1967, but a substantial recovery then followed with the original number being regained by 1977 and a new high of 147 achieved in 1982. Sales data for European firms show the same general pattern, but with a more immediate and pronounced recovery of share. Thus, following a fall from 26.7 per cent of the equalised sample sales in 1962 to 25.1 per cent in 1967, European firms reached a new high of 28.9 per cent as early as 1972, this rising to 31.5 per cent by the end of the 20-year period.

The share of equalised sample sales accounted for by German firms was virtually the same in 1982 (6.7 per cent) as in 1962 (6.8 per cent), with falls in the first and last quinquennia cancelling out a rise during the middle decade, most notably from 1967 (5.2 per cent) to 1972 (7.1 per cent). The French firms' share of equalised sample sales rose consistently over the first 15 years of the period, from 3.3 per cent to 5.3 per cent, almost retaining the latter level in

---

1   For example, if a country or industry has a larger share of the smaller firms in our sample than the average, then a substantial expansion of the rationalised sample over a five-year period (such as occurred from 1967–72 and again from 1972–77) will increase the share of that country or industry in that sample; this, then, will not necessarily be due to above-average performance by that industry or country but rather to wider data coverage.

42

1982. A factor common to both French and German firms is that their performance over the 20 years in terms of share of sample sales was superior to that in terms of numbers of firms. This suggests increasing size concentration among the largest enterprises of these countries, as compared to that of the whole equalised sample.

For UK firms, the basic picture is of a severe and sustained decline from 1967 to 1977 (from 51 firms to 38 and from 8.3 per cent of equalised sample sales to 6.3 per cent) followed by a major recovery in 1977–82, with both numbers of firms (47 in 1982) and sales share (8.0 per cent) returned to only slightly below the 1962 level. In view of the notably poor performance of the UK economy in terms of real output growth in recent years, this recovery of UK firms in our sample would appear surprising. Two possible explanations may be noted. First, the distorting influence of inflation and exchange-rate changes may have worked to the particular favour of UK firms in this period.[1] This possibility will be subjected to scrutiny in Part IV. Secondly, in view of the extensive international commitment of the UK firms in our sample, as described in Part VII, it may be that leading UK firms have performed much better in recent years than the UK economy as a whole by virtue of their overseas operations.

Finally, in relation to other European firms, the rise in numbers of firms from smaller countries, for example, Sweden, Spain and Turkey, during the decade 1967–77 should be noted, along with the modest reversal of this trend during the most recent five-year period (despite the arrival of two Norwegian firms in the sample).

The contribution of Japanese firms to our sample of the world's largest enterprises has increased dramatically during the two decades covered. In 1962, there were 29 Japanese enterprises in the equalised sample of 483 (that is, 6.0 per cent), which accounted for 3.6 per cent of the total sample sales. By 1982 the number had risen to 79 (16.4 per cent) and the share of sales to 12.1 per cent. It is, however, interesting to note that the increase in the Japanese involvement has been concentrated in the first decade and, to a lesser degree, in the last five years.

Alongside Japan, the other major source of new firms in the equalised sample is the 'other countries' group, though here, by contrast to Japan, the rise is mainly concentrated in the second decade covered. Over the whole period, the number of 'other countries' firms rose from 20 in 1962 (17 from Canada, Australia and South Africa) to 44 in 1982 (20 from Canada, Australia and South Africa). Thus the reported pattern reflects predominantly the arrival of a large number of firms from LDCs, often from the state-owned petroleum sector (though the South Korean firms included represent a more diversified range of activity). On the basis of sales, the 'other countries' group accounted for 2.2 per cent of equalised sample sales in 1962, for 2.7 per cent in 1972 and for 7.3 per cent in 1982. Within the 'other countries' group Canada, Australia and South Africa together accounted for 84.9 per cent of sales in 1962, for 63.2 per cent in 1972 and 31.5 per cent in 1982, this fall reflecting the rise of LDC enterprises.

(b) INDUSTRIAL COMPOSITION (Table 3.4)

In discussing the industrial composition of the equalised sample over the period 1962–82, attention must be first directed to the increase in the share of both numbers and sales of enterprises in the 'petroleum' industry since 1972. After generally maintaining its position in the sample between 1962 and 1972, this sector increased its number of entries from 40 in 1972 (36 in 1962) to 54 in 1977 and to 71 in 1982. Similarly the 'petroleum' industry's share of equalised sample sales rose from 15.6 per cent in 1972 (the same as in 1962) to 24.2 per cent in 1977 and 32.0 per cent in 1982. In addition to reflecting underlying trends of real economic importance, this development considerably affects our interpretation of the performance of *other* industries over the last decade. Thus, to accommodate for the doubling in the share of (what was already in 1972) the largest industry in the sample, virtually all other sectors had to suffer some decline in their contribution to total sales between 1972 and 1982. Close observation of Table 3.4 immediately suggests that several industries which would otherwise have increased their share of sales in the second decade did not do so because of the

1 By the same token these factors could have contributed to the pronounced decline from 1972–77, though this was less at variance with intuitive expectations.

immense growth in the 'petroleum' sector. Analysis of the sales figures excluding 'petroleum' will allow a less distorted impression of the relative achievements of the other industries. Thus, in the discussion below we review each industry's share of the total sales of all equalised sample industries *except* 'petroleum'.

In addition to 'petroleum', six other industries can be loosely categorised as 'increasing share industries' (ISI) over the period 1962–82. Predictably four of these industries, 'office equipment (including computers)', 'electronics and electrical appliances', 'industrial and agricultural chemicals' and 'pharmaceuticals and consumer chemicals', are 'high research intensity' (HRI) industries, whose growth has been based on the successful marketing of a sustained sequence of new products. Less predictably, and somewhat more tentatively, we also characterise as ISIs two of the 'low research intensity' (LRI) industries. The first of these is 'publishing and printing', where a number of leading firms have achieved a healthy growth through successful diversification into the computer-based collection, analysis and dissemination of business and financial information, and into radio and TV, both being activities complementary to their existing media expertise and their reporting networks. Similarly, the 'drink' sector achieved status as an ISI, again perhaps due to a successful extension of activity by several leading beverage firms into related service areas of the leisure industries.

Seven industries seem to be most suitably characterised as being 'stable share industries' (SSI). Three of the seven SSIs are from the HRI group of industries. One of them, 'measurement, scientific and photographic equipment', seems to be a clear-cut case of little change in share, but the other two, 'aerospace' and 'motor vehicles', merit some discussion. In one respect delineation of 'aerospace' as an SSI is, perhaps, the easiest compromise description of a very volatile and seemingly arbitrary series of sales share figures. However, this *is* an industry dependent on a relatively small number of very large purchasing decisions geared to defence budgets and space programmes, and to the timing of fleet renewals by quite a small number of major airlines. The allocation of 'motor vehicles' to the SSIs is based upon the relative constancy of the shares for 1962, 1967 and 1982, with the implied assumption that the significantly higher shares recorded by this industry in 1972 and 1977 represent a temporary boom, a repetition of which is not immediately likely.

Two 'medium research intensity' (MRI) industries, 'industrial and farm equipment' and 'building materials', seem to be fairly reliably allocated to the SSI group. The last two SSIs are 'paper and wood products' and 'tobacco', both of which do have notably stable shares from 1962–77, though the former has a decline, and the latter a rise, in the last quinquennium of a size which could presage a change of trend.

The remaining five industries are characterised as 'declining share industries' (DSI). In the case of 'rubber', the decline in share has persisted steadily throughout the period, while for 'textiles, apparel and leather goods' perceptible declines in share in the first decade noticeably steepened in the second half of the 20-year period. For both 'food' and 'shipbuilding, railroad and transportation equipment', the more notable declines took place between 1962 and 1972, though in both cases the 1982 share was also lower than that for 1972. Finally, in the case of 'metals', the share in 1982 was considerably lower than in 1962, though the most significant declines were concentrated in the first and last quinquennia.

With four of its seven industries characterised as ISI, and the other three as SSI, the HRI industries are clearly the most growth-oriented group. In fact, their share of 'petroleum'-excluded equalised sample sales rose from 46.2 per cent in 1962 to 54.1 per cent in 1982, with increases in each five-year period (though only marginally in that between 1967 and 1972). Further, and despite the vast rise in 'petroleum' firms, the number of HRI industry firms in the equalised sample rose by 19 over the two decades (compared with falls of 35 for MRI and 21 for LRI).

Predictably, with its three DSI and two SSI, most of the compensating decline in equalised sample sales share ('petroleum' excluded) occurred among the MRI industry grouping, in fact from 28.4 per cent in 1962 to 22.9 per cent in 1982, with the decline exceeding 1 per cent in each five-year period except 1972–77.

With two each of ISI, DSI and SSI, the sales share changes of the LRI industries are less dramatic than for the HRI and MRI industries. A fairly steady fall from 22.5 per cent in 1962 to 19.1 per cent in 1977, is partially offset by a recovery to 20.0 per cent in 1982 (mainly due to the 'drink' and 'tobacco' industries).

(c)   CHANGES IN SPECIALISATION 1962–82 (tables 3.5 to 3.8)

In interpreting the changes in industrial specialisation of particular areas or countries over the 20-year period, it is important to recognise the influence of increases or decreases in those subsamples. Any increase in the number of firms in the subsample of a particular area or country will tend to give a distorted picture by altering the industry specialisation in that country or area. Thus, if a country sample of firms increased by, say, one, the industry of that firm will receive a boost which may overstate its increased role in the activity of the largest firms in that country. Any such bias will be less the larger the size of the subsample and the smaller the change in the number of firms in that subsample. However, even in a sample of constant numbers of firms, changes in the composition of these firms at the margin may exaggerate changes in industrial specialisation. For example, the entry and/or exit of firms from a particular industry may also affect the share of the total sales accounted for by that industry. Once more this bias will be less the larger the sample. Because of this, only countries with a reasonably large number of firms in the equalised sample are analysed at all closely.

We should also note that, as in section (b) above, the most realistic assessment of the changing contribution of a particular industry to an area's activity (that is, its role in that area's industrial specialisation) is obtained after excluding the 'petroleum' sector from the total figures. Otherwise, for several areas, virtually all other industries would appear to be squeezed into a declining role.

The data of Table 3.7 show that, on a 'petroleum'-excluded basis, there was a strong tendency for the USA to increase its specialisation in the HRI industries over the 1962-82 period. Thus these seven industries accounted for 49.1 per cent of US non-'petroleum' equalised sample sales in 1962, for 53.7 per cent in 1972 and for 58.1 per cent in 1982. Six of the seven industries had a higher sales share in 1982 than 1962, the exception being 'motor vehicles', where there was a substantial decline concentrated in the second decade. For three HRI industries ('office equipment', 'measurement, scientific and photographic equipment' and 'pharmaceuticals and consumer chemicals') the increasing role was sustained throughout the period, while for 'electronics and electrical appliances' and 'industrial and agricultural chemicals' the most notable increase occurred in the first decade, the higher level of 1972 then being held in 1982. Finally, 'aerospace' manifests the type of volatility discussed in section (b), recording its highest share of equalised sample sales in 1982 after its lowest share in 1972.

For the USA, the major part of the declining specialisation occurred in the MRI industries. These five industries accounted for 26.0 per cent of non-'petroleum' equalised sample sales in 1962, for 20.5 per cent in 1972 and for only 17.0 per cent in 1982. All five industries had lower sales shares in 1982 than in 1962, the decline being considerable and sustained for all these industries, except 'industrial and farm equipment', where the fall was least and occurred entirely between 1962 and 1972.

As a whole, the LRI industries retained a virtually unchanged role in US industrial specialisation, accounting for 23.1 per cent of non-'petroleum' equalised sample sales in 1982 compared with 23.0 per cent in 1962 and 22.1 per cent in 1972. Despite this, three of the seven industries have increased their role — 'publishing and printing', whose growth in share was small but sustained; 'drink', where increase was concentrated on the period 1962–72, and 'tobacco', where the greatest growth in share occurred from 1972 to 1982. The most sustained decline was that of 'textiles, apparel and leather goods', while 'paper and wood products' had the same share in 1982 as in 1962, and 'food' a somewhat lower share, despite some recovery between 1972 and 1982.

As we have seen from Table 3.3, the US share of equalised sample sales declined from 1962 to 1982, and Table 3.8 reveals that this decline was reflected at the level of virtually every sector. In fact, over the two decade period, US firms recorded some decline in prominence in all industries except 'office equipment', though in some cases this was relatively small (for example, 'aerospace' and 'drink'), whilst in another ('pharmaceuticals and consumer chemicals') significant recovery in the period 1972–82 offset part of a 1962–72 decline.

Like the USA, Europe increased its specialisation in HRI industries over the period.1962–82. The HRI industries accounted for 42.0 per cent of non-'petroleum' equalised sample sales in 1962, 48.9 per cent in 1972 and 51.5 per cent in 1982. Among the individual countries,[1] specialisation in HRI industries increased most notably for Germany, Italy and Sweden and diminished for the UK.

The two HRI industries where European firms seem to have most strongly increased their specialisation are 'industrial and agricultural chemicals' (where a notable increase in specialisation is recorded by Germany, a marginal increase by the UK, and a decline by France) and 'motor vehicles' (with significant rises in specialisation by Germany, Italy and Sweden and a notable decline by the UK). For 'electronics and electrical appliances' there was a slight increase in specialisation by Europe as a whole, with the most perceptible trend for any individual country being an increase by France. For Europe as a whole, there was a small increase in specialisation in 'pharmaceuticals and consumer chemicals' and a very marginal decline in 'office equipment'. 'Aerospace' was, as usual, volatile, though a sustained decline in UK specialisation is suggested.

Again, as was the case for the USA, the majority of the decline in specialisation in Europe, required to compensate for the increase in specialisation in HRI industries, occurs in the MRI industries. These five industries accounted for 32.6 per cent of European non-'petroleum' equalised sample sales in 1962, for 28.6 per cent in 1972 and for 25.9 per cent in 1982. Generally this decline in specialisation persists at the national level, though least strongly for the UK.

The one MRI industry where there is some increase in European specialisation is 'building materials', which claims an increasing share of both UK and French sales. The strongest tendency towards decreasing specialisation is found in 'rubber' and 'metals' (where declining specialisation is clear for France, Germany and the UK). A much more marginal decline in European specialisation in 'industrial and farm equipment' is indicated.

In 1962, the six LRI industries accounted for 20.9 per cent of European non-'petroleum' sales, this falling to 18.6 per cent in 1972 and then partially recovering to 19.5 per cent in 1982. The most notable feature about these sectors is the strong increase in UK specialisation from an already high level of commitment in 1962. This arises primarily as a result of notable increases in specialisation in 'food', 'drink' and 'tobacco', offsetting diminished specialisation in the other three LRI industries.

For Europe as a whole, specialisation increases in 'drink' and 'tobacco', remains more or less constant in 'food', falls strongly in 'textiles, apparel and leather goods' and more marginally in 'paper and wood products' and in 'publishing and printing'.

Table 3.8 shows that, between 1962 and 1982, European firms increased their share of sales in 14 industries, and most notably in 'industrial and agricultural chemicals', 'motor vehicles' and 'building materials'. The European share of activity declined in five industries, of which the most significant falls were recorded by 'office equipment' and 'publishing and printing'.

Japan's specialisation in HRI industries increased notably between 1972 and 1982, having diminished slightly in the previous decade. In the latter year, these industries accounted for 59.2 per cent of Japan's non-'petroleum' sales compared with 50.1 per cent in 1972 and 52.4 per cent in 1962. This owes most to increasing specialisation in 'industrial and agricultural chemicals' and 'motor vehicles', offsetting a decline in specialisation in 'electronics and electrical appliances'.

The compensating decline in specialisation required to allow for the rise in HRI industries is shared between MRI and LRI industries (rather than being concentrated on the former as for USA and Europe), and in both cases occurs solely in the second decade of our period.[2] For the 11 industries in these groups pronounced declines in specialisation were recorded by 'metals' and 'textiles, apparel and leather goods', and probably for 'shipbuilding, railroad and transportation equipment' (there a notable rise in sales share between 1962 and 1972 was followed by an even larger decline between 1972 and 1982). The data of Table 3.7 suggest that 'paper and wood products' and 'publishing and printing' are areas of small, but notably increasing,

---

1   Due to the problems of small sample size noted above, extreme care must be taken in interpreting changes in industrial specialisation for individual European countries from Table 3.7. Here only the more important, and seemingly strongly documented, trends are reported.

2   MRI industries accounted for 32.1 per cent of Japan's non-'petroleum' equalised sample sales in 1962, for 32.9 per cent in 1972 and 27.4 per cent in 1982. For the LRI industries the comparable shares were 15.6 per cent, 16.9 per cent and 12.3 per cent.

specialisation for Japanese firms. Among the MRI and LRI industries in which Japan is significantly represented, there is some suggestion of increasing specialisation in 'industrial and farm equipment' and in 'food'.

Table 3.8 shows that in each of the 18 industries in which it had some representation in the equalised sample in 1982, Japan had increased its representation (in terms of share of each industry's sales) between 1962 and 1982. In three cases ('pharmaceuticals and consumer chemicals', 'shipbuilding, railroad and transportation equipment', and 'drink') some fall in share had occurred in the second decade, but not sufficiently to offset the previous increase. It is, of course, reflective of the general Japanese growth in the equalised sample that it substantially increased its share of sales in several industries which were among its own areas of decreased specialisation – notably 'electronics and electical appliances', 'metals' and 'textiles, apparel and leather goods'.

Finally, in this section, we seek an alternative perspective on the comparative specialisation of areas and countries, by grouping industries according to their changing share of equalised sample sales. Thus above we delineated seven industries which we classified as 'increasing share industries' (ISI),[1] a further seven which were 'stable share industries' (SSI),[2] and a last five which were 'declining share industries' (DSI).[3] If we consider the first group to consist of the most dynamic sectors with the most buoyant future, and the last group as comprising the least dynamic industries with a future of relative decline, then we may consider a country's relative specialisation between these groupings as an indication of its industrial health and prospects.

In 1982 the USA had a relatively high proportion (60 per cent) of its equalised sample sales in the ISIs and only 16 per cent in the DSIs. As is to be expected, the ISIs' share had risen from 38 per cent in 1962, while the DSIs' had fallen from 29 per cent. It is interesting to note that the substantial fall in US firms' overall representation in the sample (Table 3.3) has occurred despite what seems to be a basically favourable industrial specialisation, and also despite reorientation of that specialisation towards the growth industries.

For European firms, 53 per cent of sales in 1982 were in ISIs (up from 38 per cent in 1962) and 22 per cent in DSIs (down from 35 per cent). Of the individual countries, Italy had the most favourable industry mix in 1982, in the sense we have defined it, with 61 per cent of the sales of its firms in ISIs and 10 per cent in DSIs, but it should be noted that this is based on a rather small sample. The UK achieved quite a substantial rise in the share of its sales in ISIs, from 30 per cent in 1962 to 46 per cent in 1982, but was less successful in lessening its commitment to the DSIs with a fall from 27 per cent to 24 per cent. Quite similarly to the UK, France had 47 per cent of its sales in ISIs in 1982 (a somewhat smaller rise from 38 per cent) and 20 per cent of its sales in DSI (again a relatively small decline from 25 per cent). Germany's relatively small shift into ISI (up from 35 per cent to 42 per cent) over the period is seen to be more impressive once it is noted that it was achieved despite a decline in its spcialisation in 'petroleum'. Another notable change in specialisation for Germany was the fall in DSI sales from 40 per cent in 1962 to 24 per cent in 1982, which compares favourably with the relatively stable commitment to these industries reported for the UK and France.

In 1982, 43 per cent of Japanese firms' sample sales were in ISIs, following a rise from 36 per cent in 1962. The share of sales accounted for by DSIs had fallen to 25 per cent in 1982, from 43 per cent in 1962. From this we may infer that the impressive growth in Japanese representation in the equalised sample reported in Table 3.3 is mainly due to overall performance by Japanese firms rather than to a favourable industrial structure or to a particularly growth-industry-oriented reformation of that industrial structure.

1   'Office equipment (including computers)', 'electronics and electrical appliances', 'industrial and agricultural chemicals', 'pharmaceuticals and consumer chemicals', 'publishing and printing', 'drink', 'petroleum'.
2   'Aerospace', 'measurement, scientific and photographic equipment', 'motor vehicles', 'industrial and farm equipment', 'building materials', 'paper and wood products', 'tobacco'.
3   'Shipbuilding, railroad and transportation equipment', 'rubber', 'metal manufacture and products', 'textiles, apparel and leather goods', 'food'.

(d) GOVERNMENT-OWNED FIRMS (GOFs) IN THE EQUALISED SAMPLE, 1962–82

Government-owned firms (GOFs) have steadily increased their role in the sample of 483 firms. In 1962 there were 14 GOFs accounting for 2.4 per cent of the sales. By 1967 the number had risen to 21 and the share of sales to 3.2 per cent, and this was followed by a further rise to 23 firms and 3.8 per cent of sales in 1972. The second decade of the period, however, saw a much more dramatic rise in the contribution of GOFs. During the period 1972–77 their number rose to 36, and their share of sales to 6.6 per cent. In the last quinquennium this rate of growth was continued, and by 1982 there were 50 GOFs among equalised sample firms, which accounted for 10.4 per cent of the total sales.

In 1962 the GOFs were dominated by Europe, which accounted for 12 of the 14 firms and for 90 per cent of the GOF sales. Thus, 12 of Europe's 142 firms in the equalised sample (that is, 8.5 per cent) were government owned in 1962, these accounting for 8.0 per cent of European sales. France and Germany contributed three GOFs each and the UK two in 1962. The two non-European GOFs in 1962 were of Mexican and South African origin, and they accounted for 11.0 per cent of sales of the 'other countries' group.

By 1972, the European dominance of GOFs had lessened somewhat, its share now being 16 out of 23 (69.6 per cent) and 80.6 per cent of GOF sales. However, at the same time, GOFs had increased their share of the European part of the equalised sample with 16 out of 139 firms (11.5 per cent) and 10.5 per cent of sales. In 1972 France had four GOFs in the equalised sample and the UK, Germany and Italy three each. 'Other countries' GOFs increased their share not only of total GOFs but also of total 'other countries' firm sales, to 28.7 per cent in 1972. The seven 'other countries' GOFs came from seven different countries, Brazil, Argentina, India, Chile and Zambia having added representatives since 1962.

The period 1972–77 saw the number of European GOFs in the equalised sample increase from 16 to 25 (or 17.6 per cent of the 142 European firms), with sales of 14.7 per cent of total European sales. In 1977, the UK had five GOFs in the equalised sample, France four, and Germany, Italy and Spain three each. By contrast, with the increasing role of GOFs in the European subsample, the role of European firms in the GOF subsample was one of relative decline, at least in terms of sales share (68.6 per cent in 1977 compared with 80.6 per cent in 1972). The most dramatic change between 1972 and 1977 was the relative role of GOFs in the 'other countries' subsample, especially on the sales basis. Thus, the 11 'other countries' GOFs were 32.4 per cent of the 34 'other countries' firms in 1977 and accounted for 45.7 per cent of their sales. These 11 'other countries' GOFs originated from nine countries (India and Brazil each having two representatives).

The substantial rise of GOFs in the 1972–77 period persisted through the following quinquennium, though some of the underlying influences were different. In particular, in these latter years, the emphasis reverted somewhat back to Europe. Thus, European GOFs rose from 25 to 36 (or 24.5 per cent of the 147 European firms in the equalised sample); these 36 GOFs accounting for 22.3 per cent of European firm sales in the equalised sample in 1982 (compared with 14.7 per cent in 1977). As a result of this, European GOFs virtually held their share of all GOF sales (67.5 per cent in 1982 compared with 68.6 per cent in 1977) after 15 years of steady decline (from 90 per cent in 1962). The major contributing factor to this rise was, of course, the substantial nationalisation programme carried out in France. Thus, in 1982 there were 12 French GOFs in the equalised sample, accounting for 29.0 per cent of total GOF sales. In 1977 four French GOFs had accounted for 19.8 per cent of GOF sales. The UK had five GOFs in 1982, Italy four, and Germany three.

In 1982 there were 14 GOFs from 'other countries' in the equalised sample, three more than in 1977. Nevertheless, just as the substantial growth of European GOFs checked the rising proportion of 'other countries' GOFs in all GOFs, the addition of a number of extra privately owned 'other countries' enterprises to the equalised sample between 1977 and 1982 (notably from South Korea) slowed the rise of GOFs amongst total 'other countries' firms. Thus the 14 'other countries' GOFs were 31.8 per cent of all 'other countries' firms (compared with 32.4 per cent in 1977) and accounted for 47.6 per cent of all 'other countries' firm's sales (compared with 45.7 per cent in 1977). India and Brazil were still the only countries of this group with two GOFs in the equalised sample.

The two industries which dominated the GOF group during the years 1962–82 were 'metals' and 'petroleum'. In 1962, 'metals' accounted for five of the 14 GOFs (35.7 per cent) and for 19.3 per cent of GOF sales. By 1972, nine of the 23 GOFs were from the 'metals' industry (39.1 per cent), these accounting for 32.4 per cent of total GOF sales. Though 'metals' further increased its number of GOFs to 15 in 1982, the vast rise of 'petroleum' sales over the decade resulted in a *relatively* smaller contribution from 'metals', its 15 firms representing 30.0 per cent of the 50 GOFs in 1982 and 16.9 per cent of their sales. Government-owned 'metals' firms have increased their rate steadily among all 'metals' firms over the period. In 1962, the five government-owned 'metals' firms came from a total of 88 'metals' firms (5.7 per cent) and accounted for 3.2 per cent of total 'metals' firm sales. By 1982 the total number of 'metals' firms in the equalised sample had fallen to 66, but now 15 of these (22.7 per cent) were GOFs and these 15 accounted for 18.8 per cent of the sales of the 66.

In 1962 there were three government-owned 'petroleum' firms in the equalised sample (21.4 per cent of the 14 GOFs), and these accounted for 18.1 per cent of GOF sales. By 1972 the number had risen to five out of 23 GOFs (21.7 per cent) and these accounted for 29.1 per cent of GOF sales. The rise over the next decade was much more dramatic, to 12 firms in 1977 (33.3 per cent of the 36 GOFs) and to 19 in 1982 (38.0 per cent of the 50 GOFs). Government-owned 'petroleum' firms accounted for 46.4 per cent of all GOF sales in 1977 and 53.2 per cent in 1982. Similar increases in the role of GOFs in total 'petroleum' activity are found. The three government-owned 'petroleum' firms in 1962 were 8.3 per cent of the total number of 'petroleum' firms in the equalised sample (36) and accounted for 2.7 per cent of their sales. By 1972 GOFs accounted for five out of 40 'petroleum' firms (12.5 per cent) and for 7.0 per cent of their sales. By 1982 the total number of 'petroleum' firms in the equalised sample had risen to 71 of which 19 were government-owned (26.8 per cent); these 19 accounted for 17.3 per cent of the total sales.

As illustrated in the discussion above, two types of factor have contributed to the rise in GOFs. First, the share of equalised sample activity accounted for by GOFs will increase if an industry in which government ownership is already prominent increases its contribution to the equalised sample, as a result of an above-average growth rate of activity in that industry. Here firms which are *already* government owned enter the sample by displacing, mainly, privately owned firms, thus increasing the share of GOFs. The growth of 'petroleum' has operated in that way. Secondly, the share of GOFs will rise if firms already in the sample under private ownership are nationalised. The case of France in recent years has provided the most concentrated example of this influence.

(e) EMPLOYMENT OF THE EQUALISED SAMPLE

In the next part of this volume we will discuss samples of firms ranked by employment rather than by sales. However, it might be of some general interest to trace the evolution of the aggregate employment of the 483 firms in the equalised sample during the period 1962—82. The equalised sample firms employed 17.3 million workers in 1962. In the next five years the number rose steadily to 21.5 million and then to 25.2 million in 1972. This 46 per cent rise in employment over the 1962—72 period is not surprising, bearing in mind the relative fast rate of growth of the world economy during that decade and the fact that the equalised sample not only includes many of the world's most progressive enterprises but also allows for changes in its composition so that more dynamic firms enter to replace those in relative decline. However, this rate of growth did not persist far beyond 1972, though equalised-sample employment was again higher in 1977 at 26.5 million. Finally, although a fall in employment to 25.8 million occurred between 1977 and 1982, the total labour force of the world's largest industrial enterprises is still 2 per cent higher than it was at the start of the very difficult decade.

Table 3.1

Countries of origin of the rationalised sample, 1962 to 1982, numbers of firms and sales

	Number of firms					Sales $ million					Per cent distribution of sales				
	1962	1967	1972	1977	1982	1962	1967	1972	1977	1982	1962	1967	1972	1977	1982
USA	297	283	336	409	330	203,315	314,665	507,559	1,035,359	1,533,212	67.3	66.9	58.0	53.1	47.8
Europe	149	136	186	273	256	81,138	117,176	254,325	608,742	1,020,945	26.9	24.9	29.1	31.2	31.9
EEC[1]	134	121	160	203	195	74,910	108,605	230,146	517,930	869,488	24.8	23.1	26.3	26.6	27.1
Germany	36	25	43	53	52	20,618	24,584	62,758	141,392	214,187	6.8	5.2	7.2	7.3	6.7
France	27	23	31	37	38	9,975	16,804	39,777	100,069	161,869	3.3	3.6	4.5	5.1	5.1
Italy	7	8	7	10	11	4,563	8,932	13,327	37,657	64,178	1.5	1.9	1.5	1.9	2.0
Netherlands	4	5	8	12	8	2,520	4,240	13,645	31,012	34,656	0.8	0.9	1.6	1.6	1.1
Belgium	3	3	5	10	4	995	1,797	5,174	13,934	18,294	0.3	0.4	0.6	0.7	0.6
Luxembourg	1	1	1	1		700	957	1,744	941	1,073	0.2	0.2	0.2	0.0	0.0
UK	54	53	61	73	77	25,381	37,001	67,339	130,891	263,349	8.4	7.9	7.7	6.7	8.2
Denmark				4	1				2,156	794				0.1	0.0
Germany/Belgium															
Italy/Switzerland		1	1		1		354	712		4,209		0.1	0.1		0.1
UK/Italy															
UK/Netherlands	2	2	2	2	2	10,158	13,936	22,924	55,645	106,879	3.4	3.0	2.6	2.9	3.3
Other Europe	15	15	26	70	61	6,228	8,571	24,179	90,812	151,457	2.1	1.8	2.8	4.7	4.7
Austria	1	1	2	4	3	223	285	889	4,469	9,511	0.1	0.1	0.1	0.2	0.3
Finland				6	8				5,357	10,853				0.3	0.3
Greece					1					1,124					0.0
Norway					3					6,656					0.2
Sweden	8	5	13	28	20	2,485	2,585	9,758	32,199	46,942	0.8	0.5	1.1	1.7	1.5
Switzerland	6	8	8	14	12	3,520	5,420	12,040	28,840	44,155	1.2	1.2	1.4	1.5	1.4
Portugal		1	1	1	1		281	599	837	2,454		0.1	0.1	0.0	0.1
Spain			2	10	10			893	11,091	19,254			0.1	0.6	0.6
Turkey				3	3				5,487	10,508				0.3	0.3
Japan	31	43	79	116	133	10,962	27,725	87,428	206,256	409,875	3.6	5.9	10.0	10.6	12.8
Other Countries	20	21	35	67	73	6,488	11,018	25,430	98,634	240,283	2.1	2.3	2.9	5.1	7.5
Australia	2	2	4	4	6	758	1,491	3,574	5,921	14,328	0.3	0.3	0.4	0.3	0.4
Canada	13	11	20	28	26	4,307	6,102	12,919	33,305	59,857	1.4	1.3	1.5	1.7	1.9
New Zealand					1					1,524					0.0
South Africa	2	2	2	6	6	443	771	1,338	7,056	14,227	0.1	0.2	0.2	0.4	0.4
Netherlands Antilles	1	1	1	2	2	267	369	792	3,415	7,253	0.1	0.1	0.1	0.2	0.2
Israel				1	1				1,310	2,900				0.1	0.1
Argentina		2	1		1		702	917		4,455		0.1	0.1		0.1
Brazil		1	1	6	5		507	1,531	12,439	24,001		0.1	0.2	0.6	0.7
Chile			1	1	1			628	1,231	3,045			0.1	0.1	0.1
Colombia					1					2,152					0.1
India	1	1	2	3	2	173	277	1,295	4,288	10,557	0.1	0.1	0.1	0.2	0.3
Indonesia			1					600					0.1		
Kuwait				1	1				1,376	12,234				0.1	0.4
Mexico	1	1	1	2	3	540	799	1,318	3,997	16,869	0.2	0.2	0.2	0.2	0.5
Panama					1					808					0.0
Peru					1					1,396					0.0
Philippines					1					2,890					0.1
South Korea				9	9				9,900	37,135				0.5	1.2
Taiwan				1	2				1,920	7,236				0.1	0.2
Venezuela				1	2				9,628	17,416				0.5	0.5
Zambia			1	1				518	1,862				0.1	0.1	
TOTAL	497	483	636	865	792	301,903	470,584	874,742	1,948,991	3,204,315	100.0	100.0	100.0	100.0	100.0

1 The listed countries are treated as having constituted the EEC throughout the period 1962–82. See comment in Part I.

Source: *Fortune* July and August 1963; June and September 1968; May and September 1973; 8 May and 14 August 1978; 2 May and 22 August 1983.

Table 3.2

Industrial composition of the rationalised sample, 1962–82, number of firms and sales

	Number of firms					Sales $ million					Per cent distribution of sales				
	1962	1967	1972	1977	1982	1962	1967	1972	1977	1982	1962	1967	1972	1977	1982
High Research Intensity															
Aerospace	15	15	19	19	22	12,081	20,294	22,818	41,747	90,387	4.0	4.3	2.6	2.1	2.8
Office equipment (incl. computers)	8	9	12	16	20	5,665	12,552	24,194	46,174	94,376	1.9	2.7	2.8	2.4	2.9
Electronics and electrical appliances	45	45	51	60	59	28,662	48,746	91,076	164,747	285,295	9.5	10.4	10.4	8.5	8.9
Measurement, scientific and photographic equipment	1	2	6	11	13	1,056	2,764	5,588	13,353	24,943	0.3	0.6	0.6	0.7	0.8
Industrial and agricultural chemicals	36	44	52	70	66	20,868	37,904	71,324	157,895	227,242	6.9	8.1	8.2	8.1	7.1
Pharmaceuticals and consumer chemicals	23	20	32	35	36	7,313	12,638	28,101	54,591	91,878	2.4	2.7	3.2	2.8	2.9
Motor vehicles (incl. components)	40	34	43	60	53	42,926	64,657	123,294	260,436	336,989	14.2	13.7	14.1	13.8	10.5
Total	168	169	215	271	269	118,571	199,555	366,395	738,943	1,151,110	39.3	42.4	41.9	37.9	35.9
Medium Research Intensity															
Industrial and farm equipment	39	34	40	66	59	13,741	21,070	35,593	87,984	130,021	4.6	4.5	4.1	4.5	4.1
Shipbuilding, railroad and transportation equipment	7	11	9	15	8	3,779	6,785	8,529	18,088	19,547	1.3	1.4	1.0	0.9	0.6
Rubber	9	8	10	12	13	7,638	10,356	17,067	30,125	39,472	2.5	2.2	2.0	1.5	1.2
Building materials	14	10	21	32	29	4,495	5,000	14,423	33,797	51,500	1.5	1.1	1.6	1.7	1.6
Metal manufacturing and products	90	81	101	132	111	42,999	60,274	115,730	230,217	319,045	14.2	12.8	13.2	11.8	10.0
Total	159	144	181	257	220	72,652	103,485	191,342	400,211	559,585	24.1	22.0	21.9	20.5	17.5
Low Research Intensity															
Textiles, apparel and leather goods	24	23	31	40	27	8,101	12,377	22,917	41,369	44,331	2.7	2.6	2.6	2.1	1.4
Paper and wood products	22	19	29	43	38	8,190	12,351	26,503	55,604	73,688	2.7	2.6	3.0	2.9	2.3
Publishing and printing	5	6	9	17	18	1,261	2,249	4,467	14,212	30,456	0.4	0.5	0.5	0.7	1.0
Food	53	54	74	98	76	31,939	44,810	82,213	164,849	236,924	10.6	9.5	9.4	8.5	7.4
Drink	10	9	18	23	23	3,246	5,076	14,572	26,582	53,185	1.1	1.1	1.7	1.4	1.7
Tobacco	9	9	9	12	11	4,189	6,115	12,059	27,629	53,366	1.4	1.3	1.4	1.4	1.7
Total	123	120	170	233	193	56,926	82,978	162,731	330,245	491,950	18.9	17.6	18.6	16.9	15.4
Petroleum	36	39	43	69	90	46,811	74,235	127,730	419,646	935,817	15.5	15.8	14.6	21.5	29.2
Other manufacturing	11	11	27	35	20	6,943	10,331	26,544	59,946	65,852	2.3	2.2	3.0	3.1	2.1
TOTAL	497	483	636	865	792	301,903	470,584	874,742	1,948,991	3,204,314	100.0	100.0	100.0	100.0	100.0

Source: *Fortune* July and August 1963; June and September 1968; May and September 1973; 8 May and 14 August 1978; 2 May and 22 August 1983.

Table 3.3

Countries of origin of the equalised sample, 1962 to 1982, numbers of firms and sales

	Numbers of firms					Sales $ million					Per cent distribution of sales				
	1962	1967	1972	1977	1982	1962	1967	1972	1977	1982	1962	1967	1972	1977	1982
USA	292	283	256	238	213	202,515	314,665	474,971	922,382	1,401,707	67.6	66.9	58.5	54.5	49.2
Europe	142	136	139	142	147	80,022	117,176	234,987	521,650	899,652	26.7	25.1	28.9	30.9	31.5
EEC¹	128	121	120	109	118	73,952	108,605	213,551	453,936	783,976	24.6	23.2	26.2	26.9	27.5
Germany	34	25	30	29	29	20,297	24,584	57,405	124,713	189,956	6.8	5.2	7.1	7.4	6.7
France	26	23	25	23	24	9,816	16,804	37,355	89,723	146,986	3.3	3.6	4.6	5.3	5.2
Italy	7	8	7	7	7	4,563	8,932	13,327	35,793	59,830	1.5	1.9	1.6	2.1	2.1
Netherlands	4	5	5	5	4	2,520	4,240	12,424	26,279	30,417	0.8	0.9	1.5	1.6	1.1
Belgium	3	3	3	3	4	995	1,797	4,364	10,810	18,294	0.3	0.4	0.5	0.6	0.6
Luxembourg	1	1	1			700	957	1,744			0.2	0.2	0.2		
UK	51	53	45	38	47	24,903	37,001	60,550	106,740	227,405	8.3	7.9	7.5	6.3	8.0
Germany/Belgium		1	1	1	1		354	712	4,233	4,209		0.1	0.1		0.1
Italy/Switzerland															
UK/Italy			1	1				2,746					0.3	0.3	
UK/Netherlands	2	2	2	2	2	10,158	13,936	22,924	55,645	106,879	3.4	3.0	2.8	3.3	3.7
Other Europe	14	15	19	33	29	6,070	8,571	21,436	67,714	115,676	2.1	1.9	2.7	4.0	4.1
Austria	1	1	1	2	2	223	285	512	4,256	8,600	0.1	0.1	0.1	0.3	0.3
Finland					1					3,634					0.1
Norway				1	2				1,541	5,806				0.1	0.2
Sweden	7	5	9	13	7	2,327	2,585	8,178	22,514	31,294	0.8	0.5	1.0	1.3	1.1
Switzerland	6	8	7	8	9	3,520	5,420	11,613	25,108	41,127	1.2	1.2	1.4	1.5	1.4
Portugal		1	1		1		281	599		2,454		0.1	0.1		0.1
Spain			1	6	4			534	8,808	12,253			0.1	0.5	0.4
Turkey				3	3				5,487	10,508				0.3	0.4
Japan	29	43	65	69	79	10,643	27,725	81,503	171,353	346,158	3.6	5.9	10.0	10.1	12.1
Other Countries	20	21	23	34	44	6,488	11,018	20,645	76,532	203,285	2.2	2.4	2.7	4.6	7.3
Australia	2	2	2	2	3	758	1,491	2,782	4,579	10,313	0.3	0.3	0.3	0.3	0.4
Canada	13	11	11	11	15	4,307	6,102	9,416	21,814	45,229	1.4	1.3	1.2	1.3	1.6
South Africa	2	2	1	4	2	443	771	848	5,875	8,536	0.1	0.2	0.1	0.3	0.3
Netherlands Antilles	1	1	2	2	1	267	369	792	3,415	6,025	0.1	0.1	0.1	0.2	0.2
Israel				1	1				1,310	2,900				0.1	0.1
Argentina		2	1	2	1		702	917	1,862	4,455		0.1	0.1	0.1	0.2
Brazil		1	1	2	2		507	1,531	9,384	20,659		0.1	0.2	0.6	0.7
Chile			1	1	1			628	1,231	1,660			0.1	0.1	0.1
Colombia					1					2,152					0.1
India	1	1	1	1	2	173	277	1,295	3,763	10,557	0.1	0.1	0.2	0.2	0.4
Indonesia			1					600					0.1		
Kuwait				1	1				1,376	12,234				0.1	0.4
Mexico	1	1	1	1	1	540	799	1,318	3,394	14,853	0.2	0.2	0.2	0.2	0.5
Philippines					1					2,890					0.1
South Korea				4	9				6,981	37,135				0.4	1.3
Taiwan				1	2				1,920	7,236				0.1	0.3
Venezuela				1	1				9,628	16,451				0.6	0.6
Zambia			1					518					0.1		
TOTAL	483	483	483	483	483	299,668	470,584	812,106	1,691,917	2,850,802	100.0	100.0	100.0	100.0	100.0

1 The listed countries are treated as having constituted the EEC throughout the period 1962–82. See comment in Part I.

Source: *Fortune* July and August 1963; June and September 1968; May and September 1973; 8 May and 14 August 1978; 2 May and 22 August 1983.

Table 3.4

Industrial composition of the equalised sample, 1962 to 1982, numbers of firms and sales

	Number of firms					Sales $ million					Per cent distribution of sales				
	1962	1967	1972	1977	1982	1962	1967	1972	1977	1982	1962	1967	1972	1977	1982
High Research Intensity															
Aerospace	15	15	14	14	17	12,081	20,294	20,896	38,383	84,839	4.0	4.3	2.6	2.3	3.0
Office equipment (incl. computers)	8	9	10	11	12	5,665	12,552	23,367	42,947	84,858	1.9	2.7	2.9	2.5	3.0
Electronics and electrical appliances	43	45	39	38	41	28,343	48,746	86,068	149,940	265,250	9.5	10.4	10.6	8.9	9.3
Measurement, scientific and photographic equipment	1	2	2	3	3	1,056	2,764	4,037	8,389	14,817	0.4	0.6	0.5	0.5	0.5
Industrial and agricultural chemicals	33	44	42	43	44	20,387	37,904	67,280	140,278	202,729	6.8	8.1	8.3	8.3	7.1
Pharmaceuticals and consumer chemicals	19	20	23	21	24	6,673	12,638	24,418	43,831	77,881	2.2	2.7	3.0	2.6	2.7
Motor vehicles (incl. components)	39	34	39	38	36	42,767	64,657	121,638	245,756	318,479	14.3	13.7	15.0	14.5	11.2
Total	158	169	169	168	177	116,972	199,555	347,704	669,524	1,048,853	39.0	42.4	42.8	39.6	36.8
Medium Research Intensity															
Industrial and farm equipment	38	34	26	28	30	13,583	21,070	29,832	64,001	97,656	4.5	4.5	3.7	3.8	3.4
Shipbuilding, railroad and transportation equipment	7	11	8	9	5	3,779	6,785	8,076	14,703	16,362	1.3	1.4	1.0	0.9	0.6
Rubber	9	8	8	8	9	7,638	10,356	16,221	27,308	34,896	2.5	2.2	2.0	1.6	1.2
Building materials	13	10	12	10	10	4,334	5,000	10,639	18,546	28,432	1.4	1.1	1.3	1.1	1.0
Metal manufacturing and products	88	81	80	75	66	42,682	60,274	106,989	192,708	267,868	14.2	12.8	13.2	11.4	9.4
Total	155	144	134	130	120	72,016	103,485	171,757	317,266	445,214	24.0	22.0	21.1	18.8	15.6
Low Research Intensity															
Textiles, apparel and leather goods	24	23	20	15	12	8,101	12,377	18,460	25,130	28,990	2.7	2.6	2.3	1.5	1.0
Paper and wood products	22	19	21	20	17	8,190	12,351	23,265	38,773	48,763	2.7	2.6	2.9	2.3	1.7
Publishing and printing	5	6	5	7	7	1,261	2,249	2,815	8,196	17,256	0.4	0.5	0.3	0.5	0.6
Food	53	54	53	52	49	31,939	44,810	73,452	132,769	203,784	10.7	9.5	9.0	7.8	7.1
Drink	10	9	12	9	10	3,246	5,076	12,200	16,929	39,016	1.1	1.1	1.5	1.0	1.4
Tobacco	9	9	8	6	7	4,189	6,115	11,670	22,983	48,910	1.4	1.3	1.4	1.4	1.7
Total	123	120	119	109	102	56,926	82,978	141,868	244,780	386,719	19.0	17.6	17.5	14.5	13.6
Petroleum	36	39	40	54	71	46,811	74,235	126,532	409,205	912,449	15.6	15.8	15.6	24.2	32.0
Other manufacturing	11	11	21	22	13	6,943	10,331	24,245	51,142	57,567	2.3	2.2	3.0	3.0	2.0
TOTAL	483	483	483	483	483	299,668	470,584	812,106	1,691,917	2,850,802	100.0	100.0	100.0	100.0	100.0

Source: *Fortune* July and August 1963; June and September 1968; May and September 1973; 8 May and 14 August 1978; 2 May and 22 August 1983.

Table 3.5
Composition, by industry and country, of equalised samples of firms, 1962, 1972, 1982

	Aerospace			Office equipment (incl. computers)			Electronics and electrical appliances			Measurement, scientific and photographic equipment			Industrial and agricultural chemicals		
	1962	1972	1982	1962	1972	1982	1962	1972	1982	1962	1972	1982	1962	1972	1982
USA	12	11	12	7	8	10	20	17	16	1	2	2	20	22	19
Europe	3	3	5	1	1	1	15	12	12				13	15	15
EEC[1]	3	3	5	1	1	1	12	9	9				11	13	13
Germany							2	2	2				5	3	4
France	1	1	1				3	2	2				3	3	3
Italy			2	1	1	1							1	1	1
Netherlands							1	1	1					2	2
Belgium														1	1
Luxembourg															
UK	2	2	2				6	4	4				2	2	2
Germany/Belgium														1	
Italy/Switzerland															
UK/Italy															
UK/Netherlands															
Other Europe							3	3	3				2	2	2
Austria															
Finland															
Norway															
Sweden							2	2	2						
Switzerland							1	1	1				2	1	1
Portugal														1	1
Spain															
Turkey															
Japan					1	1	7	9	10			1		5	8
Other Countries							1	1	3						2
Australia							1	1	1						1
Canada															
South Africa															
Netherlands Antilles															
Israel									1						
Argentina															
Brazil															
Chile															
Colombia															
India															
Indonesia															
Kuwait															
Mexico															
Philippines															
South Korea									1						
Taiwan															
Venezuela															
Zambia															1
TOTAL	15	14	17	8	10	12	43	39	41	1	2	3	33	42	44

54

Table 3.5 (cont.)

	Pharmaceuticals and consumer chemicals			Motor vehicles (incl. components)			TOTAL HIGH RESEARCH INTENSITY			Industrial and farm equipment			Shipbuilding, railroad and transportation equipment		
	1962	1972	1982	1962	1972	1982	1962	1972	1982	1962	1972	1982	1962	1972	1982
USA	16	15	18	18	16	9	94	91	86	26	14	13	6	3	1
Europe	3	6	5	15	15	14	50	52	52	9	9	10		1	1
EEC¹	1	4	3	14	12	11	42	42	42	7	6	6		1	1
Germany		1	1	3	4	4	10	10	12	3	4	3			
France		1	1	4	3	2	11	10	10	2	1	1			
Italy				1	2	2	3	4	4						
Netherlands							1	3	3						
Belgium								1	1					1	
Luxembourg															
UK	1	2	1	6	3	3	17	13	12	2	1	2			1
Germany/Belgium								1							
Italy/Switzerland															
UK/Italy															
UK/Netherlands															
Other Europe	2	2	2	1	3	3	8	10	10	2	3	4			
Austria															
Finland															
Norway								1	1						
Sweden				1	2	2	3	4	4	2	2	3			
Switzerland	2	2	2		2	2	5	4	4		1	1			
Portugal					1	1		1	1						
Spain								1							
Turkey						1			1						
Japan		2	1	6	8	13	13	25	34	2	2	5	1	4	2
Other Countries							1	1	5	1	1	2			1
Australia							1	1	2						
Canada							1	1		1	1	1			
South Africa															
Netherlands Antilles															
Israel									1						
Argentina															
Brazil															
Chile															
Colombia															
India															
Indonesia															
Kuwait															
Mexico															
Philippines															
South Korea															
Taiwan									1						1
Venezuela									1						
Zambia															
TOTAL	19	23	24	39	39	36	158	169	177	38	26	30	7	8	5

55

Table 3.5 (cont.)

	Rubber			Building materials			Metal manufacturing and products			TOTAL MEDIUM RESEARCH INTENSITY			Textiles, apparel and leather goods		
	1962	1972	1982	1962	1972	1982	1962	1972	1982	1962	1972	1982	1962	1972	1982
USA	5	5	5	10	8	3	37	29	20	84	59	42	15	9	4
Europe	4	2	3	3	3	6	38	31	25	54	46	45	4	3	2
EEC¹	4	2	3	3	3	6	36	27	23	50	39	39	4	3	1
Germany	1	1	1				15	10	9	19	14	12			
France	1			1	2	2	7	6	5	11	10	9	1	1	
Italy	1						1	1	1	2	1	2	1		
Netherlands							1	1	1	1	2	1	1		
Belgium							2	1	1	2	1	1			
Luxembourg							1		2	1	1	2			
UK	1		1	2	1	4	9	7	4	14	9	12	2	2	1
Germany/Belgium															
Italy/Switzerland			1												
UK/Italy		1													
UK/Netherlands												1			
Other Europe							2	4	2	4	7	6			1
Austria							1	1	1	1	1	1			
Finland															
Norway															
Sweden							1	2		3	4	3			
Switzerland								1	1		2	2			
Portugal															
Spain															
Turkey		1	1		1	1						1			
Japan							6	12	11	9	20	20	5	8	5
Other Countries							7	8	10	8	9	13			1
Australia							1	1	1	1		1			1
Canada							4	4	3	5	5	4			
South Africa							1		1	1		2			
Netherlands Antilles							1								
Israel															
Argentina									1						
Brazil									1		1	1			
Chile								1			1				
Colombia								1							
India							1	1	1	1	1	1			
Indonesia															
Kuwait															
Mexico															
Philippines															
South Korea									2			3			
Taiwan															
Venezuela								1			1				
Zambia															
TOTAL	9	8	9	13	12	10	88	80	66	155	134	120	24	20	12

Table 3.5 (cont.)

	Paper and wood products			Publishing and printing			Food			Drink			Tobacco		
	1962	1972	1982	1962	1972	1982	1962	1972	1982	1962	1972	1982	1962	1972	1982
USA	16	14	11	2	2	2	42	35	27	5	7	4	5	5	3
Europe	4	3	2	2	1	1	8	12	16	2	3	3	4	3	4
EEC[1]	4	2	2	2	1	1	6	11	14	2	3	3	4	3	3
Germany													1	1	
France				1	1	1		1	3						
Italy															
Netherlands															
Belgium															
Luxembourg															
UK	4	2	2				5	9	10	2	3	3	3	2	3
Germany/Belgium															
Italy/Switzerland															
UK/Italy															
UK/Netherlands															
Other Europe															
Austria		1					1	1	1						1
Finland							2	1	2						
Norway															
Sweden		1													
Switzerland							1	1							
Portugal							1		2						
Spain															1
Turkey															
Japan		2	4	1	1	2	1	4	4						
Other Countries															
Australia	2	2		1	1	2	2	2	2		1	1			
Canada	2	2					1	1	1	3	1	2			
South Africa				1	1	2	1	1	1	3	1	2			
Netherlands Antilles															
Israel															
Argentina															
Brazil															
Chile															
Colombia															
India															
Indonesia															
Kuwait															
Mexico															
Philippines															
South Korea															
Taiwan															
Venezuela															
Zambia															
TOTAL	22	21	17	5	5	7	53	53	49	10	12	10	9	8	7

Table 3.5 (cont.)

	TOTAL LOW RESEARCH INTENSITY			Petroleum			Other manufacturing			TOTAL		
	1962	1972	1982	1962	1972	1982	1962	1972	1982	1962	1972	1982
USA	85	72	51	24	22	30	5	12	4	292	256	213
Europe	24	25	28	10	9	18	4	7	4	142	139	147
EEC[1]	22	23	24	10	9	10	4	7	3	128	120	118
Germany	1	1	1	3	2	2	1	3	2	34	30	29
France	1	2	3	3	2	2				26	25	24
Italy	1	1		1	1	1				7	7	7
Netherlands	1			1	1	1	1			4	5	4
Belgium										3	3	4
Luxembourg										1	1	
UK	17	18	19	1	2	3	2	3	1	51	45	47
Germany/Belgium											1	1
Italy/Switzerland											1	
UK/Italy												
UK/Netherlands	1	1	1	1	1	1				2	2	2
Other Europe	2	2	4			8			1	14	19	29
Austria						1				1	1	2
Finland						1						1
Norway						1						2
Sweden	1	1								7	9	7
Switzerland	1	1	2						1	6	7	9
Portugal						1						1
Spain			1			3					1	4
Turkey			1			1						3
Japan	6	16	16	1	4	7			2	29	65	79
Other Countries	8	6	7	1	5	16	2	2	3	20	23	44
Australia	1	1	1						1	2	2	3
Canada	7	5	5			3	1	1	1	13	11	15
South Africa							1	1		2	1	2
Netherlands Antilles							1	1	1	1	1	1
Israel												1
Argentina					1	1					1	1
Brazil					1	1					1	2
Chile												1
Colombia						1						1
India				1	1	1				1	2	2
Indonesia				1	1	1					1	1
Kuwait						1						1
Mexico				1	1	1				1	1	1
Philippines						1						1
South Korea						4						9
Taiwan			1			1						2
Venezuela						1						1
Zambia											1	
TOTAL	123	119	102	36	40	71	11	21	13	483	483	483

1 The listed countries are treated as having constituted the EEC throughout the period 1962–82. See comment in Part I.

Source: *Fortune* July and August 1963; May and August 1963; May and September 1973; 2 May and 22 August 1983.

Table 3.6

Sales of the equalised samples, 1962, 1972, 1982, by industry and country

	Aerospace			Office equipment (incl. computers)			Electronics and electrical appliances			Measurement, scientific and photographic equipment			Industrial and agricultural chemicals		
	1962	1972	1982	1962	1972	1982	1962	1972	1982	1962	1972	1982	1962	1972	1982
USA	10,615	18,010	70,844	5,258	21,720	78,870	16,434	42,921	98,822	1,056	4,037	12,486	12,450	31,343	72,849
Europe	1,466	2,886	13,995	407	940	2,469	8,123	26,373	86,338				7,937	28,752	103,449
EEC[1]	1,466	2,886	13,995	407	940	2,469	6,934	23,170	73,320				7,355	31,569	93,472
Germany			2,338				2,130	7,864	22,423				3,565	11,110	43,365
France	245	720	5,453				825	3,685	17,155				1,428	3,647	11,808
Italy				407	940	2,469							551	3,598	6,664
Netherlands							1,529	6,207	16,093					3,627	12,100
Belgium														1,181	3,888
Luxembourg															
UK	1,221	2,166	6,204				2,450	5,414	17,649				1,811	4,877	15,647
Germany/Belgium														712	
Italy/Switzerland															
UK/Italy															
UK/Netherlands															
Other Europe							1,189	3,203	13,018				582	2,817	9,977
Austria															
Finland															
Norway							602	1,427	8,245						3,183
Sweden							587	1,776	4,773				582	2,218	6,794
Switzerland															
Portugal														599	
Spain															
Turkey															
Japan					707	3,519	3,526	16,235	68,763			2,331		4,368	21,505
Other Countries							260	539	11,327						4,926
Australia															
Canada							260	539	2,460						3,251
South Africa															
Netherlands Antilles															
Israel									2,900						
Argentina															
Brazil															
Chile															
Colombia															
India															
Indonesia															
Kuwait															
Mexico															
Philippines															
South Korea															1,675
Taiwan									5,967						
Venezuela															
Zambia															
TOTAL	12,081	20,896	84,839	5,665	23,367	84,858	28,343	86,068	265,250	1,056	4037	14,817	20,387	67,280	202,729

Table 3.6 (cont.)

	Pharmaceuticals and consumer chemicals			Motor vehicles (incl. components)			TOTAL HIGH RESEARCH INTENSITY			Industrial and farm equipment			Shipbuilding, railroad and transportation equipment		
	1962	1972	1982	1962	1972	1982	1962	1972	1982	1962	1972	1982	1962	1972	1982
USA	5,918	17,977	63,201	30,964	72,914	124,272	82,695	208,922	521,344	9,196	18,591	43,133	3,542	3,371	2,202
Europe	755	5,114	12,554	9,927	32,456	114,093	28,615	99,338	332,898	3,455	8,243	30,790		636	1,960
EEC[1]	233	2,968	6,081	9,563	29,423	96,555	25,958	88,139	285,892	2,811	5,388	20,570		636	1,960
Germany		1,232	1,709	3,280	11,746	41,145	8,975	31,952	110,980	1,401	4,288	10,382			
France		564	1,683	2,121	7,759	27,359	4,619	16,375	63,458	676	553	5,973			
Italy				1,262	4,250	17,141	2,220	8,788	26,274						
Netherlands							1,529	9,834	28,193					636	
Belgium								1,181	3,888						
Luxembourg															
UK	233	1,172	2,689	2,900	5,668	10,910	8,615	19,297	53,099	734	547	4,215			1,960
Germany/Belgium								712							
Italy/Switzerland															
UK/Italy															
UK/Netherlands															
Other Europe	522	2,146	6,473	364	3,033	17,538	2,657	11,199	47,006	644	2,855	10,220			
Austria															
Finland															
Norway									3,183						
Sweden				364	2,499	15,005	966	3,926	23,250		764	8,044			
Switzerland	522	2,146	6,473				1,691	6,140	18,040	644	2,091	2,176			
Portugal								599							
Spain					534			534							
Turkey						2,533			2,533						
Japan		1,327	2,126	1,876	16,268	80,114	5,402	38,905	178,358	381	1,808	15,779	237	4,069	4,164
Other Countries							260	539	16,253	551	1,190	7,954			
Australia															
Canada							260	539	5,711	551	1,190	2,058			
South Africa												5,896			
Netherlands Antilles															
Israel									2,900						
Argentina															
Brazil															
Chile															
Colombia															
India															
Indonesia															
Kuwait															
Mexico															
Philippines															
South Korea									5,967						8,036
Taiwan									1,675						
Venezuela															
Zambia															
TOTAL	6,673	24,418	77,881	42,767	121,638	318,479	116,972	347,704	1,048,853	13,583	29,832	97,656	3,779	8,076	16,362

Table 3.6 (cont.)

	Rubber			Building materials			Metal manufacturing and products			TOTAL MEDIUM RESEARCH INTENSITY			Textiles, apparel and leather goods		
	1962	1972	1982	1962	1972	1982	1962	1972	1982	1962	1972	1982	1962	1972	1982
USA	5,650	11,161	19,592	3,140	6,119	6,410	22,186	40,442	81,256	43,714	79,684	152,593	4,989	8,086	9,936
Europe	1,988	4,382	12,444	1,194	3,916	19,500	15,604	40,802	102,645	22,241	57,979	167,339	1,849	3,341	5,928
EEC[1]	1,988	4,382	12,444	1,194	3,916	19,500	15,218	38,128	94,158	21,211	52,450	148,632	1,849	3,341	3,419
Germany	227						7,823	15,716	46,177	9,451	20,004	56,559			
France	425	1,636	5,567	600	3,254	10,304	2,044	7,468	17,291	3,745	12,911	39,135			
Italy	583						844	1,234	6,050	1,427	1,234	6,050	344	557	
Netherlands							248	1,954	2,224	248	2,590	2,224	552		
Belgium							460	1,618	5,197	460	1,618	5,197			
Luxembourg							700	1,744		700	1,744				
UK	753		2,668	594	662	9,196	3,099	8,394	17,219	5,180	9,603	35,258	953	2,784	3,419
Germany/Belgium															
Italy/Switzerland		2,746	4,209								2,746	4,209			
UK/Italy															
UK/Netherlands															
Other Europe							386	2,674	8,487	1,030	5,529	18,707			2,509
Austria							223	512	5,246	223	512	5,246			
Finland															
Norway							163	1,583		807	3,674	8,044			
Sweden								579			1,343				
Switzerland									3,241			5,417			
Portugal															
Spain															
Turkey															2,509
Japan		678	2,860		604	2,522	2,693	18,344	56,935	3,311	25,503	82,260	1,263	7,033	11,065
Other Countries							2,199	7,401	27,032	2,750	8,591	43,022			2,061
Australia							413	1,950	5,434	413	1,950	5,434			
Canada							1,440	3,776	8,545	1,991	4,966	10,603			
South Africa							173		2,640	173		8,536			
Netherlands Antilles															
Israel															
Argentina															
Brazil									1,654			1,654			
Chile								628	1,660		628	1,660			
Colombia															
India							173	529	2,724	173	529	2,724			
Indonesia															
Kuwait															
Mexico															
Philippines															
South Korea									4,375			12,411			
Taiwan															2,061
Venezuela															
Zambia							518	518		518	518				
TOTAL	7,638	16,221	34,896	4,334	10,639	28,432	42,682	106,989	267,868	72,016	171,757	445,214	8,101	18,460	28,990

61

Table 3.6 (cont.)

	Paper and wood products			Publishing and printing			Food			Drink			Tobacco		
	1962	1972	1982	1962	1972	1982	1962	1972	1982	1962	1972	1982	1962	1972	1982
USA	6,541	17,007	35,645	498	1,222	5,764	22,373	45,110	112,272	1,744	8,354	20,022	2,503	6,310	24,034
Europe	1,027	3,534	5,986	598	580	2,567	8,363	22,759	74,073	750	2,308	12,400	1,686	5,366	24,876
EEC[1]	1,027	2,956	5,986	598	580	2,567	5,980	18,629	58,461	750	2,308	12,400	1,686	5,366	22,789
Germany				284	580								197	662	
France						2,567		1,117	6,579						
Italy															
Netherlands															
Belgium															
Luxembourg															
UK	1,027	2,956	5,986	314			1,844	8,648	28,762	750	2,308	12,400	1,489	4,704	22,789
Germany/Belgium															
Italy/Switzerland															
UK/Italy															
UK/Netherlands							4,136	8,864	23,120						
Other Europe		578					2,383	4,130	15,612						2,087
Austria															
Finland															
Norway															
Sweden		578					554								
Switzerland							1,829	4,130	15,612						
Portugal															
Spain															
Turkey															
Japan		1,185	7,132		514	4,744	341	3,603	11,967		813	2,177			2,087
Other Countries	622	1,539		165	499	4,181	862	1,980	5,472	752	725	4,417			
Australia							345	832	3,025						
Canada	622	1,539		165	499	4,181	517	1,148	2,447	752	725	4,417			
South Africa															
Netherlands Antilles															
Israel															
Argentina															
Brazil															
Chile															
Colombia															
India															
Indonesia															
Kuwait															
Mexico															
Philippines															
South Korea															
Taiwan															
Venezuela															
Zambia															
TOTAL	8,190	23,265	48,763	1,261	2,815	17,256	31,939	73,452	203,784	3,246	12,200	39,016	4,189	11,676	48,910

Table 3.6 (cont.)

	TOTAL LOW RESEARCH INTENSITY			Petroleum			Other manufacturing			TOTAL		
	1962	1972	1982	1962	1972	1982	1962	1972	1982	1962	1972	1982
USA	38,648	86,089	207,673	34,199	85,729	504,413	3,259	14,547	15,684	202,515	474,971	1,401,707
Europe	14,273	37,888	125,830	11,746	31,724	252,827	3,147	8,058	20,758	80,022	234,987	899,652
EEC[1]	11,890	33,180	105,622	11,746	31,724	225,130	3,147	8,058	18,700	73,952	213,551	783,976
Germany	197	662	2,567	1,438	1,566	10,184	236	3,221	9,666	20,297	57,405	189,956
France	284	1,697	6,579	1,168	5,202	37,814		1,170		9,816	37,355	146,986
Italy	344	557		572	2,748	27,506				4,563	13,327	59,830
Netherlands	552						191			2,520	12,424	30,417
Belgium				535	1,565	9,209				995	4,364	18,294
Luxembourg										700	1,744	
UK	6,377	21,400	73,356	2,011	6,583	56,658	2,720	3,667	9,034	24,903	60,550	227,405
Germany/Belgium											712	
Italy/Switzerland												
UK/Italy											2,746	4,209
UK/Netherlands	4,136	8,864	23,120	6,022	14,060	83,759				10,158	22,924	106,879
Other Europe	2,383	4,708	20,208			27,697			2,058	6,070	21,436	115,676
Austria						3,354				223	512	8,600
Finland						3,634						3,634
Norway						2,623						5,806
Sweden	554	578								2,327	8,178	31,294
Switzerland	1,829	4,130	15,612						2,058	3,520	11,613	41,127
Portugal						2,454					599	2,454
Spain			2,087			10,166					534	12,253
Turkey			2,509			5,466						10,508
Japan	1,604	13,148	37,085	326	3,947	45,169	537	1,640	3,286	10,643	81,503	346,158
Other Countries	2,401	4,743	16,131	540	5,132	110,040			17,839	6,488	20,645	203,285
Australia	345	832	3,025						1,854	758	2,782	10,313
Canada	2,056	3,911	11,045			7,910			9,960	4,307	9,416	45,229
South Africa							270	848		443	848	8,536
Netherlands Antilles							267	792	6,025	267	792	6,025
Israel												2,900
Argentina					917	4,455					917	4,455
Brazil					1,531	19,005					1,531	20,659
Chile											628	1,660
Colombia						2,152						2,152
India					766	7,833				173	1,295	10,557
Indonesia					600						600	
Kuwait						12,234						12,234
Mexico			2,061	540	1,318	14,853				540	1,318	14,853
Philippines						2,890						2,890
South Korea						16,696						37,135
Taiwan						5,561						7,236
Venezuela						16,451					518	16,451
Zambia												
TOTAL	56,926	141,868	386,719	46,811	126,532	912,449	6,943	24,245	57,567	299,668	812,106	2,850,802

1 The listed countries are treated as having constituted the EEC throughout the period 1962–82. See comment in Part I.

Source: *Fortune* July and August 1963; May and September 1973; 2 May and 22 August 1983.

63

Table 3.7

Percentage industrial distribution of sales of equalised samples, by area and country, 1962, 1972, 1982

	USA			Europe (total)			EEC (total)[1]			Germany			France		
	1962	1972	1982	1962	1972	1982	1962	1972	1982	1962	1972	1982	1962	1972	1982
High Research Intensity															
Aerospace	5.2	3.8	5.1	1.8	1.2	1.6	2.0	1.4	1.8			1.2	2.5	1.9	3.7
Office equipment (incl. computers)	2.6	4.6	5.6	0.5	0.4	0.3	0.6	0.4	0.3						
Electronics and electrical appliances	8.1	9.0	7.1	10.2	11.2	9.6	9.4	10.8	9.4	10.5	13.7	11.8	8.4	9.9	11.7
Measurement, scientific and photographic equipment	0.5	0.8	0.9												
Industrial and agricultural chemicals	6.1	6.6	5.2	9.9	13.4	11.5	9.9	13.5	11.9	17.6	19.4	22.8	14.5	9.8	8.0
Pharmaceuticals and consumer chemicals	2.9	3.8	4.5	0.9	2.2	1.4	0.3	1.4	0.8		2.1	0.9		1.5	1.1
Motor vehicles (incl. components)	15.3	15.4	8.9	12.4	13.8	12.7	12.9	13.8	12.3	16.2	20.5	21.7	21.6	20.8	18.6
Total	40.8	44.0	37.2	35.8	42.3	37.0	35.1	41.3	36.5	44.2	55.7	58.4	47.1	43.8	43.2
Medium Research Intensity															
Industrial and farm equipment	4.5	3.9	3.1	4.3	3.5	3.4	3.8	2.5	2.6	6.9	7.5	5.5	6.9	1.5	4.1
Shipbuilding, railroad and transportation equipment	1.7	0.7	0.2		0.3	0.2		0.3	0.3						
Rubber	2.8	2.3	1.4	2.5	1.9	1.4	2.7	2.1	1.6	1.1			4.3	4.4	3.8
Building materials	1.6	1.3	0.5	1.5	1.7	2.2	1.6	1.8	2.5				6.1	8.7	7.0
Metal manufacturing and products	11.0	8.5	5.8	19.5	17.4	11.4	20.6	17.9	12.0	38.5	27.4	24.3	20.8	20.0	11.8
Total	21.6	16.8	10.9	27.8	24.7	18.6	28.7	24.6	19.0	46.6	34.8	29.8	38.2	34.6	26.6
Low Research Intensity															
Textiles, apparel and leather goods	2.5	1.7	0.7	2.3	1.4	0.7	2.5	1.6	0.4						
Paper and wood products	3.2	3.6	2.5	1.3	1.5	0.7	1.4	1.4	0.8						
Publishing and printing	0.2	0.3	0.4	0.7	0.2	0.3	0.8	0.3	0.3						
Food	11.0	9.5	8.0	10.5	9.7	8.2	8.1	8.7	7.5				2.9	3.0	4.5
Drink	0.9	1.8	1.4	0.9	1.0	1.4	1.0	1.1	1.6					1.6	
Tobacco	1.2	1.3	1.7	2.1	2.3	2.8	2.3	2.5	2.9	1.0	1.2	1.4			
Total	19.1	18.1	14.8	17.8	16.1	14.0	16.1	15.5	13.5	1.0	1.2	1.4	2.9	4.6	4.5
Petroleum	16.9	18.0	36.0	14.7	13.5	28.1	15.9	14.9	28.7	7.1	2.7	5.4	11.9	13.9	25.7
Other manufacturing	1.6	3.1	1.1	3.9	3.4	2.3	4.3	3.8	2.4	1.2	5.6	5.1		3.1	
TOTAL	100.0	100.0	100.0	100.0	100.0	100.0	100.0	100.0	100.0	100.0	100.0	100.0	100.0	100.0	100.0

Table 3.7 (cont.)

	Italy 1962	Italy 1972	Italy 1982	UK 1962	UK 1972	UK 1982	Other Europe (total) 1962	1972	1982	Sweden 1962	1972	1982	Japan 1962	1972	1982
High Research Intensity															
Aerospace				4.9	3.6	2.7								0.9	1.0
Office equipment (incl. computers)	8.9	7.1	4.1	9.8	8.9	7.8	19.6	14.9	11.3	25.9	17.4	26.3	33.1	19.9	19.9
Electronics and electrical appliances															0.7
Measurement, scientific and photographic equipment														5.4	6.2
Industrial and agricultural chemicals	12.1	27.0	11.1	7.3	8.1	6.9	9.6	13.1	8.6					1.6	0.6
Pharmaceuticals and consumer chemicals				0.9	1.9	1.2	8.6	10.0	5.6						
Motor vehicles (incl. components)	27.7	31.9	28.6	11.6	9.4	4.8	6.0	14.1	15.2	15.6	30.6	47.9	17.6	20.0	23.1
Total	48.7	65.9	43.9	34.6	31.9	23.3	43.8	52.2	40.6	41.5	48.0	74.3	50.8	47.7	51.5
Medium Research Intensity															
Industrial and farm equipment	12.8			2.9	0.9	1.9	10.6	13.3	8.8	27.7	25.6	25.7	3.6	2.2	4.6
Shipbuilding, railroad and transportation equipment						0.9							2.2	5.0	1.2
Rubber				3.0		1.2								0.8	0.8
Building materials				2.4	1.1	4.0								0.7	0.7
Metal manufacturing and products	18.5	9.3	10.1	12.4	13.9	7.6	6.4	12.5	7.3	7.0	19.4		25.3	22.5	16.4
Total	31.3	9.3	10.1	20.8	15.9	15.5	17.0	25.8	16.2	34.7	44.9	25.7	31.1	31.3	23.8
Low Research Intensity															
Textiles, apparel and leather goods	7.5	4.2		3.8	4.6	1.5			2.2				11.9	8.6	3.2
Paper and wood products				4.1	4.9	2.6		2.7		23.8	7.1			1.5	2.1
Publishing and printing				1.3										0.6	1.4
Food				7.4	14.3	12.6	39.3	19.3	13.5				3.2	4.4	3.5
Drink				3.0	3.8	5.5								1.0	0.6
Tobacco				6.0	7.8	10.0			1.8						
Total	7.5	4.2		25.6	35.3	32.3	39.3	22.0	17.5	23.8	7.1		15.1	16.1	10.7
Petroleum	12.5	20.6	46.0	8.1	10.9	24.9			23.9				3.1	4.8	13.0
Other manufacturing				10.9	6.1	4.0			1.8						0.9
TOTAL	100.0	100.0	100.0	100.0	100.0	100.0	100.0	100.0	100.0	100.0	100.0	100.0	100.0	100.0	100.0

Table 3.7 (cont.)

	Other Countries (total) 1962	1972	1982	Canada 1962	1972	1982	TOTAL 1962	1972	1982
High Research Intensity									
Aerospace							4.0	2.6	3.0
Office equipment (incl. computers)							1.9	2.9	3.0
Electronics and electrical appliances	4.0	2.6	5.6	6.0	5.7	5.4	9.5	10.6	9.3
Measurement, scientific and photographic equipment							0.4	0.5	0.5
Industrial and agricultural chemicals			2.4			7.2	6.8	8.3	7.1
Pharmaceuticals and consumer chemicals							2.2	3.0	2.7
Motor vehicles (incl. components)							14.3	15.0	11.2
Total	4.0	2.6	8.0	6.0	5.7	12.6	39.0	42.8	36.8
Medium Research Intensity									
Industrial and farm equipment	8.5	5.8	3.9	12.8	12.6	4.6	4.5	3.7	3.4
Shipbuilding, railroad and transportation equipment			4.0				1.3	1.0	0.6
Rubber							2.5	2.0	1.2
Building materials							1.4	1.3	1.0
Metal manufacturing and products	33.9	35.8	13.3	33.4	40.1	18.9	14.2	13.2	9.4
Total	42.4	41.6	21.2	46.2	52.7	23.4	24.0	21.1	15.6
Low Research Intensity									
Textiles, apparel and leather goods	9.6	7.5	1.0	14.4	16.3		2.7	2.3	1.0
Paper and wood products	2.5	2.4	2.1	3.8	5.3		2.7	2.9	1.7
Publishing and printing							0.4	0.3	0.6
Food	13.3	9.6	2.7	12.0	12.2	9.2	10.7	9.0	7.1
Drink	11.6	3.5	2.2	17.5	7.7	5.4	1.1	1.5	1.4
Tobacco						9.8	1.4	1.4	1.7
Total	37.0	23.0	7.9	47.7	41.5	24.4	19.0	17.5	13.6
Petroleum	8.3	24.9	54.1			17.5	15.6	15.6	32.0
Other manufacturing	8.3	7.9	8.8			22.0	2.3	3.0	2.0
TOTAL	100.0	100.0	100.0	100.0	100.0	100.0	100.0	100.0	100.0

1 EEC treated as Germany, France, Italy, Netherlands, Belgium, Luxembourg, UK, Denmark, throughout the period 1962–82. See comment in Part I.

Source: derived from Table 3.6.

Table 3.8

Percentage geographical distribution of sales of equalised samples, by industry, 1962, 1972, 1982

	USA			Europe (total)			EEC (total)[1]			Germany			France		
	1962	1972	1982	1962	1972	1982	1962	1972	1982	1962	1972	1982	1962	1972	1982
High Research Intensity															
Aerospace	87.9	86.2	83.5	12.1	13.8	16.5	12.1	13.8	16.5			2.8	2.0	3.4	6.4
Office equipment (incl. computers)	92.8	93.0	92.9	7.2	4.0	2.9	7.2	4.0	2.9				2.9	4.3	6.5
Electronics and electrical appliances	58.0	49.9	37.3	28.7	30.6	32.5	24.5	26.9	27.6	7.5	9.1	8.5	7.0	5.4	5.8
Measurement, scientific and photographic equipment	100.0	100.0	84.3												
Industrial and agricultural chemicals	61.1	46.6	35.9	38.9	46.9	51.0	36.1	42.7	46.1	17.5	16.5	21.4			
Pharmaceuticals and consumer chemicals	88.7	73.6	81.0	11.3	20.9	16.1	3.5	12.2	7.8		5.0	2.2		2.3	2.2
Motor vehicles (incl. components)	72.4	59.9	39.0	23.2	26.7	35.8	22.4	24.2	30.3	7.7	9.7	12.9	5.0	6.4	8.6
Total	70.7	60.1	49.7	24.5	28.6	31.7	22.2	25.3	27.3	7.7	9.2	10.6	3.9	4.7	6.1
Medium Research Intensity															
Industrial and farm equipment	67.7	62.3	44.2	25.4	27.6	31.5	20.7	18.1	21.1	10.3	14.4	10.6	5.0	1.9	6.1
Shipbuilding, railroad and transportation equipment	93.7	41.7	13.5		7.9	12.0		7.9	12.0						
Rubber	74.0	68.8	56.1	26.0	27.0	35.7	26.0	27.0	35.7	3.0			5.6	10.1	16.0
Building materials	72.5	57.5	22.5	27.5	36.8	68.6	27.5	36.8	68.6				13.8	30.6	36.2
Metal manufacturing and products	52.0	37.8	30.3	36.6	38.1	38.3	35.7	35.6	35.2	18.3	14.7	17.2	4.8	7.0	6.5
Total	60.7	46.4	34.3	30.9	33.8	37.6	29.5	30.5	33.4	13.1	11.6	12.7	5.2	7.5	8.8
Low Research Intensity															
Textiles, apparel and leather goods	61.6	43.8	34.3	22.8	18.1	20.4	22.8	18.1	11.8						
Paper and wood products	79.9	73.1	73.1	12.5	15.2	12.3	12.5	12.7	12.3						
Publishing and printing	39.5	43.4	33.4	47.4	20.6	14.9	47.4	20.6	14.9			14.9	22.5	20.6	3.2
Food	70.0	61.4	55.1	26.2	31.0	36.3	18.7	25.4	28.7						
Drink	53.7	68.5	51.3	23.1	18.9	31.8	23.1	18.9	31.8					1.5	
Tobacco	59.8	54.0	49.1	40.2	46.0	50.9	40.2	46.0	46.6	4.7	5.7				
Total	67.9	60.7	53.7	25.1	26.7	32.5	20.9	23.4	27.3	0.3	0.5	0.7	0.5	1.2	1.7
Petroleum	73.1	67.8	55.3	25.1	25.1	27.7	25.1	25.1	24.7	3.1	1.2	1.1	2.5	4.1	4.1
Other manufacturing	46.9	60.0	27.2	45.3	33.2	36.1	45.3	33.2	32.5	3.4	13.3	16.8		4.8	
TOTAL	67.6	58.5	49.2	26.7	28.9	31.5	24.6	26.2	27.5	6.8	7.1	6.7	3.3	4.6	5.2

Table 3.8 (cont.)

	Italy			UK			Other Europe (total)			Sweden			Japan		
	1962	1972	1982	1962	1972	1982	1962	1972	1982	1962	1972	1982	1962	1972	1982
High Research Intensity															
Aerospace				10.1	10.4	7.3								3.0	4.1
Office equipment (incl. computers)	7.2	4.0	2.9	8.6	6.3	6.7	4.2	3.7	4.9				12.4	18.9	25.9
Electronics and electrical appliances										2.1	1.7	3.1			15.7
Measurement, scientific and photographic equipment				8.9	7.2	7.7								6.5	10.6
Industrial and agricultural chemicals	2.7	5.3	3.3	3.5	4.8	3.5	2.9	4.2	4.9						
Pharmaceutical and consumer chemicals	3.0	3.5					7.8	8.8	8.3					5.4	2.7
Motor vehicles (incl. components)	3.0	3.5	5.4	6.8	4.7	3.4	0.9	2.5	5.5	0.9	2.1	4.7	4.4	13.4	25.2
Total	1.9	2.5	2.5	7.4	5.5	5.1	2.3	3.2	4.5	0.8	1.1	2.2	4.6	11.2	17.0
Medium Research Intensity															
Industrial and farm equipment				5.4	1.8	4.3	4.7	9.6	10.5	4.7	7.0	8.2	2.8	6.1	16.2
Shipbuilding, railroad and transportation equipment						12.0							6.3	50.4	25.4
Rubber	7.6			9.9	6.2	7.6								4.2	8.2
Building materials				13.7		32.3								5.7	8.9
Metal manufacturing and products	2.0	1.2	2.3	7.3	7.8	6.4	0.9	2.5	3.2	0.4	1.5		6.3	17.1	21.3
Total	2.0	0.7	1.4	7.2	5.6	7.9	1.4	3.2	4.2	1.1	2.1	1.8	4.6	14.8	18.5
Low Research Intensity															
Textiles, apparel and leather goods	4.2	3.0		11.8	15.1	11.8			8.7				15.6	38.1	38.2
Paper and wood products				12.5	12.7	12.3		2.5		1.7	2.5			5.1	14.6
Publishing and printing				24.9										18.3	27.5
Food				5.8	11.8	14.1	7.5	5.6	7.7				1.1	4.9	5.9
Drink				23.1	18.9	31.8								6.7	5.6
Tobacco				35.5	40.3	46.6			4.3						
Total	0.6	0.4		11.2	15.1	19.0	4.2	3.3	5.2	1.0	0.4		2.8	9.3	9.6
Petroleum	1.2	2.2	3.0	4.3	5.2	6.2			3.0				0.7	3.1	5.0
Other manufacturing				39.2	15.1	15.7			3.6						5.7
TOTAL	1.5	1.6	2.1	8.3	7.5	8.0	2.1	2.7	4.1	0.8	1.0	1.1	3.6	10.0	12.1

68

Table 3.8 (cont.)

	Other countries (total) 1962	1972	1982	Canada 1962	1972	1982	TOTAL 1962	1972	1982
High Research Intensity									
Aerospace							100.0	100.0	100.0
Office equipment (incl. computers)							100.0	100.0	100.0
Electronics and electrical appliances	0.9	0.6	4.3	0.9	0.6	0.9	100.0	100.0	100.0
Measurement, scientific and photographic equipment			2.4			1.6	100.0	100.0	100.0
Industrial and agricultural chemicals							100.0	100.0	100.0
Pharmaceuticals and consumer chemicals							100.0	100.0	100.0
Motor vehicles (incl. components)							100.0	100.0	100.0
Total	0.2	0.2	1.5	0.2	0.2	0.5	100.0	100.0	100.0
Medium Research Intensity									
Industrial and farm equipment	4.1	4.0	8.1	4.1	4.0	2.1	100.0	100.0	100.0
Shipbuilding, railroad and transportation equipment			49.1				100.0	100.0	100.0
Rubber							100.0	100.0	100.0
Building materials							100.0	100.0	100.0
Metal manufacturing and products	5.2	6.9	10.1	3.4	3.5	3.2	100.0	100.0	100.0
Total	3.8	5.0	9.7	2.8	2.9	2.4	100.0	100.0	100.0
Low Research Intensity									
Textiles, apparel and leather goods			7.1				100.0	100.0	100.0
Paper and wood products	7.6	6.6		7.6	6.6		100.0	100.0	100.0
Publishing and printing	13.1	17.7	24.2	13.1	17.7	24.2	100.0	100.0	100.0
Food	2.7	2.7	2.7	1.6	1.6	1.2	100.0	100.0	100.0
Drink	23.2	5.9	11.3	23.2	5.9	11.3	100.0	100.0	100.0
Tobacco							100.0	100.0	100.0
Total	4.2	3.3	4.2	3.6	2.8	2.9	100.0	100.0	100.0
Petroleum	1.2	4.1	12.1			0.9	100.0	100.0	100.0
Other manufacturing	7.7	6.8	31.0			17.3	100.0	100.0	100.0
TOTAL	2.2	2.7	7.3	1.4	1.2	1.6	100.0	100.0	100.0

1 EEC treated as Germany, France, Italy, Netherlands, Belgium, Luxembourg, UK, Denmark throughout the period 1962–82. See comment in Part I.

Source: derived from Table 3.6.

PART IV Employment of the world's largest enterprises

Ideally we would hope that the changes in the composition of $ values of sales of the equalised sample, as discussed in Part III, were a reasonable reflection of the relative changes in *real* output of the world's largest firms between countries and industries. In practice, however, differential rates of inflation, between countries and/or industries, and changes in exchange rates may reduce the likelihood of this parity. During the first decade of the study these problems were probably not too serious. Rates of inflation were low, and exchange rates changed only rarely, and mainly as a response to sustained differences in inflation rates. During the second decade none of this remained viable. Both prices and exchange rates were very much more volatile and the latter were influenced by speculative factors to a degree that ruled out any conviction that they would offset differential price changes in any reasonably systematic manner.

To get an alternative perspective on this we have constructed samples based on employment levels rather than $ sales values. This we do for two reasons:

(i)   because levels of employment, and changes in employment, are an important economic indicator, and are of particular interest to governments in their quest for full employment; and

(ii)   because employment changes may reflect real output changes more closely than do changes in $ value of sales, and provide some indication of the nature of any distortion involved in sales data.

A problem with the employment samples is that to construct them from *Fortune* data in the same form as the sales samples, that is, to have a sample of the X largest employers in each year, we have to work with much smaller numbers of firms than for sales. The reason for this is that employment/sales ratios at the firm level vary widely, especially for the non-US sample, and it is likely that some firms with very high employment/sales ratios will be excluded entirely from the sales-ranked *Fortune* samples, which would have featured in quite a high position in an employment-ranked sample. To eliminate this danger we chose a cut-off level for employment which seems to preclude the possibility of firms with employment above that level being omitted from the *Fortune* sample.

Two samples were eventually derived:

(i)   a 100-firm sample (that is, 100 largest employers) for all the years 1962–82; and

(ii)   following the expanded *Fortune* coverage of non-US firms (see Part I) we can use a 251-firm sample for the period 1972–82 only (the target sample size was 250, but three firms tied for 249th position in one of the years!).

(a)   THE EMPLOYMENT SAMPLES 1962–82 (tables 4.1 to 4.4)

Table 4.1 sets out data on the distribution of the firms in the 100-firm sample, and of their employment, by country of origin over the period 1962–82. Table 4.3 provides similar data for the 251-firm sample, for 1972–82. Comparison of developments over the decade common to these two tables does not reveal sustained consistency between them. One obvious factor likely to underlie such discrepancies is the difference in sample size.[1] Also, with relatively small samples, the entry and exit of firms at the margin may be reflected in quite large changes in employment composition between countries. This factor can help explain both relative volatility of country shares between years (most notably for the 100-firm sample), and the occasional contrasts between the two tables.

Bearing in mind the above qualifications, it is still possible to discern a number of trends in the employment samples. The US share of the employment in these samples has declined somewhat over the period 1962–82. The European share was also lower in 1982 than in 1962, with a notable decline over the decade 1972–82. Of the leading individual European countries, France provides clearest evidence of having an increasing share of employment over the two decades, and the UK the clearest evidence of a declining share. For Germany, an upward trend in the share from 1967 to 1982 is suggested. A modest rise in employment share, concentrated in the earlier part of the period, seems the most plausible interpretation of the Japanese data. Much less equivocal is the rising share of employment accounted for by 'other countries' firms where the rate of increase rose substantially and persistently between 1972 and 1982.

Information on the industrial composition of the 100 and 251-firm employment samples are given in tables 4.2 and 4.4 respectively. Industries which have clearly increased their share of employment over the 20 years include 'office equipment', 'electronics and electrical appliances' (though the rise seems to be concentrated in the first decade), 'industrial and agricultural chemicals' (though again the rise was concentrated in the period 1962–72), 'petroleum' (where a predictably strong rise in the second decade offsets an earlier fall in share) and 'tobacco'. Two industries, for which we have no data for 1962–72, but which increased their share of employment between 1972 and 1982, were 'pharmaceuticals and consumer chemicals' and 'drink'. A modest rising trend in employment is also evident in the 'building materials' sector share between 1962 and 1982.

The most notable declines in employment shares are recorded by 'rubber', 'metal manufacture and products' and 'textiles, apparel and leather goods'. 'Paper and wood products' also showed a decline from 1972–82, as did 'motor vehicles' in the period 1977–82 after being on a rising trend over the previous 15 years. The shares of the 'food' industry are particularly volatile, though around a fairly stable trend.

(b) RATES OF CHANGE OF EMPLOYMENT 1962–82 (Table 4.5)

Here we seek a rather different perspective on the evolution of employment levels over the two decades period. Growth rates in employment are calculated for each successive five-year period. Thus, for each quinquennium a sample of firms is derived consisting of all firms from the *rationalised* samples for which employment data was available for both the first and last years of the period. From these firms the employment growth rates quoted in Table 4.5 are derived.

Overall, the rate of growth of employment declined consistently over the two decades, from 23 per cent in 1962–67, to 14 per cent in 1967–72, 5 per cent in 1972–77 and finally a slight fall in employment of 0.4 per cent in 1977–82. Using these sample averages as a norm, we can attempt to identify those industries which have tended to do better or worse than average in terms of employment growth.

Three industries record consistently above-average growth rates, two from the HRI group – 'measurement, scientific and photographic equipment' and 'pharmaceuticals and consumer chemicals' – and one from the LRI group, 'drink'. Two more LRI industries also have above-average growth rates of employment from 1967 to 1982, namely 'publishing and

---

1   This point should make it clear that the discrepancies between the two tables do not represent 'inaccuracies'. Thus if the national composition of firms ranked between 101 and 251 evolved differently from that of those ranked 1 to 100, over the period 1972–82, tables 4.1 and 4.3 would reveal different patterns, with each accurately reflecting the changes in its own sample.

printing' (following average growth in 1962–67) and 'tobacco' (where employment growth had been well below average in 1962–67). Three other HRI industries record predominantly, but inconsistently, above-average growth of employment – 'aerospace' (where the below-average rate in 1967–72 involves an actual fall in employment level), 'office equipment' and 'electronics and electrical appliances' (which, like 'aerospace', has one quinquennium in which employment falls, 1972–77 in this case). The case of 'motor vehicles' is an unusual one in as much as employment growth rates are above average in 1962–77, whereas a major fall in employment levels occurs from 1977 to 1982. 'Industrial and agricultural equipment' shows the same type of pattern in a less extreme form.

In two industries – 'industrial and agricultural chemicals' and 'paper and wood products' – employment growth rates were above average in the first decade, but below average in the second. By contrast, 'petroleum' follows a decade of below-average employment growth with consistently above-average increases during the period 1972–82.

Two industries, 'rubber' and 'metals', both from the MRI group of industries, have below-average employment growth throughout the period, whilst 'textiles, apparel and leather goods' (from LRI) is below average from 1967 to 1982, and also is the only industry to have falls in employment levels in both parts of the last decade.

At the country level, trends in employment growth are less easily categorised than those for industries. US-owned firms recorded a very high and substantially above-average rise in employment from 1962 to 1967. They experienced slightly below-average rates in the years 1967–72 and 1977–82, and marginally above the average between 1972 and 1977. Growth rates of European firms were below average in all periods except 1967–72, and most notably so in the period 1962–67. Germany followed a considerably below-average growth of employment in the first quinquennium with a relatively high average between 1967 and 1972; it also alternated below- and above-average performance in the subsequent decade. France sustained above-average growth rates of employment throughout the 20 years, but most notably in the first decade. By contrast, the UK's employment growth rates were below average throughout the period, considerably so in all periods except 1972–77, and with a major decline in employment levels between 1977 and 1982. Sweden achieved above-average employment growth rates from 1967 to 1982, following a below-average performance in the first quinquennium. Japan achieved above-average growth rates of employment during the years 1962–67 and again (though quite marginally) between 1967 and 1972. However, from 1972 to 1977, Japan was the only one of the leading countries identified in Table 4.5 to suffer a decline in employment level. By contrast, that country returned to a positive, and above-average, growth in employment levels between 1977 and 1982, when a number of other countries slipped into employment decline. Thus, Japan, in employment terms at least, seems to have been hit by the recessionary developments of the last decade most dramatically in the first five years but to have achieved a relative recovery by the second quinquennium, when other countries were suffering from a further slowing of employment growth.

(c)   COMPARATIVE CHANGES IN EMPLOYMENT AND SALES SHARES (Table 4.6)

As noted earlier, one of the reasons for presenting the employment samples discussed in section (a) is to attempt a check on the reliability of $ values of sales as an indicator of real changes in economic activity. So if changes in $ values of sales do accurately reflect changes in real output, we would expect reasonable consistency between changes in the composition of employment and that of sales in the samples. To make such a comparison realistically, samples whose composition is initially determined by employment are much preferred, since changes in the composition of sales-based samples will be directly influenced by the potentially distorting influences with which we are concerned.

Even so, we should note that differences in employment shares and sales shares may still occur for two reasons other than exchange-rate changes and differential rates of inflation. These reasons are:

(i)   Employment may not accurately reflect changes in real output due to differential rates of productivity growth.

(ii) Employment and sales may respond differently to marginal changes in the composition of the sample in ways which do not reflect the types of distortion that mainly concern us. For example, if the *number* of firms from a given country remained the same but a firm from a high-employment/sales industry left the sample to be replaced by one from a low-employment/sales industry, then that country's share of employment might decline but its share of sales might not. This would not, however, warrant the conclusion that, for the time period in question, $ sales tended to overstate real output changes for that country. This problem is likely to be more relevant in the 100-firm sample than the 251-firm sample.

In Table 4.6 the country shares of both employment and sales of the 100 and 251-firm employment samples are given. Taking due account of the two other factors just discussed, we nevertheless consider that any major differences between changes in employment share (believed to fairly closely approximate changes in *real* output share) and changes in $ value of sales share will reflect the distorting influences of differential rates of inflation and exchange-rate changes.

Overall, the figures in Table 4.6 suggest that the sales figures for US firms tend to overstate the real decline in their performance, since the decline in employment share is much less pronounced. For the UK it would seem that sales figures hide a real decline during the period 1962–72, and between 1977 and 1982 misrepresent a continuing decline as a quite substantial recovery. In the case of Germany, sales figures seem to somewhat overstate real performance between 1962 and 1977, and seriously understate it from 1977 to 1982. France, however, seems to be a case where sales figures and employment figures follow basically similar patterns, suggesting that here sales figures are a reasonable approximation for real activity. For Japan, sales share rises much more substantially between 1962 and 1972 than does employment share, which may mean that sales overstate performance in this period, though productivity rises could also be a substantial explanatory factor. Less difference is to be found in the latter decade.

This brief summary serves to suggest that $ value sales figures may give a distorted picture of relative changes in economic performance between countries. However, we would urge some caution in drawing too firm a conclusion from the data set out in this chapter as the sample size was quite small, this especially applies to the first of the two decades analysed.

(d) EMPLOYMENT CONCENTRATION RATIOS

During the period 1962–82, there seem to have been modest declines in concentration in the employment samples. Thus, in 1962 the 25 largest employers accounted for 48.6 per cent of the employment of the largest 100 employers. This value fell to 47.5 per cent in 1972 and 45.0 per cent in 1982.

Similarly in 1972, the 25 largest employers accounted for 31.5 per cent of the total employment of the 251 largest employers, this falling to 31.2 per cent in 1977 and 29.5 per cent in 1982.

Finally, the 100 largest employers accounted for 66.3 per cent of the employment of the 251 largest employers in 1972, for the same proportion in 1977, and for 65.5 per cent in 1982.

Table 4.1
Countries of origin of the small employment sample,[1] 1962 to 1982, number of firms and employment

	Number of firms					Employment					Percentage distribution of employment				
	1962	1967	1972	1977	1982	1962	1967	1972	1977	1982	1962	1967	1972	1977	1982
USA	39	40	35	36	37	4,187,936	5,670,984	5,511,502	5,862,757	5,531,252	41.9	47.2	40.0	39.9	39.0
Europe	54	52	57	54	50	5,278,192	5,634,726	7,421,583	7,713,370	7,076,382	52.9	46.9	53.8	52.5	49.9
EEC[2]	51	49	53	50	44	5,064,697	5,400,485	7,068,611	7,322,834	6,510,601	50.7	44.9	51.3	49.9	46.0
Germany	17	15	13	13	13	1,477,043	1,453,829	1,779,014	1,929,873	1,986,242	14.8	12.1	12.9	13.1	14.0
France	5	7	10	11	9	352,973	653,611	1,101,996	1,400,087	1,277,796	3.5	5.4	8.0	9.5	9.0
Italy	7	4	4	3	3	489,495	425,917	508,793	580,397	491,981	4.9	3.5	3.7	4.0	3.5
Netherlands	2	1	3	3	3	289,000	241,000	546,600	546,000	409,900	2.9	2.0	4.0	3.7	2.9
UK	18	20	20	17	15	1,938,486	2,150,128	2,451,208	2,215,227	1,898,682	19.4	17.9	17.8	15.1	13.4
UK/Italy			1	1				170,000	169,250				1.2	1.2	
UK/Netherlands	2	2	2	2	2	517,700	476,000	511,000	482,000	446,000	5.2	4.0	3.7	3.3	3.1
Other Europe	3	3	4	4	6	213,495	234,241	352,972	390,536	565,781	2.1	1.9	2.6	2.7	4.0
Austria				1	1				80,047	75,223				0.5	0.5
Sweden	1	1	1		2	55,570	64,759	70,638		175,536	0.6	0.5	0.5		1.2
Switzerland	2	2	3	3	3	157,925	169,482	282,334	310,489	315,022	1.6	1.4	2.0	2.1	2.2
Japan	5	5	6	6	6	394,289	473,096	648,875	595,668	649,135	3.9	3.9	4.7	4.1	4.6
Other Countries	2	3	2	4	7	121,755	241,250	202,791	509,499	910,939	1.2	2.0	1.5	3.5	6.4
Canada	1	1		1	1	49,855	59,195		91,700	127,000	0.5	0.5		0.6	0.9
South Africa					1					149,818					1.1
Netherlands Antilles					1					75,000					0.5
India	1	1	1	1	1	71,900	119,383	127,382	208,582	199,737	0.7	1.0	0.9	1.4	1.4
Mexico		1	1	1	1		62,672	75,409	104,838	125,000		0.5	0.5	0.7	0.9
South Korea					2					234,384					1.7
Zambia				1					104,379					0.7	
TOTAL	100	100	100	100	100	9,982,172	12,020,056	13,784,751	14,681,294	14,167,708	100.0	100.0	100.0	100.0	100.0

1 Covers the 100 largest firms, by employment levels, in each year.
2 The listed countries are treated as having constituted the EEC throughout the period 1962–82. See comment in Part I.

Source: *Fortune* July and August 1963; June and September 1968; May and September 1973; 8 May and 14 August 1978; 2 May and 22 August 1983. Organised as described in text.

Table 4.2

Industrial composition of the small employment sample,[1] 1962 to 1982, number of firms and employment

	Number of firms					Employment					Percentage distribution of employment				
	1962	1967	1972	1977	1982	1962	1967	1972	1977	1982	1962	1967	1972	1977	1982
High Research Intensity															
Aerospace	6	8	3	2	5	527,444	828,162	247,658	253,749	544,039	5.3	6.9	1.8	1.7	3.8
Office equipment (incl. computers)	5	5	7	5	5	346,352	572,217	796,174	669,656	732,518	3.5	4.8	5.8	4.6	5.2
Electronics and electrical appliances	17	18	18	16	20	2,090,176	2,584,442	3,230,930	2,891,662	3,214,544	20.9	21.5	23.4	19.7	22.7
Measurement, scientific and photographic equipment	1	1	1	1	1	47,800	105,600	114,800	123,700	136,500	0.5	0.9	0.8	0.8	1.0
Industrial and agricultural chemicals	8	9	12	11	12	673,747	936,899	1,368,485	1,349,939	1,266,573	6.7	7.8	9.9	9.2	8.9
Pharmaceuticals and consumer chemicals					1					79,700					0.6
Motor vehicles (incl. components)	13	17	17	16	13	1,752,844	2,605,177	3,167,254	3,506,777	2,710,268	17.6	21.7	23.0	23.9	19.1
Total	50	58	58	51	57	5,438,363	7,632,497	8,925,301	8,795,483	8,684,142	54.5	63.5	64.7	59.9	61.3
Medium Research Intensity															
Industrial and farm equipment	5	3	3	5	3	355,187	247,719	270,314	442,871	344,722	3.6	2.1	2.0	3.0	2.4
Shipbuilding, railroad and transportation equipment	1	1	1	1	1	84,500	103,196		73,268	137,000	0.8	0.9		0.5	1.0
Rubber	6	5	4	4	2	450,768	440,690	513,201	552,140	262,096	4.5	3.7	3.7	3.8	1.8
Building materials	1	1	1	1	1	60,000	64,600	129,000	160,000	138,407	0.6	0.5	0.9	1.1	1.0
Metal manufacturing and products	17	14	11	15	9	1,312,103	1,249,503	1,244,709	1,688,115	1,008,274	13.1	10.4	9.0	11.5	7.1
Total	30	24	19	26	16	2,262,558	2,105,708	2,157,224	2,916,394	1,890,499	22.7	17.5	15.6	19.9	13.3
Low Research Intensity															
Textiles, apparel and leather goods	4	4	3	1	1	228,000	329,000	310,000	112,009	80,000	2.3	2.7	2.2	0.8	0.6
Paper and wood products	1		1	1		50,405		79,600	86,300		0.5		0.6	0.6	
Food	5	4	5	5	7	542,965	543,482	711,252	721,009	866,695	5.4	4.5	5.2	4.9	6.1
Drink			1	1	3			82,300	76,000	337,609			0.6	0.5	2.4
Tobacco	1	1	2	2	3	100,000	90,000	203,000	247,600	379,169	1.0	0.7	1.5	1.7	2.7
Total	11	9	12	10	14	921,370	962,482	1,386,152	1,242,918	1,663,473	9.2	8.0	10.1	8.5	11.7
Petroleum	7	6	8	7	8	721,981	619,245	769,223	864,887	1,199,215	7.2	5.2	5.6	5.9	8.5
Other manufacturing	2	3	3	6	5	637,900	700,124	546,851	861,612	726,379	6.4	5.8	4.0	5.9	5.1
TOTAL	100	100	100	100	100	9,982,172	12,020,056	13,784,751	14,681,294	14,167,708	100.0	100.0	100.0	100.0	100.0

1 Covers the 100 largest firms, by employment levels, in each year.

Source: *Fortune* July and August 1963; June and August 1968; May and September 1973; 8 May and 14 August 1978; 2 May and 22 August 1983. Organised as described in text.

Table 4.3
Countries of origin of the large employment sample,[1] 1972 to 1982, number of firms and employment

	Number of firms			Employment			Percentage distribution of employment		
	1972	1977	1982	1972	1977	1982	1972	1977	1982
USA	117	119	118	9,423,191	9,896,807	9,495,604	45.3	44.7	43.9
Europe	105	98	101	9,569,192	9,901,436	9,577,369	46.0	44.7	44.3
EEC[2]	92	84	87	8,853,393	9,018,581	8,646,022	42.6	40.7	40.0
Germany	18	16	17	2,045,312	2,063,252	2,164,438	9.8	9.3	10.0
France	16	16	17	1,380,325	1,631,084	1,666,632	6.6	7.4	7.7
Italy	7	6	7	632,839	744,347	676,990	3.0	3.4	3.1
Netherlands	3	3	2	546,600	546,000	409,900	2.6	2.5	1.9
Belgium	2	2	2	103,201	92,821	84,760	0.5	0.4	0.4
UK	43	38	39	3,464,116	3,289,827	3,128,222	16.6	14.9	14.5
Italy/Switzerland			1			69,080			0.3
UK/Italy	1	1		170,000	169,250		0.8	0.8	
UK/Netherlands	2	2	2	511,000	482,000	446,000	2.5	2.2	2.1
Other Europe	13	14	14	715,799	882,855	931,347	3.4	4.0	4.3
Austria	1	1	1		80,047	75,223		0.4	0.3
Sweden	7	7	6	322,973	380,473	385,147	1.6	1.7	1.8
Switzerland	5	6	7	352,472	422,335	470,977	1.7	1.9	2.2
Portugal	1			40,354			0.2		
Japan	19	16	15	1,232,583	1,080,262	1,099,913	5.9	4.9	5.1
Other Countries	10	18	17	580,648	1,263,623	1,465,140	2.8	5.7	6.8
Australia	1	1	1	55,000	62,000	70,000	0.3	0.3	0.3
Canada	2	4	3	107,488	277,173	236,000	0.5	1.3	1.1
South Africa	1	3	3	44,655	159,272	273,618	0.2	0.7	1.3
Netherlands Antilles	1	1	1	39,000	47,513	75,000	0.2	0.2	0.3
Argentina	1			37,474			0.2		
Brazil	1	1	2	34,240	57,813	122,435	0.2	0.3	0.6
India	1	2	1	127,382	262,182	199,737	0.6	1.2	0.9
Indonesia	1			60,000			0.3		
Mexico	1	1	1	75,409	104,838	125,000	0.4	0.5	0.6
South Korea		4	4		188,453	318,936		0.9	1.5
Venezuela			1			44,414			0.2
Zambia		1			104,379			0.5	
TOTAL	251	251	251	20,805,614	22,142,128	21,638,026	100.0	100.0	100.0

1   Covers the 251 largest firms, by employment levels, in each year.

2   The listed countries are treated as having constituted the EEC throughout the period 1972–82. See comment in Part I.

Source: *Fortune* May and September 1973; 8 May and 14 August 1978; 2 May and 22 August 1983. Organised as described in text.

76

Table 4.4

Industrial composition of the large employment sample,[1] 1972 to 1982, number of firms and employment

	Number of firms			Employment			Percentage distribution of employment		
	1972	1977	1982	1972	1977	1982	1972	1977	1982
High Research Intensity									
Aerospace	11	9	15	690,497	687,152	1,053,463	3.3	3.1	4.9
Office equipment (incl. computers)	9	11	12	880,039	964,406	1,147,250	4.2	4.4	5.3
Electronics and electrical appliances	25	27	30	3,603,360	3,528,281	3,740,476	17.3	15.9	17.3
Measurement, scientific and photographic equipment	1	2	1	114,800	158,700	136,500	0.6	0.7	0.6
Industrial and agricultural chemicals	20	18	20	1,716,311	1,695,475	1,615,665	8.2	7.7	7.5
Pharmaceuticals and consumer chemicals	8	8	11	327,004	389,919	517,468	1.6	1.8	2.4
Motor vehicles (incl. components)	23	24	23	3,434,034	3,881,252	3,257,210	16.5	17.5	15.1
Total	97	99	112	10,766,045	11,305,185	11,468,032	51.7	51.1	53.0
Medium Research Intensity									
Industrial and farm equipment	17	18	15	917,430	1,092,883	887,842	4.4	4.9	4.1
Shipbuilding, railroad and transportation equipment	4	3	2	184,450	189,343	206,486	0.9	0.9	1.0
Rubber	7	7	5	665,765	684,714	455,176	3.2	3.1	2.1
Building materials	3	4	5	223,600	290,162	300,427	1.1	1.3	1.4
Metal manufacturing and products	41	44	35	2,683,523	3,046,335	2,324,020	12.9	13.8	10.7
Total	72	76	62	4,674,768	5,303,437	4,173,951	22.5	24.0	19.3
Low Research Intensity									
Textiles, apparel and leather goods	11	8	5	635,594	453,279	277,965	3.1	2.0	1.3
Paper and wood products	7	6	5	333,327	303,530	219,660	1.6	1.4	1.0
Food	26	24	26	1,663,644	1,636,718	1,762,832	8.0	7.4	8.1
Drink	4	5	7	233,941	280,376	528,345	1.1	1.3	2.4
Tobacco	4	5	6	285,000	391,305	535,969	1.4	1.8	2.5
Total	52	48	49	3,151,506	3,065,208	3,324,771	15.1	13.8	15.4
Petroleum	18	17	21	1,190,718	1,354,013	1,858,229	5.7	6.1	8.6
Other manufacturing	12	11	7	1,022,577	1,114,285	813,063	4.9	5.0	3.8
TOTAL	251	251	251	20,805,614	22,142,128	21,638,026	100.0	100.0	100.0

1 Covers the 251 largest firms, by employment levels, in each year.

Source: *Fortune* May and September 1973; 8 May and 14 August 1978; 2 May and 22 August 1983. Organised as described in text.

Table 4.5

Rates of growth of employment, 1962/67, 1967/72, 1972/77, 1977/82, for constant samples[1] of firms, by industry and country

	USA				Europe (total)			
	1962/67 1962 = 100	1967/72 1967 = 100	1972/77 1972 = 100	1977/82 1977 = 100	1962/67 1962 = 100	1967/72 1967 = 100	1972/77 1972 = 100	1977/1982 1977 = 100
High Research Intensity								
Aerospace	136.7	70.7	115.6	114.8	114.6	76.4	94.8	103.6
Office equipment (incl. computers)	171.8	120.9	106.0	121.3	106.6	124.1	98.3	86.4
Electronics and electrical appliances	144.7	130.3	95.8	97.1	108.0	128.2	100.9	102.2
Measurement, scientific and photographic equipment	218.9	118.2	123.6	114.7			103.6	91.3
Industrial and agricultural chemicals	143.6	104.6	105.8	100.7	109.9	131.1	100.7	90.7
Pharmaceuticals and consumer chemicals	167.4	134.6	122.3	107.6	157.5	136.5	107.5	103.4
Motor vehicles (incl. components)	137.5	109.5	106.9	76.4	132.2	134.0	109.3	92.0
Total	146.0	111.4	106.1	98.9	116.6	127.5	103.2	95.7
Medium Research Intensity								
Industrial and farm equipment	147.5	116.5	116.2	86.1	94.7	112.7	94.2	99.2
Shipbuilding, railroad and transportation equipment	120.6	76.9	107.5	101.6			101.5	100.7
Rubber	108.2	112.6	98.6	69.7	114.4	116.3	106.9	113.8
Building materials	116.3	129.6	101.8	83.9	107.4	132.6	112.1	99.7
Metal manufacturing and products	114.7	102.9	98.6	82.0	103.5	95.6	106.6	89.7
Total	121.1	107.8	103.8	81.8	103.2	102.4	104.9	94.5
Low Research Intensity								
Textiles, apparel and leather goods	131.3	114.7	89.9	97.3	130.8	118.2	85.1	72.4
Paper and wood products	124.7	121.7	101.8	93.1	174.2	129.7	99.5	82.3
Publishing and printing	142.3	127.5	114.7	142.5	107.2	105.0	97.9	104.5
Food	120.8	135.4	110.5	107.2	113.3	116.1	95.8	96.1
Drink	146.6	142.6	139.3	160.5	138.5	135.0	119.3	97.1
Tobacco	144.9	168.7	131.3	152.9	98.9	147.6	115.7	111.5
Total	126.8	128.4	106.9	111.4	118.8	121.6	98.5	94.1
Petroleum	126.3	108.6	122.0	112.4	81.4	105.9	111.2	126.8
Other Manufacturing	142.9	121.6	114.6	89.8	74.8	70.2	100.7	96.7
TOTAL	135.1	113.4	107.1	98.7	107.4	115.5	103.3	96.6

Table 4.5 (cont.)

	EEC[2]				Germany			
	1962/67 1962=100	1967/72 1967=100	1972/77 1972=100	1977/82 1977=100	1962/67 1962=100	1967/72 1967=100	1972/77 1972=100	1977/82 1977=100
High Research Intensity								
Aerospace	114.6	76.4	94.8	103.6			107.5	
Office equipment (incl. computers)	106.6	124.1	98.3	86.4				
Electronics and electrical appliances	107.9	128.5	98.8	100.7	99.5	127.9	97.6	92.9
Measurement, scientific and photographic equipment			103.6	85.5			103.6	85.5
Industrial and agricultural chemicals	108.8	130.1	100.7	89.0	106.3	155.3	130.2	102.4
Pharmaceuticals and consumer chemicals	125.1	122.7	104.3	100.5			79.4	101.4
Motor vehicles (incl. components)	132.2	131.6	107.7	90.7	118.5	146.1	104.1	112.8
Total	116.0	126.1	101.9	94.0	107.0	140.9	107.3	102.8
Medium Research Intensity								
Industrial and farm equipment	89.1	110.3	90.2	101.0	94.6	124.8	88.5	105.7
Shipbuilding, railroad and transportation equipment			101.5					
Rubber	114.4	116.3	106.9	113.8			83.7	113.5
Building materials	107.4	132.6	112.0	99.3				
Metal manufacturing and products	103.2	94.7	105.2	88.1	104.7	91.1	107.0	103.7
Total	102.8	100.8	104.1	93.6	103.1	96.8	101.8	104.5
Low Research Intensity								
Textiles, apparel and leather goods	130.8	118.2	85.1	69.3			92.7	95.0
Paper and wood products	174.2	129.7	105.7	72.2				108.1
Publishing and printing	107.2	105.0	97.9	99.1				110.9
Food	114.2	113.8	92.5	95.1				
Drink	138.5	135.0	119.3	97.1				
Tobacco	98.9	147.6	115.7	111.9			54.1	96.6
Total	119.8	120.8	97.4	92.7			75.0	104.1
Petroleum	81.4	105.9	111.4	128.1	62.5	44.1	133.3	136.9
Other Manufacturing	74.8	70.2	100.7	94.3			87.8	97.8
TOTAL	106.8	114.1	101.9	95.4	103.4	121.6	103.5	103.5

79

Table 4.5 (cont.)

	France				UK			
	1962/67 = 100	1967/72 = 100	1972/77 = 100	1977/82 = 100	1962/67 = 100	1967/72 = 100	1972/77 = 100	1977/82 = 100
High Research Intensity								
Aerospace	113.4		89.4	110.9	115.2	76.4	93.1	99.2
Office equipment (incl. computers)	130.0	217.7	101.9	121.2			116.1	89.6
Electronics and electrical appliances				150.7	115.2	95.4	94.4	95.7
Measurement, scientific and photographic equipment								
Industrial and agricultural chemicals	112.9	125.7	91.2	81.0	120.0	117.6	81.3	82.4
Pharmaceuticals and consumer chemicals	178.5	145.6	106.3	116.9	125.1	122.7	124.1	96.9
Motor vehicles (incl. components)			121.9	97.9	127.5	110.1	101.0	63.4
Total	141.3	155.7	107.5	106.5	119.6	100.3	96.3	83.9
Medium Research Intensity								
Industrial and farm equipment	88.3	103.8		104.8	79.6	84.4	91.7	89.1
Shipbuilding, railroad and transportation equipment								
Rubber	151.4	105.4	129.2	113.9	99.5			
Building materials	107.7		124.3	89.4	106.3	132.6	94.1	112.7
Metal manufacturing and products	109.2	102.3	108.7	85.7	96.4	108.3	105.8	73.5
Total	110.1	113.9	119.4	95.8	95.2	104.8	102.0	82.5
Low Research Intensity								
Textiles, apparel and leather goods				74.6	187.5	115.9	82.7	70.0
Paper and wood products				65.6	174.2	129.7	105.7	68.9
Publishing and printing	114.6	105.0	97.9	77.5	103.3	116.4	90.2	105.3
Food			85.2	78.9	129.6	135.0	119.3	104.6
Drink					138.5	147.6	122.0	95.6
Tobacco					98.9			113.9
Total	114.6	105.0	87.9	75.5	135.9	124.3	98.9	96.1
Petroleum	156.7	114.7	183.5	129.3	75.0	110.0	104.7	150.9
Other manufacturing		67.9	83.6		74.8	70.8	116.2	91.9
TOTAL	127.8	125.9	109.9	101.9	107.9	103.6	100.3	90.6

Table 4.5 (cont.)

	Other Europe				Sweden			
	1962/67 1962 = 100	1967/72 1967 = 100	1972/77 1972 = 100	1977/82 1977 = 100	1962/67 1962 = 100	1967/72 1967 = 100	1972/77 1972 = 100	1977/82 1977 = 100
High Research Intensity								
Aerospace								
Office equipment (incl. computers)								
Electronics and electrical appliances	109.3	125.6	117.2	112.5	109.5	154.3	128.3	122.8
Measurement, scientific and photographic equipment	128.7	142.0	99.2	106.8				106.8
Industrial and agricultural chemicals	207.8	150.0	115.4	113.3				91.1
Pharmaceuticals and consumer chemicals	127.7	197.4	127.7	110.7				
Motor vehicles (incl. components)				104.5	127.7	197.4	135.9	112.7
Total	125.3	143.2	116.5	109.8	116.2	173.8	131.5	116.9
Medium Research Intensity								
Industrial and farm equipment	109.3	116.7	100.5	96.2	109.3	106.4	103.0	93.8
Shipbuilding, railroad and transportation equipment				100.7				87.9
Rubber								
Building materials			111.1	108.3				
Metal manufacturing and products	113.8	114.2	125.0	100.5			122.9	96.6
Total	110.0	116.4	108.8	98.7	109.3	106.4	110.1	93.7
Low Research Intensity								
Textiles, apparel and leather goods			85.5	109.2			85.5	86.2
Paper and wood products				99.8				
Publishing and printing				146.8				146.8
Food	106.8	133.3	120.7	101.8				116.4
Drink								
Tobacco				98.7				
Total	106.8	133.4	110.5	103.8			85.5	101.3
Petroleum			105.7	104.7				91.0
Other manufacturing				154.6				
TOTAL	117.2	133.4	113.3	105.1	112.0	137.6	116.3	105.1

Table 4.5 (cont.)

	Japan				Other Countries			
	1962/67 1962 = 100	1967/72 1967 = 100	1972/77 1972 = 100	1977/82 1977 = 100	1962/67 1962 = 100	1967/72 1967 = 100	1972/77 1972 = 100	1977/82 1977 = 100
High Research Intensity								
Aerospace								
Office equipment (incl. computers)	116.8	113.0	94.7	129.4	133.4	85.8	129.0	201.2
Electronics and electrical appliances			96.9	115.0				
Measurement, scientific and photographic equipment	117.4	116.6	89.7	176.6				121.8
Industrial and agricultural chemicals	135.5	128.7	86.4	89.2				
Pharmaceuticals and consumer chemicals	231.4	131.3	102.8	80.7				
Motor vehicles (incl. components)				113.3				
Total	141.2	119.6	97.8	111.9	133.4	85.8	129.0	185.4
Medium Research Intensity								
Industrial and farm equipment	125.0	134.2	103.9	86.6	113.2	101.8	146.3	145.7
Shipbuilding, railroad and transportation equipment	169.4	125.2	91.3	81.1			132.2	193.3
Rubber			110.9	124.0			81.3	112.5
Building materials			95.5	131.1				
Metal manufacturing and products	108.3	110.4	92.0	88.1	123.2	107.1	122.3	101.6
Total	114.3	115.1	95.5	91.4	121.1	106.6	123.0	114.9
Low Research Intensity								
Textiles, apparel and leather goods	117.2	99.3	77.2	81.0	119.4	113.2	108.0	83.2
Paper and wood products			86.9	103.2	145.8	116.1	164.6	96.9
Publishing and printing			92.8	106.5			86.6	119.9
Food	102.9	96.7	90.4	93.9	105.4	134.4	107.3	102.2
Drink		148.6	101.3	95.5	102.9	143.5	127.4	
Tobacco								
Total	115.0	101.4	83.0	90.6	116.0	123.7	109.2	95.7
Petroleum	107.5	122.6	97.9	96.4	133.3	107.2	144.3	129.7
Other manufacturing			129.8	98.8	114.2	154.2	111.9	140.8
TOTAL	129.1	115.6	95.0	103.0	121.4	110.7	122.3	122.7

82

Table 4.5 (cont.)

	Canada				TOTAL			
	1962/67 1962 = 100	1967/72 1967 = 100	1972/77 1972 = 100	1977/82 1977 = 100	1962/67 1962 = 100	1967/72 1967 = 100	1972/77 1972 = 100	1977/82 1977 = 100
High Research Intensity								
Aerospace					131.0	72.0	110.7	112.6
Office equipment (incl. computers)					163.5	121.2	105.0	118.0
Electronics and electrical appliances	133.4	85.8	129.0	136.0	124.6	126.7	98.2	103.9
Measurement, scientific and photographic equipment					218.9	118.2	121.3	114.7
Industrial and agricultural chemicals					125.1	118.5	102.2	94.3
Pharmaceuticals and consumer chemicals					164.3	134.7	116.3	105.3
Motor vehicles (incl. components)					140.1	120.0	107.3	87.3
Total	133.4	85.8	129.0	136.0	134.2	117.6	104.3	99.4
Medium Research Intensity								
Industrial and farm equipment	113.2	101.8	146.3	44.3	124.7	115.1	108.6	95.5
Shipbuilding, railroad and transportation equipment					127.2	92.0	104.9	130.8
Rubber					110.5	113.9	101.6	84.6
Building materials					113.5	129.9	106.3	95.0
Metal manufacturing and products	120.4	104.7	128.7	86.3	109.6	101.5	103.3	89.7
Total	118.0	104.1	132.8	74.9	113.5	106.6	104.6	92.3
Low Research Intensity								
Textiles, apparel and leather goods	119.4	113.2	108.0	83.2	128.6	112.8	86.1	84.5
Paper and wood products	145.8	116.1	164.6	96.9	132.6	122.7	101.2	89.9
Publishing and printing	100.0	115.4	114.1	100.0	122.3	120.6	114.4	119.4
Food	102.9	143.5	107.3	102.2	116.5	124.7	102.5	101.7
Drink			127.4		139.2	140.5	124.1	119.1
Tobacco					110.9	154.8	121.5	125.0
Total	116.7	118.6	115.8	92.4	122.5	124.0	102.1	101.9
Petroleum					107.0	107.8	120.2	118.9
Other manufacturing				138.5	90.2	91.2	107.5	102.0
TOTAL	118.8	105.9	125.8	95.3	122.9	114.2	105.0	99.6

1 For each 5 year period all firms from the rationalised sample for which employment data were available for both years of the period are included.

2 EEC treated as Germany, France, Italy, Netherlands, Belgium, Luxembourg, UK, Denmark throughout the period 1962–82. See comment in Part I.

Source: *Fortune* July and August 1963; June and September 1968; May and September 1973; 8 May and 14 August 1978; 2 May and 22 August 1983.

Table 4.6
Geographical distribution of employment and sales of the employment samples

	Percentage distribution of employment					Percentage distribution of sales				
	1962	1967	1972	1977	1982	1962	1967	1972	1977	1982
[A] 100 Firm Sample[1]										
USA	41.9	47.2	40.0	39.9	39.0	62.5	62.8	52.2	48.6	45.6
Europe (total)	52.9	46.9	53.8	52.5	49.9	34.2	33.3	41.1	44.4	43.9
Germany	14.8	12.1	12.9	13.1	14.0	9.5	8.7	10.7	11.9	10.6
France	3.5	5.4	8.0	9.5	9.0	2.2	3.3	5.6	6.9	5.5
Italy	4.9	3.5	3.7	4.0	3.5	3.0	2.7	2.8	3.7	3.8
Netherlands	2.9	2.0	4.0	3.7	2.9	1.4	1.1	2.8	2.6	1.6
UK	19.4	17.9	17.8	15.1	13.4	10.0	9.9	10.2	9.4	10.8
Switzerland	1.6	1.4	2.0	2.1	2.2	1.6	1.1	2.1	2.0	1.9
Japan	3.9	3.9	4.7	4.1	4.6	2.4	3.2	6.2	5.6	6.4
Other Countries (total)	1.2	2.0	1.5	3.5	6.4	0.5	0.9	0.5	1.4	4.0
TOTAL	100.0	100.0	100.0	100.0	100.0	100.0	100.0	100.0	100.0	100.0
[B] 251 Firm Sample[2]										
USA			45.3	44.7	43.9			57.4	55.2	52.1
Europe (total)			46.0	44.7	44.3			33.3	35.0	35.5
Germany			9.8	9.3	10.0			7.9	8.1	7.2
France			6.6	7.4	7.7			4.5	6.3	6.2
Italy			3.0	3.4	3.1			2.2	2.7	2.8
Netherlands			2.6	2.5	1.9			1.7	1.6	1.0
UK			16.6	14.9	14.5			9.5	8.1	9.5
Sweden			1.6	1.7	1.8			1.1	1.2	1.4
Switzerland			1.7	1.9	2.2			1.7	1.8	1.7
Japan			5.9	4.9	5.1			7.5	6.5	7.0
Other Countries (total)			2.8	5.7	6.8			1.6	3.3	5.3
Canada			0.5	1.3	1.1			0.4	1.0	0.7
TOTAL			100.0	100.0	100.0			100.0	100.0	100.0

1 Covers the 100 largest firms, by employment levels, in each year.
2 Covers the 251 largest firms, by employment levels, in each year.

Source: *Fortune* July and August 1963; June and September 1968; May and September 1973; 8 May and 14 August 1978; 2 May and 22 August 1983. Organised as described in text.

PART V Concentration, size and diversification

How concentrated are the world's largest companies? Is competition between them increasing or decreasing? In which sectors is concentration the most — and the least? Which are the largest enterprises of all, and how is their role changing over time? To what extent have the world's leading enterprises spread their activity into more than one industry? Which are the most strongly established diversification links between industries? Is diversification increasing or decreasing as leading firms battle to maintain their position in a difficult economic environment? These are some of the questions this part of our study tries to answer.

(a) CONCENTRATION (tables 5.1 to 5.3)

Table 5.1 presents data on the proportion of the sales of the largest 20 firms in each of a number of industries[1] accounted for by the three largest firms in that industry, from 1962 to 1982. In effect, this gives a world concentration ratio. Where 20 firms were not available, in some or all years, the ratio is given as three of a smaller number of firms, with the latter number being kept constant over the period, so that while concentration in these industries cannot be strictly compared with that in other industries in a given year, the change over time can be isolated. Of the eight industries treated in this way in Table 5.1, our usual 'three out of 20 firm' concentration ratios *could* be calculated for 1982 in five cases, due to increases in rationalised sample size.[2]

In 1982, the unweighted average for the 14 industries for which 'three out of 20 firm' concentration ratios could be calculated was 33.2 per cent. Most notably above this average were 'office equipment (including computers)', 'motor vehicles' and 'drink'. Industries of significantly below average concentration were 'industrial and agricultural equipment', 'textiles, apparel and leather goods', 'paper and wood products', 'industrial and agricultural chemicals', and 'electronics and electrical appliances'. We can also get a general impression of the level of concentration in the three other industries covered in Table 5.1 by calculating a hypothetical minimum 'three out of 20 firm' concentration ratio. This we do by assuming that each of the firms needed to bring the sample up to 20 firms is of the same size as the smallest firm in the 1982 rationalised sample. On this basis, it is clear that 'tobacco' is very highly concentrated (the hypothetical minimum ratio is higher than any of the 14 industries already discussed) and 'rubber' and 'shipbuilding, railroad and transportation equipment' are also well above average with ratios of just over 40 per cent.

If we turn to look at the trends in concentration suggested by Table 5.1, it seems clear that the most pervasive tendency was towards *declining* concentration. First, five industries

---

1   Three industries are totally excluded either because they do not have enough firms in some years to make the exercise viable, or, in the case of 'other manufacturing', because the exercise would be meaningless, given the miscellaneous nature of the group.

2   'Drink', 39.1 per cent; 'paper and wood products', 25.6 per cent; 'building materials', 33.6 per cent; 'aerospace', 33.9 per cent; 'office equipment (including computers)', 51.3 per cent.

('textiles, apparel and leather goods', 'petroleum', 'electronics and electrical appliances', 'motor vehicles', and 'industrial and farm equipment') suggest a sustained tendency towards lessening concentration throughout the 20-year period. In addition, five more industries showed declines in concentration from 1962 to 1972 followed by some tendency to renewed concentration from 1972 to 1982 ('food', 'industrial and agricultural chemicals', 'metal manufacture and products', 'shipbuilding, railroad and transportation equipment', and 'aerospace'). This U-shaped pattern in concentration was also demonstrated by 'tobacco', though here the decline from 1962 to 1972 was more marginal and the rise from 1972 to 1982 more substantial, and again by 'drink', where the upturn occurred in 1967. Finally, 'paper and wood products' and 'pharmaceuticals and consumer chemicals' also had declines in concentration from 1962 to 1972, with no strongly perceptible trend in the remainder of the period.

Two industries which run somewhat contrary to the tendencies outlined are 'rubber' and 'building materials', where rises in concentration from 1962 to 1972 are offset (but in both cases only partially) by falls from 1972 to 1982. The concentration ratio of the remaining industry, 'office equipment', shows no obvious pattern.

As a result of these evolutionary patterns in concentration over two decades, 11 industries finished with lower concentration ratios in 1982 than they had had in 1962, whilst five had higher ratios and in one case the change was negligible.

A pattern often detected at the industry level in Table 5.1, of an initial tendency towards lower concentration being halted or reversed, is clearly revealed in Table 5.2(a). Here we present data of the sales of the 483 firms in the equalised sample for each year. In 1962 the largest 25 firms accounted for 31.0 per cent of the total equalised sample sales; by 1967 their share had fallen to 28.6 per cent and by 1972 to 27.5 per cent, but this was followed by a substantial rise over the next five years to 30.2 per cent, this level being repeated in 1982. Similarly, the share of the 50 largest firms in the equalised sample also fell and then recovered, in this case the increase in concentration persisting through the second decade to achieve a marginally higher level in 1982 (43.0 per cent) than in 1962 (42.8 per cent).

In Table 5.3 (a) we perform a similar type of exercise for US and non-US firms separately, and examine the shares of the X largest firms in each area as a percentage of the sales of the 200 largest firms from that sector. An interesting contrast with the picture set out in Table 5.2 (a) emerges immediately, since it can be seen that for both US and non-US firms the renewed increase in the share of sales accounted for by the largest 25 firms begins after 1967 rather than after 1972. For US firms, this rise in concentration persists steadily after 1967 to reach a level of 50.3 per cent in 1982 compared with 46.4 per cent in 1962. For non-US firms, however, the rise in concentration ends in 1977 and the 1982 value of 39.7 per cent is only 1.2 per cent above that for 1962. Rather different emphasis emerges when we look at the case where X = 50 (that is, the sales of the 50 largest firms as a proportion of the sales of the 200 largest). Here the upturn in US concentration does not occur until after 1972 but is then strong enough to lead to a higher level in 1982 than 1962 (64.6 per cent compared with 62.4 per cent). However, for non-US firms, the period of increased concentration in the X = 50 case was between 1967 and 1977, though the 1982 value (virtually unchanged from 1977) was again higher, at 57.4 per cent, than 1962, 54.7 per cent.

(b)   SIZE (tables 5.4 to 5.6)

In tables 5.4 to 5.6, we explore various aspects of the size distribution of the world's largest industrial enterprises. Thus, in Table 5.4, the sales of a particular number of US firms [either the largest X firms in Table 5.4 (a), or those ranked X_i to X_j in Table 5.4 (b)] are compared with the sales of an equal number (or comparably ranked) non-US firms. Two conclusions clearly emerge from this table. First the USA has the largest average firm size and its size superiority is most pronounced among the very large firms. In 1982, for example, the sales of the 25 largest US firms were 33 per cent greater than those of the 25 largest non-US firms; while the sales of the 50 largest US firms exceeded those of an equal number of non-US firms by only 18 per cent and, indeed, sales of US firms ranked 26–50 were 15 per cent smaller than the non-US firms similarly ranked. Secondly, the size superiority of the USA has fallen markedly and persistently over the period, this decline being perhaps most notable for firms ranked 26–50.

Table 5.5 sets out the geographical origins of the X largest firms [5.5 (a)], or those ranked X_i to X_j [5.5 (b)], in 1962, 1972 and 1982. It can be seen that, although the USA still had the largest share of the biggest firms, its relative decline in these groups was greater than its overall decline in the sample. While the US share of the equalised sample fell from 292 firms (61 per cent) in 1962 to 213 (44 per cent) in 1982, its share of the largest 25 fell from 20 (80 per cent) to 14 (56 per cent) and of the largest 50 from 38 (76 per cent) to 20 (40 per cent). Again, while in 1962 the USA dominated the 100 largest firms (with 67 entries) more completely than any succeeding 100, by 1982 it had fewer firms in the largest 100 (43) than between 101–200 (50) or 201–300 (52).

The European pattern is somewhat the reverse of that of the USA. Whereas the number of European firms in the 483 of the equalised sample only increased by five between 1962 and 1982, the number in the top 50 rose from 12 to 19. Again, in 1982, the contribution of European firms to the largest 100 firms (37) was larger than for any subsequent 100.

Although Japan has clearly made the strongest impact on the equalised sample over the period covered, the full strength of this growth had not quite reached the very largest firms by 1982. Thus in that year Japan had 17 per cent of its sample firms in the largest 100 compared with 20 per cent for the USA and 25 per cent for Europe. The same comment can be made of the firms of 'other countries', though it is interesting to note, as is suggested by Table 5.5 (b), that a number of new 'other countries' entrants between 1972 and 1982 had taken quite a considerable step into the ranking by 1982. This reflects the large proportion of new 'other countries' entrants in 'petroleum'.

Table 5.6 gives details of the sales of the five largest firms in each industry. It may be worth recalling at this point that the firms are classified to the industry which accounts for the largest part of their output though, as we shall document shortly, many of them are quite extensively diversified into several areas of activity. This means, first, that in Table 5.6 the sales recorded for many of the firms do not exclusively represent production in the industry to which the enterprise is allocated. Secondly, Table 5.6 excludes sources of products where these are the subsidiary activity of firms classified, on balance, to another industry.[1] Obviously a preferable approach would be to list the leading suppliers of each industry's product irrespective of the industry to which the firms are classified. Unfortunately our knowledge of diversification at the firm level is not sufficiently detailed or reliable (though an exercise along these lines is performed in Table 5.10 on a sample basis).

With the qualifications just outlined in mind, Table 5.6 gives a picture of relative stability (but by no means ossification) at the top of each industry. Of the 100 firms covered, 28 had entered the largest five in their industry between 1977 and 1982 (eight of these reaching the top three). While 10 industries had two (or more) new entrants in the top five in 1982 (compared with 1977), five other industries retained the same top five (though in only one case in unchanged order). Of the 20 industries, 14 had the same leading firm in 1982 as in 1977, and in five of the other industries the new leading firm had ranked second in 1977. Nevertheless, only five of the industries had the same three firms occupying the top three positions as in 1977, though in three of these cases the order was unchanged. Further, in only 11 cases were all of 1977's top three still in the top five in 1982.

There is no consistent suggestion in Table 5.6 that the growth performance of the largest firms in each industry between 1977 and 1982 had been notably better or worse than the industry average. In nine industries the leading firms' growth performance had been clearly better than average, and in 10 it had been worse. By contrast, 13 firms ranked second in 1982 had above-average growth rates over the preceding five years, and only seven below average. In only three of the 18 cases for which the comparison is possible did all the top three ranked firms in an industry in 1982 have above-average growth rates over the previous five years ('metals', 'publishing and printing', 'tobacco'), and in only two cases ('office equipment' and 'petroleum') did all of the top three have below-average growth rates.

---

1   As an illustration, Du Pont was ranked second in 'industrial and agricultural chemicals' in 1977 but subsequently became classified to 'petroleum' as a result of its takeover of Conoco. It nevertheless remains very prominent amongst the major producers of chemical products.

Of the 100 firms covered by Table 5.6, 53 come from the USA, 30 from Europe (the UK 11[1], Germany 10), 12 from Japan and five from 'other countries'. Compared with the largest 100 firms in the equalised sample in 1982, as shown in Table 5.5 (a), this suggests a notably more above-average representation of US firms, slightly lower than average for Japan and 'other countries' and significantly lower than average for Europe.

(c) INDUSTRIAL DIVERSIFICATION (tables 5.7 to 5.11)

An important characteristic common to the majority of the firms in our sample is the wide scope of their activity. Few of them limit their activity to one industry and to their home-country market. In Part VII we shall discuss, in some detail, the ways in which the world's largest enterprises have spread their activity by diversifying geographically, that is, by selling and producing outside their home country. Here we provide some evidence on their industrial diversification, that is, their tendency to be active in more than one industry.

A number of sources proved useful in deriving firm-level evidence on the nature and extent of industrial diversification:

1 company reports and accounts;
2 J. M. Stopford, *The World Directory of Multinational Enterprises 1982–83*, Macmillan, London 1983; and
3 *Standard and Poors' Register of Corporations, Directors and Executives*, vol. 1, Standard and Poors, New York 1983.

From these sources we were able to locate, for 636 of the 792 firms in the 1982 rationalised sample, which industries these enterprises were active in other than that characterised as their main industry.

This information is set out in Table 5.7. Here the first column gives the number of firms covered in each main industry, while the next 20 columns give the number of firms from the main industry to have diversifications into each subsidiary industry. Thus, 20 firms allocated to the 'aerospace' industry are covered, of which nine are also active in 'office equipment', 10 in 'electronics and electrical appliances', etc. The final row of Table 5.7 attempts a summary measure of diversification by giving the *average* number of other industries each firm in the main industry is active in, that is, 'aerospace' firms are, on average, active in 3.65 other industries.

In addition to these measures of diversification, we are also interested in the extent to which particular industries are penetrated, that is, the extent to which firms from other industries have diversified *into* a particular industry. It will be seen from Table 5.7 that 65 firms from industries other than 'aerospace' have subsidiary interests in that industry (that is, have penetrated 'aerospace'), whilst 77 have penetrated 'office equipment' etc. Two summary measures of penetration are given in the last two rows of Table 5.7.

'Penetration Ratio (A)' [PR(A)] is measured as x/n where x is the number of firms not classified to the industry which do have a subsidiary interest in it and n is the number of firms classified to that industry. Thus, for 'aerospace', where $x = 65$ and $n = 20$, PR(A) = 3.25. The purpose of PR(A) is to summarise the relationship between the extent of outside interest in the industry (x) and mainstream interest in the industry (n).

'Penetration Ratio (B)' [PR(B)] is defined as $x/636 - n$, where x and n are the same as for PR(A). PA(B) then measures the number of firms with a subsidiary interest in an industry as a proportion of those which could have a subsidiary interest in the industry, that is, those not classified to that industry as their main area of activity. Thus, for 'aerospace', 65 firms have a subsidiary interest in 'aerospace' out of the 616 firms, in our sample of 636, classified to other industries, that is PR(B) = 0.11. PR(B) thus provides a measure of the relative attractiveness of each industry for the diversifications of firms from other industries.

At this point we should mention a very basic problem in analysing industrial diversification, namely, that for any system of classification, some industries will be defined to be much

---

1 Excluding those jointly owned with the Netherlands.

wider in scope than others. Any attempt to derive a system of industrial classification which appears logical along the lines of such factors as products sold, processes used, raw materials embodied, etc., is likely to incorporate some quite broad industries and some which are much more narrowly specified. This is, of course, quite inevitable. Conceptually there is no way in which the full range of productive industry can be operationally divided into a number of equally wide subunits. Now, other things being equal, it would be expected that the most widely defined industries would have low degrees of diversification and high degrees of penetration, and vice versa for the most narrowly defined. However, in practice, we do not think this likely. It is in the nature of the types of diversification links which emerge between industries that certain industries will rank highly in terms of both diversification and penetration. On the other hand, the characteristics of some other industries (such as their basic technology) may encourage a high level of exclusivity, providing little basis for the successful diversification of firms in that industry but also making penetration difficult. We have some check on this from Table 5.7. Thus, if industry 'width' *were* the preponderant cause of different levels of diversification between industries, we would expect that those industries ranked highest in terms of diversification (final column of Table 5.7) would be systematically the ones ranked lowest in terms of PR(B) (final row in Table 5.7). This is, in fact, not the case, so we may conclude that the distinctive characteristics of particular industries substantially affect their diversification and penetration, in addition to the influence of the breadth of coverage of each industry.

Before discussing Table 5.7 in more detail, let us first introduce some further measures of industrial diversification. While the information in Table 5.7 helps us to delineate the industries into which firms have diversified, it does not tell us how large these diversifications are in relation to the firms' main activity, nor which are the most significant diversifications. Table 5.8 attempts to supply some information along these lines by providing data on the percentage of firms' sales made outside the main industry. It will thus be seen that, on average, the 513 firms covered in Table 5.8 had their activity divided in the proportion of 75 per cent in their main industry and 25 per cent in other industries. Table 5.9 covers 356 firms for which the type of information given in Table 5.8 is available for both 1977 and 1982, with the aim of seeing if any notable changes in the extent of their diversification have occurred.

The information in Table 5.10 extends our knowledge of diversification further by showing the amount of the total sales of each industry which is accounted for by each subsidiary industry. Thus, for example, the firms in 'aerospace' have 72.5 per cent of their sales in that industry, 2.2 per cent in 'office equipment', 5.0 per cent in 'electronics and electrical appliances', etc. The first total row in this table relates to the distribution of the output of the 469 firms in this sample by *product*, for example, the total output of 'aerospace' products (whether from the 'aerospace' industry itself or as the subsidiary activity of other firms) is 2.4 per cent of sample output. The second total reverts to the basis of categorising all the output of each firm to its main industry. Finally, the last row of Table 5.10 introduces a further penetration ratio, expressing the percentage of the total supply of the product which is accounted for by firms which are not allocated to the industry (that is, firms for which the product in question represents a subsidiary activity). Finally, Table 5.11 presents the same type of information as Table 5.10 for the 341 firms for which the data are available for both 1977 and 1982.

The data of tables 5.7 and 5.8 suggest that six industries are clearly above average in terms of diversification, whether the measure used is the number of diversifications (Table 5.7) or sales (Table 5.8). These are 'aerospace', 'electronics and electrical appliances', 'industrial and agricultural chemicals', 'industrial and farm equipment', 'metals', and 'tobacco'. Four more industries ('shipbuilding, railroad and transportation equipment', 'building materials', 'publishing and printing', and 'drink') are of noticeably above-average diversification in terms of the sales measure, but not in terms of numbers of diversifications, suggesting that the firms in these industries tend to be oriented to a relatively small number of quite substantial diversifications. By contrast, firms in 'rubber' and 'motor vehicles' are somewhat above average in terms of the numbers of diversifications measure, but below average by the sales index; this suggests an extensive range of small subsidiary activities. Five industries are below average by both measures, namely, 'office equipment', 'textiles, apparel and leather goods', 'paper and wood products', 'food' and 'petroleum'.

In terms of penetration, eight industries[1] are of above-average penetration by both numbers [PR(A)] and sales [PR(C)], and another eight[2] below average by both measures. 'Pharmaceuticals and consumer chemicals' and 'drink' are below average in terms of PR(A) but above in terms of PR(C) (suggesting a relatively small number of penetrations which are nevertheless of substantial magnitude compared to the size of firms in the industry), whilst 'paper and wood products' has an average value of PR(C) but well below average value of PR(A).

Tables 5.7 and 5.10 provide detailed information on the diversification links that exist between industries. In discussing these tables, we do not seek to elaborate on each of these links, but rather select a few of the more prominent ones in an attempt to delineate some of the different types of motivations for diversification illustrated.

A number of the diversification links between the more R and D intensive industries may be attributed to *technological complementarity and spillover*, which will occur where a firm from one industry undertakes a subsidiary interest in another industry in order to make use of technology (relevant to that industry) created as a spin-off of R and D undertaken in its main industry. Likely examples here are 'electronics and electrical appliances' links with 'office equipment' and 'aerospace', and 'motor vehicles' links with 'aerospace' and 'industrial and farm equipment'.

A familiar factor contributing to diversification links between industries is *vertical integration*, where the fact that the output of one industry is an input to another leads some firms to have interests in both sectors. Thus while several of our industries (for example, 'petroleum' and 'metals') are defined to cover the whole of a sustained vertically integrated production process, there are others where we find similar vertical links involving diversification. Thus, although the 'petroleum' industry is defined to run from oil extraction to fuel marketing, a subsidiary vertical link, which often involves diversification, is that in which oil serves as the basic input to the petrochemical industry. Similarly the fact that basic industrial chemicals provide the bases for pharmaceutical products underlies the diversification links between our 'industrial and agricultural chemicals' and 'pharmaceutical and consumer chemicals' industries. The links between 'industrial and agricultural chemicals' and 'textiles, apparel and leather goods' are of a similar type. In a comparable way many 'metals' firms have diversifications forward into 'industrial and farm equipment' by producing heavy mechanical equipment (for example, generating plant) which incorporates metal components cast by them.

Other diversifications may derive from *product complementarity*. One form of this will emerge when a firm produces a hybrid or multicomponent good which uses parts from different industries. The links between 'industrial and farm equipment' and 'electronics and electrical appliances' illustrate this. Here we have two industries which are clearly defined by their two distinct types of technology (electrical engineering and mechanical engineering) and each of which produces a range of products which is unequivocally based on its own technology. But there also exists a range of products which combines substantial elements of both mechanical and electrical engineering, but which has to be classified to one or other industry. Where a firm in one industry produces a hybrid product which, on balance, has been allocated to the other industry, diversification of this type will occur. Product complementarity also underlies the diversification links between 'pharmaceuticals and consumer chemicals' and 'measurement, scientific and photographic equipment'. Here a number of 'pharmaceuticals' firms undertake the manufacture of the instruments necessary for the diagnosis and administration procedures involved in the use of the drugs they produce.

Finally, *marketing complementarities* may contribute to diversification links, for example, between 'food', 'tobacco' and 'drink' and also between 'food' and 'pharmaceuticals and consumer chemicals'. In such cases, firms may have been encouraged to produce goods from

1   'Aerospace', 'office equipment', 'measurement, scientific and photographic equipment', 'industrial and agricultural chemicals', 'industrial and farm equipment', 'shipbuilding, railroad and transportation equipment', 'building materials', 'textiles, apparel and leather goods'.
2   'Electronics and electrical appliances', 'motor vehicles', 'rubber', 'metals', 'publishing and printing', 'food', 'tobacco', 'petroleum'.

these various industries in response to their frequently shared sales outlets and similar marketing techniques.

The changes in the pattern of diversification and penetration between 1977 and 1982 are set out in tables 5.9 and 5.11. Though the majority of industries have shown some tendency towards increasing diversification during the five-year period, we here discuss a few of the more significant changes.[1] In fact, it can be seen that the industries where the firms have opted to increase diversified activity most significantly are either those of medium- or low-research intensity or those which have proved most vulnerable to the recession of recent years.

Thus the only HRI industry to rank among those with appreciable rises in diversification is the one with the least impressive recent growth performance, namely 'motor vehicles'. In fact, while US and European 'motor vehicles' firms increased their diversification, the opposite was the case for Japanese firms. It can also be seen that several industries decreased the extent of their diversification *into* 'motor vehicles', (for example, 'aerospace', 'rubber' and 'industrial and farm equipment').

Two resource-based MRI industries, 'building materials' and 'metals', increased their diversification significantly between 1977 and 1982. In both cases, 'industrial and farm equipment' was a leading recipient of the extra subsidiary activity of these industries.

'Textiles, apparel and leather goods' is another industry which shows a general tendency to increased diversification (substantial rises for US, European and Japanese firms) in response to the vulnerability of its traditional activity. Probably more positively oriented are the rises in diversification of 'publishing and printing' firms, and most notably of US firms in this industry. One increased area of activity here is into 'paper and wood products', which has clear complementarities with the main activities of 'publishing and printing' firms. The other increasing diversification is into operations classified under our 'other manufacturing industries' grouping, these being into radio, TV and the provision of financial and business information, which are activities making extended use of reporting networks and communications expertise already basic to the 'publishing and printing' industry.

Finally, there is evidence of increased interpenetration among firms in the 'food'-'drink'-'tobacco' nexus of industries. Rises in diversification are notable for both 'drink' and 'tobacco' industries, the former increasing activity in 'food' (as well as in 'petroleum') and the latter in both 'drink' and 'food'.

The most notable case of declines in diversification is that of 'aerospace', which decreases its interest in 'motor vehicles' and, to a lesser extent, in 'electronics and electrical appliances'.

As Table 5.11 shows, the tendency to increased diversification also results in increased penetration in the majority of industries.[2] The most substantial rises in PR(C) have occurred in 'office equipment', 'industrial and agricultural chemicals', 'industrial and farm equipment', 'paper and wood products' and 'food'.

1   Of course rising diversification need not represent a positive decision by firms to acquire new assets in other industries. If a firm in an industry with an especially low growth rate already has subsidiary activity in other much faster-growing sectors, these subsidiary operations will inevitably increase their share of the enterprises's overall sales. Nevertheless, it is likely that the more substantial diversification changes in our tables represent conscious managerial decisions.

2   Rises in penetration are not an inevitable corollary of rises in diversification. If demand for a product grows substantially, this may result in extensive diversification into its supply by firms from other industries, but if supply from its main industry grows faster than from external sources the penetration ratio will still decline.

Table 5.1
Largest firm concentration ratios,[1] 1962, 1967, 1972, 1977, 1982 by industry

	1962	1967	1972	1977	1982
Food	38.8	36.3	34.6	34.9	35.1
Drink[2]	50.0	47.3	52.0	52.8	53.2
Tobacco[2]	58.2	57.0	56.2	59.8	68.9
Textiles, apparel and leather goods	29.0	28.5	27.8	26.7	24.8
Paper and wood products[3]	29.5	27.1	26.6	28.6	26.3
Industrial and agricultural chemicals	32.7	29.1	24.8	26.4	27.7
Pharmaceuticals and consumer chemicals	48.6	35.2	30.2	32.8	31.8
Petroleum	47.7	43.2	41.4	38.8	35.9
Rubber[4]	52.3	55.8	58.6	56.0	56.1
Building materials[5]	44.6	46.9	54.8	52.6	50.1
Metal manufacturing and products	31.7	29.1	27.1	27.3	31.4
Electronics and electrical appliances	41.8	38.2	35.2	35.4	28.8
Shipbuilding, railroad and transportation equipment[6]	74.0	68.3	57.6	58.8	67.2
Motor vehicles	66.7	63.2	56.2	50.5	41.3
Aerospace[7]	42.7	40.7	35.5	39.4	37.3
Office equipment (incl. computers)[4]	65.4	72.1	66.0	68.3	67.7
Industrial and farm equipment	34.7	32.2	32.1	29.6	24.0

1   Except where otherwise specified the sales of the 3 largest firms in the world as a percentage of the sales of the 20 largest firms in the world.
2   Sales of 3 largest firms in the world as a percentage of 9 largest firms in world.
3   Sales of 3 largest firms in the world as a percentage of 19 largest firms in world.
4   Sales of 3 largest firms in the world as a percentage of 8 largest firms in world.
5   Sales of 3 largest firms in the world as a percentage of 10 largest firms in world.
6   Sales of 3 largest firms in the world as a percentage of 7 largest firms in world.
7   Sales of 3 largest firms in the world as a percentage of 15 largest firms in world.

Source: *Fortune*, July and August 1963; June and September 1968; May and September 1973; 8 May and 14 August 1978; 2 May and 22 August 1983.

Table 5.2 (a)
Sales of x largest firms in world as a percentage of sales of equalised sample 1962–82

	1962	1967	1972	1977	1982
x = 25	31.0	28.6	27.5	30.2	30.2
x = 50	42.8	40.4	38.7	42.2	43.0
x = 100	57.5	55.0	53.9	57.1	57.9
x = 150	67.4	65.6	64.8	67.3	67.8
x = 200	75.3	73.9	73.3	75.1	75.4
x = 250	81.5	80.6	80.0	81.4	81.6
x = 300	86.7	86.1	85.6	86.4	86.7
x = 350	91.2	90.7	90.3	90.8	91.1
x = 400	95.0	94.6	94.3	94.6	94.9
x = 483	100.0	100.0	100.0	100.0	100.0

Table 5.2 (b)
Sales of firms ranked x_i to x_j as a percentage of equalised sample 1962–82

	1962	1967	1972	1977	1982
x_i to x_j = 1 to 25	31.0	28.6	27.5	30.2	30.2
x_i to x_j = 26 to 50	11.8	11.7	11.2	12.1	12.8
x_i to x_j = 51 to 100	14.7	14.6	15.2	14.8	14.9
x_i to x_j = 101 to 150	9.9	10.6	10.9	10.3	9.9
x_i to x_j = 151 to 200	7.9	8.4	8.6	7.8	7.6
x_i to x_j = 201 to 250	6.3	6.7	6.7	6.2	6.2
x_i to x_j = 251 to 300	5.2	5.4	5.6	5.1	5.1
x_i to x_j = 301 to 350	4.4	4.6	4.7	4.3	4.4
x_i to x_j = 351 to 400	3.8	3.9	4.0	3.8	3.8
x_i to x_j = 401 to 483	5.0	5.4	5.7	5.4	5.1

Source: *Fortune*, July and August 1963; June and September 1968; May and September 1973; 8 May and 14 August 1978; 2 May and 22 August 1983.

Table 5.3 (a)
Sales of x largest firms as a percentage of sales of 200 largest firms for US and non-US samples 1962–82

	US					Non-US				
	1962	1967	1972	1977	1982	1962	1967	1972	1977	1982
x = 25	46.4	43.8	44.5	48.2	50.3	38.5	35.4	36.4	39.9	39.7
x = 50	62.4	60.0	58.9	62.6	64.6	54.7	52.6	54.8	57.5	57.4
x = 100	80.6	79.1	78.1	80.5	81.3	76.5	75.5	76.7	78.0	77.9
x = 150	92.0	91.4	91.0	91.9	92.4	90.6	89.9	90.1	90.7	90.6
x = 200	100.0	100.0	100.0	100.0	100.0	100.0	100.0	100.0	100.0	100.0

Table 5.3 (b)
Sales of firms ranked x_i to x_j as a percentage of sales of 200 largest firms for US and non-US samples 1962–82

	US					Non-US				
	1962	1967	1972	1977	1982	1962	1967	1972	1977	1982
x_i to x_j = 1 – 25	46.4	43.8	44.5	48.2	50.3	38.5	35.4	36.4	39.9	39.7
x_i to x_j = 26 – 50	16.0	16.2	14.4	14.4	14.3	16.2	17.2	18.4	17.6	17.7
x_i to x_j = 51 – 100	18.1	19.1	19.2	17.9	16.7	21.8	23.0	21.8	20.5	20.5
x_i to x_j = 101 – 150	11.4	12.3	12.9	11.4	11.2	14.1	14.4	13.5	12.7	12.7
x_i to x_j = 151 – 200	8.0	8.6	9.0	8.1	7.6	9.4	10.1	9.9	9.3	9.4

Source: *Fortune* July and August 1963; June and September 1968; May and September 1973; 8 May and 14 August 1978; 2 May and 22 August 1983.

Table 5.4 (a)

Sales of x largest US firms as a percentage of sales of x largest non-US firms 1962–82

Non-US = 100

	1962	1967	1972	1977	1982
x = 25	224.6	227.7	167.3	147.7	132.7
x = 50	212.5	209.7	147.0	133.0	117.9
x = 100	196.2	192.3	139.4	126.1	109.2
x = 150	189.1	186.7	138.2	123.8	106.8
x = 200	186.3	183.6	136.9	122.2	104.7
x = 250	NA	NA	135.7	120.6	102.7
x = 300	NA	NA	134.6	119.0	100.9

Table 5.4 (b)

Sales of firms ranked x_i to x_j in US sample as a percentage of firms ranked x_i to x_j in non-US sample 1962–82

Non-US = 100

	1962	1967	1972	1977	1982
x_i to x_j = 1 – 25	224.6	227.7	167.3	147.7	132.7
x_i to x_j = 26 – 50	184.0	172.8	106.9	99.8	84.7
x_i to x_j = 51 – 100	155.3	152.4	120.3	106.6	85.0
x_i to x_j = 101 – 150	150.3	157.4	131.1	109.9	92.0
x_i to x_j = 151 – 200	159.8	155.8	125.4	106.5	84.4
x_i to x_j = 201 – 250	NA	NA	120.4	99.2	75.6
x_i to x_j = 251 – 300	NA	NA	115.1	91.8	68.3

Source: *Fortune*, July and August 1963; June and September 1968; May and September 1973; 8 May and 14 August 1978; 2 May and 22 August 1983.

Table 5.5 (a)
Number of firms of a given area in largest x firms, 1962, 1972, 1982

	USA 1962	1972	1982	Europe 1962	1972	1982	Japan 1962	1972	1982	Other Countries 1962	1972	1982
x = 25	20	16	14	5	7	7	–	2	2	–	–	2
x = 50	38	26	20	12	18	19	–	6	7	–	–	4
x = 100	67	53	43	31	38	37	2	9	13	–	–	7
x = 200	124	118	93	63	62	65	8	16	26	5	4	16
x = 300	182	170	145	91	89	94	16	30	38	11	11	23
x = 400	241	218	178	123	116	126	21	50	61	15	16	35
x = 483	292	256	213	142	139	147	29	65	79	20	23	44

Table 5.5 (b)
Number of firms of a given area in firms ranked x_i to x_j, 1962, 1972, 1982

	USA 1962	1972	1982	Europe 1962	1972	1982	Japan 1962	1972	1982	Other Countries 1962	1972	1982
x_i to x_j = 1 to 25	20	16	14	5	7	7	–	2	2	–	–	2
x_i to x_j = 26 to 50	18	10	6	7	11	12	–	4	5	–	–	2
x_i to x_j = 51 to 100	29	27	23	19	20	18	2	3	6	–	–	3
x_i to x_j = 101 to 200	57	65	50	32	24	28	6	7	13	5	4	9
x_i to x_j = 201 to 300	58	52	52	28	27	29	8	14	12	6	7	7
x_i to x_j = 301 to 400	59	48	33	32	27	32	5	20	23	4	5	12
x_i to x_j = 401 to 483	51	38	35	19	23	21	8	15	18	5	7	9

Source: *Fortune* July and August 1963; June and September 1973; 2 May and 22 August 1983.

Table 5.6

The largest five firms in each industry, 1982 and their five year growth rates 1962–82

| | Sales 1982 $ m | Growth of sales | | | | Rank position 1977[3] |
		1977/82 1977 = 100	1972/77 1972 = 100	1967/72 1967 = 100	1962/67 1962 = 100	
Aerospace						
United Technologies (USA)	13,577	244.6	244.3	91.5	190.7	2
Boeing (USA)	9,035	224.8	169.6	82.3	162.8	3
Rockwell International (USA)	7,395	126.2	217.7	–	–	1
McDonnell Douglas (USA)	7,331	206.8	130.1	92.9	257.3	4
General Dynamics (USA)	6,352	219.0	188.5[2]	68.3[2]	118.7[2]	–
Whole of industry[1]	90,387	186.0	187.1	99.7	165.2	
Office equipment (incl. computers)						
IBM (USA)	34,364	189.5	190.2	178.3	277.7	1
Xerox (USA)	8,456	166.6	209.9	345.1	674.0	2
Sperry (USA)	5,571	170.4	179.3	122.6	125.8	4
Honeywell (USA)	5,490	188.6	137.0	203.5	175.5	5
Litton Industries (USA)	4,942	143.6	134.5	163.9	397.2	3
Whole of industry[1]	94,376	196.7	181.4	180.5	217.5	
Electronics and electrical appliances						
General Electric (USA)	26.500	151.3	171.1	132.3	161.5	1
Siemens (Germany)	16,963	159.4	225.8	237.5	147.0	4
Hitachi (Japan)	16,262	197.8	188.9	248.9	183.1	5
Philips (Netherlands)	16,093	126.7	204.7	258.4	157.1	3
ITT (USA)	15,958	121.4	153.6	310.0	253.2	2
Whole of industry[1]	285,295	173.4	174.5	196.3	168.9	
Measurement, scientific and photographic equipment						
Eastman Kodak (USA)	10,815	181.2	171.6	145.4	226.4	1
Canon (Japan)	2,331	320.6	–	–	–	–
Baxter Travenol Labs (USA)	1,671	198.0	302.5	–	–	4
Polaroid (USA)	1,294	121.8	189.9	150.3	361.2	3
Tektronix (USA)	1,196	262.9	–	–	–	–
Whole of industry[1]	24,943	191.0	189.6	151.5	238.3	
Industrial and agricultural chemicals						
Hoechst (Germany)	14,409	143.5	246.4	247.0	191.0	1
Bayer (Germany)	14,346	155.6	278.1	227.1	130.3	3
BASF (Germany)	12,960	142.2	245.1	295.5	176.3	4
ICI (UK)	12,873	158.2	192.1	157.4	166.1	5
Dow Chemical (USA)	10,618	170.3	259.3	173.8	149.4	–
Whole of industry[1]	227,242	150.7	210.0	174.3	163.1	
Pharmaceuticals and consumer chemicals						
Procter and Gamble (USA)	11,994	164.7	207.3	144.1	150.6	1
Johnson and Johnson (USA)	5,761	197.7	221.1	255.9	147.1	3
Colgate Palmolive (USA)	4,888	127.4	212.2	176.4	152.1	2
American Home Products (USA)	4,582	170.7	169.2	160.8	196.2	4
Bristol Myers (USA)	3,600	164.3	182..4	164.7	366.8	–
Whole of industry[1]	91,878	164.6	189.9	177.2	187.0	

Table 5.6 (cont.)

	Sales 1982 $ m	Growth of sales 1977/82 1977 = 100	Growth of sales 1972/77 1972 = 100	Growth of sales 1967/72 1967 = 100	Growth of sales 1962/67 1962 = 100	Rank position 1977[3]
Motor vehicles						
General Motors (USA)	60,026	109.2	180.6	152.0	136.8	1
Ford Motor (USA)	37,067	98.0	187.4	192.0	130.0	2
Toyota Motor (Japan)	18,800	195.8	229.3	332.8	271.1	–
Nissan Motor (Japan)	16,465	214.5	194.0	310.8	324.7	–
Daimler Benz (Germany)	16,022	154.7	249.3	286.7	123.3	–
Whole of industry[1]	336,989	134.3	194.9	182.6	156.2	
Industrial and farm equipment						
Caterpillar Tractor (USA)	6,469	110.6	224.8	176.8	178.2	2
Gutehoffnungshutte (Germany)	6,386	157.2	174.5	235.3	118.1	3
Schneider (France)	5,973	160.6	–	92.2	117.2	4
Barlow Rand (South Africa)	5,896	437.4	–	–	–	–
International Harvester (USA)	4,725	79.1	171.0	137.5	138.3	1
Whole of industry[1]	130,021	148.8	192.8	165.2	163.8	
Shipbuilding, railroad and transportation equipment						
Hyundai Group (South Korea)	8,036	310.2	–	–	–	2
Hitachi Zosen (Japan)	2,402	194.8	175.4	216.3	–	–
Ogden (USA)	2,202	138.3	148.4	131.7	–	4
British Shipbuilders (UK)	1,960	–	–	–	–	–
Mitsui Engineering and Ship-building (Japan)	1,762	158.5	186.9	211.7	–	–
Whole of industry[1]	19,547	203.8	185.7	120.6	151.8	
Rubber						
Goodyear Tire and Rubber (USA)	8,689	131.1	162.8	154.4	165.6	1
Michelin (France)	5,567	156.9	216.9	250.2	153.9	4
Pirelli (Italy/Switzerland)	4,209	–	–	–	153.3	–
Firestone Tire and Rubber (USA)	3,869	87.4	164.6	143.5	146.8	2
B F Goodrich (USA)	3,005	135.2	147.5	149.8	123.9	–
Whole of industry[1]	39,472	125.5	168.6	150.1	139.8	
Building materials						
Saint-Gobain (France)	7,805	120.5	250.1	–	133.3	1
Thomas Tilling (UK)	3,915	276.5	–	–	–	5
Asahi Glass (Japan)	2,522	193.4	215.9	–	–	–
Lafarge Coppee (France)	2,499	194.3	193.4	–	–	–
Owens Corning Fibreglass (USA)	2,373	160.3	240.7	163.6	148.6	3
Whole of industry[1]	51.500	154.7	182.0	184.9	137.1	
Metal manufacturing and products						
US Steel (USA)	18,375	191.2	177.9	134.9	115.5	1
Nippon Steel (Japan)	14,425	161.9	166.1	211.4	–	2
Thyssen (Germany)	12,947	155.5	251.9	186.8	171.9	3
Nippon Kokon (Japan)	7,167	150.1	181.7	259.2	220.4	–
Krupp (Germany)	6,886	153.3	213.1	171.0	118.6	–
Whole of industry[1]	319,045	149.1	185.9	166.6	146.3	

Table 5.6 (cont.)

	Sales 1982 $ m	Growth of sales				Rank position 1977[3]
		1977/82 1977 = 100	1972/77 1972 = 100	1967/72 1967 = 100	1962/67 1962 = 100	
Textiles, apparel and leather goods						
Courtaulds (UK)	3,419	130.5	137.2	182.8	201.2	2
Toray Inds (Japan)	3,229	188.9	156.2	174.2	163.1	–
Burlington Inds (USA)	2,876	120.4	131.5	133.1	135.2	3
Interco (USA)	2,674	170.8	159.6	183.0	176.9	–
Levi Strauss (USA)	2,572	165.0	309.3	–	–	–
Whole of industry[1]	44,331	136.2	149.7	164.0	157.2	
Paper and wood products						
Georgia Pacific (USA)	5,402	147.0	190.5	237.6	250.6	1
Weyerhaeser (USA)	4,186	127.5	196.0	189.1	163.2	4
International Paper (USA)	4,015	109.4	175.3	148.0	129.1	2
Champion International (USA)	3,737	108.6	184.0	178.4	–	3
Reed International (UK)	3,246	125.8	175.8	222.1	255.2	5
Whole of industry[1]	73.688	137.5	180.9	177.1	157.2	
Publishing and printing						
Time Inc. (USA)	3,564	285.1	202.9	121.7	155.2	1
Bertelsmann (Germany)	2,567	218.8	–	–	–	3=
Dai Nippon Printing (Japan)	2,470	210.6	228.2	–	–	3=
Int. Thomson Organisation (Canada)	2,334	–	–	–	–	–
Toppan Printing (Japan)	2,274	199.8	240.1	–	–	–
Whole of industry[1]	30.456	196.9	192.9	149.6	161.8	
Food						
Unilever (UK–Netherlands)	23,120	144.8	180.1	159.5	134.4	1
Nestle (Switzerland)	13,611	162.2	203.2	230.1	98.1	2
Dart and Kraft (USA)	9,974	145.8	–	–	–	–
Beatrice Foods (USA)	9,024	170.6	221.9	262.3	168.6	3
General Foods (USA)	8,351	170.1	202.6	146.7	138.9	–
Whole of industry[1]	236,924	155.3	181.8	161.4	138.2	
Drink						
Pepsi Cola (USA)	7,499	211.5	253.3	210.5	348.2	2
Coca Cola (USA)	6,250	175.6	189.8	179.9	184.0	1
Grand Metropolitan (UK)	6,088	–	–	–	–	–
Anheuser-Busch (USA)	4,576	249.0	188.1	176.4	169.4	3
Allied Lyons (UK)	3,807	139.7	–	–	–	–
Whole of industry[1]	53,185	190.1	178.2	179.2	168.7	
Tobacco						
BAT Industries (UK)	15,478	233.9	257.4	194.7	149.7	1
RJ Reynolds Industries (USA)	10,906	226.5	232.4	170.7	134.9	2
Philip Morris (USA)	9,102	236.5	273.4	239.5	162.9	3
Imperial Group (UK)	5,146	151.1	159.6	317.6	171.4	4
American Brands (USA)	4,026	139.2	166.8	182.1	145.3	5
Whole of industry[1]	53,366	199.7	205.0	204.9	144.5	

Table 5.6 (cont.)

	Sales 1982 $ m	Growth of sales				Rank position 1977[3]
		1977/82 1977 = 100	1972/77 1972 = 100	1967/72 1967 = 100	1962/67 1962 = 100	
Petroleum						
Exxon (USA)	97,173	179.5	266.5	153.1	139.1	1
Royal Dutch/Shell Group						
(UK–Netherlands)	83,759	211.1	282.2	167.9	139.1	2
Mobil (USA)	59,946	186.6	350.5	158.8	146.7	3
BP (UK)	51,322	245.1	366.7	192.0	147.9	5
Texaco (USA)	46,986	168.3	321.2	169.7	156.5	4
Whole of industry[1]	935,817	217.9	307.0	172.0	151.6	
Other manufacturing						
Canadian Pacific (Canada)	9,960	225.2	–	–	–	3
National Coal Board (UK)	9,034	214.7	165.9	104.1	98.0	4
Ruhrkohle (Germany)	7,246	153.2	228.8	–	–	2
Schlumberger (Neth. Antilles)	6,025	278.9	272.4	214.6	138.2	–
Gulf and Western Inds. (USA)	5,486	150.6	218.1	258.9	–	5
Whole of industry[1]	65,852	179.0	193.4	152.6	134.3	

1   Total sales figure for 1982 from Table 3.2 (rationalised samples) and growth of sales figures from Table 6.1.
2   Classified to another industry in these years.
3   If in top 5.

Source: *Fortune* 2 May and 22 August 1983.

Table 5.7

Numbers of diversifications by main and subsidary industries 1982[1]

	Number of firms in main industry	Subsidiary industry – number of firms from main industry with diversifications in each subsidiary industry					
		Aerospace	Office equipment (incl. computers)	Electronics and electrical appliances	Measurement scientific and photographic equipment	Industrial and agricultural chemicals	Pharmaceuticals and consumer chemicals
Aerospace	20	–	9	10	7	4	1
Office equipment (incl. computers)	19	4	–	6	6	5	3
Electronics and electrical appliances	51	18	31	–	20	4	3
Measurement, scientific and photographic equipment	12	1	8	6	–		25
Industrial and agricultural chemicals	54		5	11	10	–	
Pharmaceuticals and consumer chemicals	34			1	18	24	–
Motor vehicles (incl. components)	38	13	2	13	6	2	2
Industrial and farm equipment	56	12	5	29	6	12	
Shipbuilding, railroad and transportation equipment	6		1		1		
Rubber	12	4		1		6	1
Building materials	22	2	1	5	2	8	4
Metal manufacturing and products	80	7	3	18	4	38	3
Textiles, apparel and leather goods	20		1	1	2	7	2
Paper and wood products	34		3	2	1	14	
Publishing and printing	16		2	1			
Food	61	1		7	1	22	20
Drink	21				1	4	1
Tobacco	8		1			2	3
Petroleum	55		3	7	3	36	7
Other manufacturing	17	3	2	11	5	4	
TOTAL	636	65	77	129	93	192	75
Penetration Ratio (A)[2]	–	3.25	4.05	2.53	7.75	3.57	2.21
Penetration Ratio (B)[3]	–	0.11	0.13	0.22	0.15	0.33	0.13

101

Table 5.7 (cont.)

	Number of firms in main industry	Subsidiary industry – number of firms from main industry with diversifications in each subsidiary industry						
		Motor vehicles (incl. components)	Industrial and farm equipment	Shipbuilding, railroad and transportation equipment	Rubber	Building materials	Metal manufacturing and products	Textiles apparel and leather goods
Aerospace	20	6	12	6		2	7	
Office equipment (incl. computers)	19	1	4	2				
Electronics and electrical appliances	51	11	27	11		6	15	2
Measurement, scientific and photographic equipment	12	1	3			1	1	
Industrial and agricultural chemicals	54	3	12		1	15	13	15
Pharmaceuticals and consumer chemicals	34		2		9	4	3	5
Motor vehicles (incl. components)	38	—	30	12	1	7	8	
Industrial and farm equipment	56	18	—	21		12	25	3
Shipbuilding, railroad and transportation equipment	6		5	—			4	
Rubber	12	7	2		—	2	3	6
Building materials	22	5	7	1	1	—		3
Metal manufacturing and products	80	14	52	15	1	4	—	5
Textiles, apparel and leather goods	20	1	4	2	1	28	2	—
Paper and wood products	34		7	1	1	3	5	5
Publishing and printing	16		2	2		11	6	
Food	61	5	11			1		9
Drink	21		1			7	1	1
Tobacco	8		1			1		1
Petroleum	55	3	6	1	1	10	15	3
Other manufacturing	17	4	7	2	2	5	4	2
TOTAL	636	79	195	76	18	119	112	60
Penetration Ratio (A)[2]	—	2.08	3.45	12.67	1.50	5.41	1.40	3.00
Penetration Ratio (B)[3]	—	0.13	0.34	0.12	0.03	0.19	0.20	0.10

Table 5.7 (cont.)

	Number of firms in main industry	Subsidiary industry – number of firms from main industry with diversifications in each subsidiary industry							Average number of diversifications per firm
		Paper and wood products	Publishing and printing	Food	Drink	Tobacco	Petroleum	Other manufacturing	
Aerospace	20	1	2					6	3.65
Office equipment (incl. computers)	19	1	4					5	1.74
Electronics and electrical appliances	51	3	3	1	1		2	19	3.49
Measurement, scientific and photographic equipment	12	1						6	2.92
Industrial and agricultural chemicals	54	4	2	9	1		13	19	3.09
Pharmaceuticals and consumer chemicals	34	3	1	14	4			14	2.77
Motor vehicles (incl. components)	38		1	1	1		1	15	2.95
Industrial and farm equipment	56	2	1	1	1	1		14	2.95
Shipbuilding, railroad and transportation equipment	6			1				3	2.83
Rubber	12		1		1		1	6	3.17
Building materials	22	6	2					12	2.68
Metal manufacturing and products	80	9	2	1	2		14	45	3.28
Textiles, apparel and leather goods	20		1	3	1			7	1.85
Paper and wood products	34	–	7			1	5	17	2.44
Publishing and printing	16	9	–				2	13	1.94
Food	61	4	2	–	15	1	2	29	2.38
Drink	21	4	1	10	–	1	1	10	1.48
Tobacco	8		2	6	6	–	1	7	4.63
Petroleum	55	5	1	6			–	36	2.62
Other manufacturing	17	3	4	2		1	3	–	3.65
TOTAL	636	55	37	55	33	5	45	283	2.84
Penetration Ratio (A)[2]	–	1.62	2.31	0.90	1.57	0.62	0.82	16.65	–
Penetration Ratio (B)[3]	–	0.09	0.06	0.10	0.05	0.01	0.08	0.46	

1 Data cover 636 firms from the 1982 rationalised sample for which information was available from the sources listed in the text.

2 Penetration Ratio A is x/n where x is the number of firms not classified to the industry with a subsidiary interest in the industry and n is the number of firms classified to the industry. Thus it attempts to estimate the relationship between outside interest in the industry (x) and mainstream interest in the industry (n).

3 Penetration Ratio B is x/636−n, where x and n are defined as in footnote 2. Thus the ratio relates the number of firms from outside the industry which *do* have a subsidiary interest in the industry (x) to the number of firms that *could* have a subsidiary interest in the industry (636−n).

Table 5.8
Industrial diversification,[1] 1982, by industry and area[2]

	USA	Europe	Japan	Other	TOTAL
Aerospace	37.6	10.1			33.5
Office equipment (incl. computers)	18.6	11.1	21.9		18.5
Electronics and electrical appliances	49.1	34.2	36.3	40.0	40.2
Measurement, scientific and photographic equipment	23.0		40.3		26.1
Industrial and agricultural chemicals	38.2	39.7	32.6	21.0	38.4
Pharmaceuticals and consumer chemicals	27.1	32.3	31.2		28.4
Motor vehicles (incl. components)	13.0	20.2	15.2		16.1
Industrial and farm equipment	21.3	34.8	40.9	52.4	31.0
Shipbuilding, railroad and transportation equipment	43.0	46.0	41.7		42.6
Rubber	25.0	6.5	3.1		15.8
Building materials	32.1	38.4	41.4	28.0	36.5
Metal manufacturing and products	33.2	36.9	15.9	20.2	29.6
Textiles, apparel and leather goods	9.1	16.1	25.0		17.0
Paper and wood products	11.9	44.9		14.0	18.6
Publishing and printing	34.1	52.8	13.4	41.8	35.2
Food	21.1	22.6	18.4	47.4	22.3
Drink	36.5	31.6		37.2	34.4
Tobacco	41.3	41.6		49.5	41.9
Petroleum	15.7	15.0		10.4	15.5
Other manufacturing	51.6	29.3	46.0	43.1	41.5
TOTAL	23.2	27.0	24.6	35.8	25.0

1　Percentage of firms sales made outside their main industry.
2　Data cover 513 firms for which information was available from the sources listed in the text. These 513 firms accounted for 80 per cent of the sales of the 792 firms in the 1982 rationalised sample.

Table 5.9

Industrial diversification,[1] 1982 and 1977, for a constant sample of firms,[2]
by industry and area

	USA		Europe		Japan		Other		TOTAL	
	1982	1977	1982	1977	1982	1977	1982	1977	1982	1977
Aerospace	38.5	40.9	2.0	2.0					35.6	38.5
Office equipment (incl. computers)	18.9	19.1	11.1	6.9	28.0	28.0			18.9	18.8
Electronics and electrical appliances	50.5	47.9	34.7	32.5	37.1	36.2	40.0	23.0	41.7	40.1
Measurement, scientific and photographic equipment	25.0	26.0			53.0	37.0			30.0	27.2
Industrial and agricultural chemicals	40.4	37.1	39.4	37.2	34.2	32.1			39.3	36.7
Pharmaceuticals and consumer chemicals	28.1	29.9	40.0	38.5	41.0	36.0			30.3	31.4
Motor vehicles (incl. components)	12.8	9.5	21.0	16.9	19.5	22.9			16.9	13.2
Industrial and farm equipment	17.0	20.7	35.1	31.6	48.0	46.2	52.4	26.1	28.6	26.1
Shipbuilding, railroad and transportation equipment	43.0	44.0	46.0	33.1	43.0	51.0			43.4	45.0
Rubber	25.0	25.8							25.0	25.8
Building materials	34.5	30.9	32.0	25.0	37.0	37.0			33.5	29.1
Metal manufacturing and products	35.3	29.8	42.5	35.5	14.9	12.4	20.2	22.0	29.8	25.6
Textiles, apparel and leather goods	10.6	5.4	21.3	16.3	24.1	17.2			17.9	12.1
Paper and wood products	13.2	12.1	55.3	48.7	0	0	14.0	16.1	19.2	18.1
Publishing and printing	40.2	28.1	61.0	55.0	13.4	13.5	10.0	5.0	30.1	21.8
Food	18.9	17.9	24.5	21.2	13.8	18.0	17.0	17.0	20.6	19.0
Drink	55.9	55.0	15.5	7.2			37.2	30.5	38.7	34.8
Tobacco	41.3	35.3	41.6	34.0					41.4	34.7
Petroleum	12.8	13.3	15.1	14.2					13.6	13.6
Other manufacturing	51.6	47.8	73.0	64.0	46.0	45.0	43.1	33.2	48.0	41.2
TOTAL	22.3	21.3	26.7	24.8	26.2	25.2	34.7	25.0	24.4	22.8

1   Percentage of firms sales made outside their main industry.
2   Data covers 356 firms for which information for both 1982 and 1977 was available from the sources listed in the text.
The 356 firms accounted for 65 per cent of the sales of the 792 firms in the 1982 rationalised sample.

Table 5.10
Industrial distribution of production by main industry and subsidiary industries, 1982[1]

Percentage industrial distribution of production

Main industry of firm	Aerospace	Office equipment (incl. computers)	Electronics and electrical appliances	Measurement, scientific and photographic equipment	Industrial and agricultural chemicals	Pharmaceuticals and consumer chemicals	Motor vehicles (incl. components)
Aerospace	72.5	2.2	5.0	0.9	0.7		6.7
Office equipment (incl. computers)	3.7	81.5	3.8	2.3		0.4	0.2
Electronics and electrical appliances	4.5	7.4	59.8	2.5	0.7	0.9	1.8
Measurement, scientific and photographic equipment		10.9	0.9	72.5	13.5	8.7	
Industrial and agricultural chemicals	0.1	1.1	2.9	0.9	62.4	70.9	0.3
Pharmaceuticals and consumer chemicals			0.1	5.3	7.4		
Motor vehicles (incl. components)	1.7	0.3	1.3	0.1	0.3	0.2	84.2
Industrial and farm equipment	1.3	0.1	6.5	0.2	3.2		4.4
Shipbuilding, railroad and transportation equipment		0.3		0.5			
Rubber	1.9		1.4		5.4	0.1	5.4
Building materials	0.1	2.0	1.5	1.1	5.2	0.7	2.4
Metal manufacturing and products	0.3	neg	0.5	0.2	4.5	3.5	1.1
Textiles, apparel and leather goods	neg	0.1	0.1	0.3	7.0	0.5	
Paper and wood products		0.1	0.2	0.1	2.6		
Publishing and printing		1.2	1.3				0.5
Food	0.1			0.1	2.8	4.6	
Drink				0.1	1.3	0.2	
Tobacco		0.3			0.2	1.5	
Petroleum		0.3	0.3	0.1	7.6	0.5	0.5
Other manufacturing	1.0	1.0	12.9	3.6	0.2		1.5
TOTAL	2.4	4.2	7.6	1.2	8.6	3.6	11.0
TOTAL (Main industry only[2])	2.0	3.8	10.4	0.6	8.0	3.2	12.0
Penetration ratio C[3]	39.1	27.2	17.8	62.1	42.2	38.1	8.2

106

Table 5.10 (cont.)

Percentage industrial distribution of production

Main industry of firm	Industrial and farm equipment	Shipbuilding, railroad and transportation equipment	Rubber	Building materials	Metal manufacturing and products	Textiles, apparel and leather goods	Paper and wood products
Aerospace	6.9	1.4		0.8	2.0		0.3
Office equipment (incl. computers)	2.9	1.8		0.6	2.4	0.1	0.4
Electronics and electrical appliances	11.0	2.0					
Measurement, scientific and photographic equipment	0.4		1.1	2.0	1.5	5.5	0.5
Industrial and agricultural chemicals	1.7			0.3	0.8	1.0	0.5
Pharmaceuticals and consumer chemicals	0.1		neg	0.6	0.9		
Motor vehicles (incl. components)	5.6	1.1		2.3	5.4	0.4	neg
Industrial and farm equipment	69.1	3.7		2.3	9.9		
Shipbuilding, railroad and transportation equipment	22.3	57.4		0.5			
Rubber	1.6		82.3			1.5	
Building materials	6.7	1.8		64.0	2.0	1.0	4.6
Metal manufacturing and products	10.1	1.2	0.1	1.4	71.0	0.4	1.4
Textiles, apparel and leather goods	0.3			0.4	0.5	82.9	
Paper and wood products	1.5	0.8		4.9	0.3	1.0	81.4
Publishing and printing	0.9	0.1		0.5			10.2
Food	0.4	0.3	0.1	0.8	0.6	1.7	0.8
Drink	neg			0.6		0.4	
Tobacco	0.5	0.1	0.1	0.3		0.1	3.3
Petroleum	0.5	0.6	neg	1.7	1.0	0.7	0.4
Other manufacturing	5.3				14.9	1.9	3.1
TOTAL	6.2	0.9	1.1	1.8	5.9	1.8	2.5
TOTAL (Main industry only²)	4.2	0.3	1.2	1.5	6.4	1.1	2.4
Penetration ratio C³	53.7	81.9	10.2	47.0	22.7	51.3	24.6

Table 5.10 (cont.)

Percentage industrial distribution of production

Main industry of firm	Publishing and printing	Food	Drink	Tobacco	Petroleum	Other manufacturing	TOTAL
Aerospace	0.2					0.3	100.0
Office equipment (incl. computers)	0.5					3.2	100.0
Electronics and electrical appliances	0.1	0.5	0.1		0.2	5.7	100.0
Measurement, scientific and photographic equipment						0.8	100.0
Industrial and agricultural chemicals	0.1	0.8	0.3		4.5	5.6	100.0
Pharmaceuticals and consumer chemicals	neg	8.5	0.5			4.7	100.0
Motor vehicles (incl. components)	0.1	0.2	neg		1.7	2.2	100.0
Industrial and farm equipment	neg		neg			3.0	100.0
Shipbuilding, railroad and transportation equipment		2.8		0.2		4.5	100.0
Rubber						1.4	100.0
Building materials	0.6					7.0	100.0
Metal manufacturing and products	neg	neg	0.4		1.0	4.7	100.0
Textiles, apparel and leather goods		0.4	0.1			4.1	100.0
Paper and wood products	3.2			0.1	0.3	3.0	100.0
Publishing and printing	64.8				3.8	18.4	100.0
Food	neg	78.1	2.7	neg	0.1	4.9	100.0
Drink	0.2	14.7	65.6	1.3	3.0	13.2	100.0
Tobacco	0.6	7.0	8.9	58.3	2.7	15.7	100.0
Petroleum		0.6			84.5	2.6	100.0
Other manufacturing	0.5	1.2			2.0	48.5	100.0
TOTAL	0.8	7.1	1.6	1.2	25.8	4.6	100.0
TOTAL (Main industry only)[2]	1.0	7.8	1.7	2.0	29.5	1.1	100.0
Penetration ratio C[3]	21.5	14.1	29.1	3.0	3.2	88.9	24.7

1   Data covers 469 firms for which information was available from the sources listed in the text. These 469 firms accounted for 75 per cent of the sales of the 792 firms in the 1982 rationalised sample.

2   Distribution of sales of this sample on the basis of all the sales of each firm being allocated to its main industry.

3   Percentage of the total supply of the product accounted for by firms not allocated to this industry.

neg − negligible is less than 0.05 per cent.

108

Table 5.11

Industrial distribution of production, by main industry and subsidiary industries for a constant sample of firms,[1] 1982 and 1977

Percentage industrial distribution of production

Main industry of firm	Aerospace		Office equipment (incl. computers)		Electronics and electrical appliances		Measurement, scientific and photographic equipment		Industrial and agricultural chemicals		Pharmaceuticals and consumer chemicals		Motor vehicles (incl. components)	
	1982	1977	1982	1977	1982	1977	1982	1977	1982	1977	1982	1977	1982	1977
Aerospace	73.5	68.1	1.8	1.9	6.7	7.9	1.0	1.4					5.3	8.2
Office equipment (incl. computers)	3.8	2.9	81.1	81.2	3.9	4.2	2.3	1.9					0.2	0.2
Electronics and electrical appliances	5.0	4.2	6.7	5.0	58.3	59.9	2.5	2.3	0.9	1.1	0.5	1.0	2.1	2.6
Measurement, scientific and photographic equipment	0.1	0.1	12.5	8.2	1.1	0.2	70.0	72.8	15.6	17.8	0.8	0.9	0.3	0.3
Industrial and agricultural chemicals			0.6	0.5	2.3	1.4	0.9	0.7	61.6	64.0	8.2	7.6		
Pharmaceuticals and consumer chemicals					0.1	0.1	5.3	4.2	7.6	7.8	69.4	68.0		
Motor vehicles (incl. components)	1.9	1.5	0.4	0.1	1.3	1.6	0.2	0.2	0.4	0.3	0.1		81.4	85.6
Industrial and farm equipment	1.4	1.0			7.1	5.0	0.1	0.1	1.9	1.9			5.2	6.4
Shipbuilding, railroad and transportation equipment													8.3	10.5
Rubber	2.5	1.7			1.5	1.7	1.5	0.8	8.3	8.8	0.1		1.5	1.9
Building materials	0.1	0.1			1.7	2.1	0.3	0.1	4.3	3.7	0.8	0.7	1.3	1.1
Metal manufacturing and products	0.4	0.4					0.4	0.2	4.9	4.7				
Textiles, apparel and leather goods			0.2	0.1			0.1	0.2	10.2	8.6				
Paper and wood products	neg	neg	0.2		0.1	0.1			2.8	2.2	0.6	0.5	0.1	0.1
Publishing and printing			0.5		0.3	0.3								
Food					1.2	0.6	0.1	0.2	3.4	3.8	5.3	5.2		
Drink			0.3	0.4			0.2		1.3	0.3	0.4			
Tobacco			0.2	0.1					0.2	0.6	1.6	0.9		
Petroleum	1.0	0.8	1.0	0.8	0.1		0.1	0.1	6.8	6.7	0.4	0.2	0.5	0.6
Other manufacturing					12.9	8.7	3.6	4.3	0.2	0.2			1.5	2.5
TOTAL	2.1	1.8	4.6	3.8	7.3	7.3	1.2	1.1	8.4	9.1	3.8	3.8	9.9	13.1
TOTAL (Main industry only[2])	1.4	1.3	4.5	3.9	10.2	10.2	0.7	0.6	7.8	8.9	3.6	3.6	11.0	14.0
Penetration ratio C[3]	49.3	48.6	21.5	17.8	18.0	16.3	61.9	61.4	42.8	37.1	34.4	35.4	9.2	8.8

Table 5.11 (cont.)

Percentage industrial distribution of production

Main industry of firm	Industrial and farm equipment		Shipbuilding, railroad and transportation equipment		Rubber		Building materials		Metal manufacturing and products		Textiles, apparel and leather goods		Paper and wood products	
	1982	1977	1982	1977	1982	1977	1982	1977	1982	1977	1982	1977	1982	1977
Aerospace	10.0	10.8	0.6	0.5					0.5	0.7				
Office equipment (incl. computers)	3.0	3.0	1.9	2.7										0.3
Electronics and electrical appliances	11.2	11.1	2.4	2.0			0.7	0.6	2.3	1.8	0.1	0.1	0.5	0.8
Measurement, scientific and photographic equipment					0.3	0.3								
Industrial and agricultural chemicals	1.6	2.1					2.4	2.4	1.6	2.5	6.5	7.7	0.6	0.7
Pharmaceuticals and consumer chemicals	0.1	0.1			neg	neg	0.3	0.4	0.8	1.1	1.0	1.2	0.5	0.7
Motor vehicles (incl. components)	6.9	6.2	1.4	1.4			0.1	0.1	0.9	0.7	0.1	0.1		0.2
Industrial and farm equipment	71.4	73.9	2.8	2.8			2.6	1.8	5.1	6.5				
Shipbuilding, railroad and transportation equipment	19.5	18.9	56.6	55.0			2.4	0.9	11.9	14.0				
Rubber	2.6	1.3			75.0	74.2	0.5	0.4			2.1	2.4		
Building materials	6.9	4.2	3.1	4.3			67.5	71.8	0.8	0.9	1.6	2.9	3.7	2.5
Metal manufacturing and products	9.9	7.8	0.7	0.8	0.2	0.1	1.5	1.3	69.2	73.5	0.4	0.5	1.6	1.6
Textiles, apparel and leather goods	0.5	0.5					0.7	0.3	0.8	0.7	81.8	87.1		
Paper and wood products	1.2	1.6	1.0	0.5			6.1	7.0	0.4	0.6	0.5	0.5	80.8	81.9
Publishing and printing	1.2	0.8	0.1	0.1			0.7	0.8					12.9	10.1
Food	0.3	0.3	0.2	0.3	0.1	0.1	0.3	0.2	0.2	0.3	1.8	1.2	0.6	0.3
Drink					0.1	0.1					0.7	1.0		
Tobacco	0.5	0.8			neg	neg	0.7	0.1			0.1	neg	3.4	3.4
Petroleum	0.6	0.6	0.1	0.2			0.4	0.4	1.1	1.3	0.1	0.1	0.4	0.6
Other manufacturing	5.3	5.4	0.6	0.7			1.7	1.8	14.9	9.5	1.9	1.8	3.1	1.8
TOTAL	6.3	6.9	0.9	1.0	0.7	1.1	1.5	1.6	5.8	6.7	1.5	1.8	2.4	2.9
TOTAL (Main industry only[2])	4.0	4.7	0.3	0.3	0.9	1.3	1.1	1.1	6.5	7.2	0.8	0.9	2.2	2.7
Penetration ratio C[3]	54.7	49.9	83.1	84.6	7.7	5.5	53.2	52.4	22.6	21.1	57.6	57.0	27.4	23.6

Table 5.11 (cont.)

Percentage industrial distribution of production

Main industry of firm	Publishing and printing		Food		Drink		Tobacco		Petroleum		Other manufacturing		TOTAL	
	1982	1977	1982	1977	1982	1977	1982	1977	1982	1977	1982	1977	1982	1977
Aerospace	0.4	0.5									3.3	3.1	100.0	100.0
Office equipment (incl. computers)	0.6	0.6	0.6	1.0							5.7	6.0	100.0	100.0
Electronics and electrical appliances	0.1	0.1			0.1	0.2			0.2	0.3	5.9	5.5	100.0	100.0
Measurement, scientific and photographic equipment	0.2	0.2	1.0	1.1	0.3	0.4					5.1	5.2	100.0	100.0
Industrial and agricultural chemicals	neg	0.1	9.2	11.1	0.5	0.2			5.5	2.6	2.6	2.1	100.0	100.0
Pharmaceuticals and consumer chemicals	0.1	0.1	0.2		0.1						2.3	0.5	100.0	100.0
Motor vehicles (incl. components)					neg	neg			2.2		6.0	7.0	100.0	100.0
Industrial and farm equipment											0.7	0.7	100.0	100.0
Shipbuilding, railroad and transportation equipment			3.7	4.3							6.4	4.0	100.0	100.0
Rubber	1.0	1.2									5.4	4.3	100.0	100.0
Building materials	0.1	0.1	neg	neg	0.4	0.4			1.1	0.3	5.2	2.6	100.0	100.0
Metal manufacturing and products											2.1	2.2	100.0	100.0
Textiles, apparel and leather goods					0.2				0.4	0.3	13.8	9.7	100.0	100.0
Paper and wood products	3.7	2.4				0.1	0.1	0.1	0.6		4.0	3.3	100.0	100.0
Publishing and printing	69.9	78.2									16.0	17.0	100.0	100.0
Food	neg	neg	80.0	81.9	2.2	1.8	neg	neg	5.5	0.6	14.9	12.5	100.0	100.0
Drink	0.3	0.3	14.4	13.1	61.3	65.2			2.8	2.9	2.4	2.4	100.0	100.0
Tobacco	0.7	0.1	7.0	5.4	9.2	7.0	58.6	65.3		3.2			100.0	100.0
Petroleum			0.5	0.1					86.5	86.5			100.0	100.0
Other manufacturing	0.5	0.5	1.2	0.9	1.2				2.0	1.8	48.5	58.5	100.0	100.0
TOTAL	0.7	0.7	6.8	7.4	1.2	1.0	1.4	1.3	28.8	23.6	4.6	4.3	100.0	100.0
TOTAL (Main industry only²)	0.8	0.6	7.2	7.9	1.2	0.9	2.4	1.9	32.2	26.8	1.3	1.2	100.0	100.0
Penetration ratio C³	25.1	25.9	14.8	11.8	40.1	37.5	0.3	0.3	3.3	1.9	86.3	83.1	24.4	23.0

1 Data cover 341 firms for which information for both 1982 and 1977 was available from the sources listed in the text. The 341 firms accounted for 61 per cent of the sales of the 792 firms in the 1982 rationalised sample.

2 Distribution of the sales of this sample on the basis of all sales of each firm being allocated to its main industry.

3 Percentage of the total supply of the product accounted for by firms not allocated to this industry.

neg – negligible is less than 0.05 per cent.

PART VI Profitability and growth 1962-82

(a) PROFITABILITY (tables 6.1 to 6.3)

Profitability data for the world's largest firms, for the period 1962–82, are set out in tables 6.1 to 6.3. A number of reservations should be noted concerning these figures. First, as we noted in Part II, the results may be influenced significantly by national differences in reporting and accounting practices. Also, changes in these practices may limit the validity of performance comparisons over time. Secondly, it should be noted that the results in these tables cover all firms from each year's rationalised sample for which profit data are available. This means that there will be considerable changes between years in the size of country and industry subsamples, which could bias the results in a manner which does not fully reflect real changes in profitability. We tend to feel that systematic distortion from this source is unlikely. Thus, since the rate-of-return figures in tables 6.1 to 6.3 are weighted averages, they will be most strongly influenced by the largest firms, most of which will have been in the sample throughout the 20-year period. Also, changes in sample size would only be likely to have a systematic effect on profitability if there were a direct link between firm size and rate of return. An econometric study of the data for 1972 and 1977 has shown there to be no significant statistical relationship between firm size and profitability for our samples.[1] Thirdly, using data for only five individual years, spread over a 20-year period, may produce results which do not accurately reflect trends (at least for individual countries and industries).

In discussing the profitability performance reflected in these tables we concentrate on rate of return on sales. Though the rate of return on asset figures reveals different points of emphasis in some cases, the overall picture is very similar, and concentration on one ratio greatly facilitates ease of exposition.

Of our groupings of industries by research intensity, it is the HRI industries which have the best profitability performance over the 20 years, generally achieving rate-of-return figures somewhat above the average. In line with the predominant tendency, the profitability of this group of industries declines over time, this decline being most sustained and pronounced for European firms and for Japanese firms between 1962 and 1967.

Generally, the most profitable of the HRI industries has been 'measurement, scientific and photographic equipment', though, unlike several of the other more successful industries (for example, 'office equipment' and 'pharmaceuticals'), it did suffer a sustained decline in profitability during the period 1967–82. The successful firms in this industry were the US ones, the few European and Japanese entrants never achieving remotely comparable profitability levels. 'Office equipment (including computers)' is another US-dominated industry where profitability levels have been consistently well above average. Once again the exceptional performances in this industry are mainly by US firms, the fledgling European and Japanese entrants struggling to achieve competitiveness. 'Aerospace' has been of below-average

---

1   P. J. Buckley, J. H. Dunning and R. D. Pearce, 'An analysis of the Growth and Profitability of the World's Largest Firms, 1972 to 1977', *Kyklos*, vol. 37, 1984, Fasc. 1, pp. 3–26.

profitability throughout the period (until 1982). US 'aerospace' firms recorded somewhat higher levels of profitability in 1972—82 than in the previous decade, by contrast with European firms where losses have become frequent in recent years. The profitability performance of the 'electronics and electrical appliances' industry has been healthy rather than spectacular during the 20 years, mainly somewhat below average for HRI industries, but avoiding the more serious declines suffered by some others in recent years.

An interesting contrast in performance between two substantially complementary industries is shown by 'industrial and agricultural chemicals' and 'pharmaceuticals and consumer chemicals'. The former industry has suffered a sustained and severe decline in performance during the period 1962—82, this also being generalised by area, with the USA, Europe and Japan all showing a basic tendency towards diminished profitability. By contrast, 'pharmaceuticals' has levels of profitability consistently above the average for HRI, and though (unlike the USA) European and Japanese firms in this industry do show a tendency towards declining profitability, it still remains among the most successful in both areas. 'Motor vehicles' ranks alongside 'industrial and agricultural chemicals' as the most troubled of the HRI industries; indeed for US firms the decline in profitability has been the most serious, especially since 1977. European firms in 'motor vehicles' have always been of below-average profitability and reported overall losses in 1982. The profitability of Japanese 'motor vehicles' firms also showed a tendency to fall, though not so markedly as that for US or European firms.

As a group, the MRI sector proved to be the most vulnerable in terms of profitability, recording not only consistently below-average rates of return but, from 1967 to 1982, the most sustained decline. Also, all the industries in this group (except 'shipbuilding, railroad and transportation equipment') proved subject to major profit collapse between 1977 and 1982, a phenomenon which was much less pervasive in HRI or LRI industries.

In 'industrial and farm equipment', US firms sustained profitability at a relatively high level between 1962 and 1977, but suffered a severe decline in the most recent quinquennium. In Europe, by contrast, declining profitability had persisted from 1962 to 1977 (though at levels above average for the MRI industries) before worsening to a slump comparable with that of the USA between 1977 and 1982. Profitability levels in 'industrial and farm equipment' in Japan also declined after 1967, but nevertheless in 1982 were at healthier levels than for Europe or the USA. Though never a notably profitable industry, 'shipbuilding, railroad and transportation equipment' seems to have weathered its most severe storms in the mid 1970s, and was the most successful MRI in 1982. This is partly due to some restructuring of the industry, and of firms within the industry. Profitability levels in 'rubber' remained consistently healthy, though never high, until the last part of the period when general problems in the industry hit European firms particularly hard, with substantial losses being made by several leading firms. In the 'building materials' industry, US firms held generally healthy levels of profits from 1962 to 1977 before a severe fall in 1982, whereas for Europe the industry was consistently of above-average profitability, though this did not preclude a sustained decline between 1972 and 1982. Profitability in 'metal manufacturing and products' has generally been low and also subject to sustained declines, during the period 1962—82 for Europe (where losses were reported overall in both 1977 and 1982) and Japan, and between 1967 and 1982 for the USA (where, in 1982, it reported aggregate losses, the only US industry to do so in any of the years covered by our data).

Though the LRI industries recorded overall profitability levels similar to those of MRI industries earlier in the period, they were generally successful in avoiding the serious declines which hit the other group from 1967 to 1982. Indeed in 1982, the average rate of return on sales of the six LRI industries was slightly above that for HRI and, for the first time, above the overall sample average.

For 1962—77, there were signs that 'textiles, apparel and leather goods' was subject to seriously sustained decline in profitability, but a certain amount of restructuring in the industry (including diversification into other areas of activity by leading firms) reversed the trend, at least for US and Japanese enterprises. By contrast, 'paper and wood products' firms, having generally sustained profit levels quite effectively for most of the period, suffered notable declines in the latter years. In the 'publishing and printing' industry profit levels have held up very impressively during the period, especially for US firms where, as we saw in Part V, improved performance probably owed something to the ability to make additional use of

113

the industry's established expertise in activities complementary to its traditional operations. Profitability levels in 'food', though always relatively low in absolute terms, have proved immune to the types of major slump seen elsewhere. For both 'drink' and 'tobacco', profit levels have been well above the general average throughout the period, though declining fairly substantially.

During the period 1962–72, profitability in the 'petroleum' industry was generally (except for Japan) well above average, though subject to decline from 1967 to 1972. This picture generally continued in the later 1970s, though in a notably changed context. Thus, the falling rate of return on sales figures between 1972 and 1982, when taken in the context of the vast sales growth of the industry over the period, does not reflect a serious decline in the industry's ability to make profits.

Looking at profitability by region or country of origin of firms, we find the USA has recorded consistently above-average rates of return, despite a persistent decline since 1967. European profitability has, by contrast, been below average throughout with declining rates of return persisting throughout the two decades. Between 1962 and 1977 Japanese rates of return on sales levels were quite close to those for Europe, but in the most recent five years Japan resisted the further declines in profitability suffered by the USA and Europe.

It is interesting to speculate on the extent to which the differences in overall profitability for various countries reported in Table 6.1 represent *nationality* effects, and the degree to which they might merely reflect the differing *industry* composition of a country's firms, that is, the nature of its industrial specialisation. Thus, the differences in profitability for the USA *vis-à-vis* Europe and Japan, reported in tables 6.1 and 6.3, do not *prove* that US firms are inherently more profitable simply because they are American; the overall difference could reflect the fact that the USA might have a greater proportion of its total sales in highly profitable industries. Casual observation of Table 6.3 tends to discount this explanation, since US firms seem to have a superior rate of return on sales figures in almost all industries. The similar proposition that differences in average industry profitability result from the country composition of the industry sample, that is, that industries reporting high profits may do so because a large proportion of their firms are from highly profitable countries, is less obviously disproved by Table 6.3.

In a recently published study[1] we investigated the above propositions, using econometric techniques, for samples of largest-firm data for 1972 and 1977 organised in a manner similar to that used here. From this we can derive strong support for the proposition that, when the influence of other factors[2] has been removed, the nationality of a firm remains a strong influence on its profitability. Similarly, the effect of industry on a firm's profitability, after the removal of other influences, was explored, and, though less strongly than for the effect of nationality, the evidence again suggested a significant influence.

(b)   GROWTH (tables 6.4 and 6.5)

In tables 6.4 and 6.5 we set out figures for the rate of growth of sales for each of the five-year periods 1962–67 (1962 = 100), 1967–72 (1967 = 100), 1972–77 (1972 = 100) and 1977–82 (1977 = 100). In each case, the data covers all firms from the rationalised sample for which sales data were available for both years. Once again a number of points need to be borne in mind in interpreting these tables. Firstly, it is necessary to reiterate that the sales growth rates will be influenced by both differences in inflation rates between countries, and by exchange-rate changes. These factors were subjected to scrutiny in Part IV. Though such distortions are most likely to be most visible in the country figures of Table 6.4, they will also be important in Table 6.5 for those industries which are dominated by firms of one nationality (for example, the pre-eminence of the USA in 'office equipment', 'aerospace' and 'measurement, scientific and photographic equipment'). Secondly, because of the particularly high and world-wide level of inflation between 1972 and 1977, there is a general tendency for the table to

1   Buckley, Dunning and Pearce, op. cit.
2   For example, industry of firm; firm size and extent of overseas production (see Part VII).

114

reveal a superior growth performance in that period for most industries and countries. Generally, a better impression of performance for a given industry or country in a particular period is, therefore, to be obtained from comparison with the average for that period, rather than merely deriving a favourable (or unfavourable) impression from a change *vis-à-vis* the previous period. Thirdly, because of the vast rise in value of 'petroleum' sales from 1972 to 1982, most other industries (while often revealing high rates of growth) record below-average performances during that period. Thus, we make a practice of comparing each industry with 'petroleum'-excluded average growth rates for 1972–82.[1] These are 187 for 1972–77 (1972 = 100) and 156 for 1977–82 (1977 = 100). We do not need to do this for the two earlier periods because the growth rate of 'petroleum' was close to the average in those cases. So the growth rates used as norms in the following discussion are 156 for 1962–67 (1962 = 100), 170 for 1967–72 (1967 = 100) and for 1972–82 those whose derivation was explained above.

The sales growth performance of the HRI industries was above average throughout the 1962–82 period, though decreasingly so. The only industry in this group to retain above-average growth rates through the period was 'pharmaceuticals and consumer chemicals'. Each of the six other HRI industries had just one quinquennium of below-average growth performance, this being 1967–72 for 'aerospace' and 'measurement, scientific and photographic equipment'; 1972–77 for 'office equipment' and 'electronics and electrical appliances' and 1977–82 for 'industrial and agricultural chemicals' and 'motor vehicles'.

By contrast with HRI, the MRI industries as a group recorded below-average growth performance throughout the two decades. The 'metal manufacturing and products' industry had below-average growth rates over the whole period 1962–82, though the recent troubles of the industry are perhaps less starkly displayed by growth rates than in the profit performance discussed earlier in this part. 'Rubber', whose growth rates had already been notably below average from 1962–77, reported the lowest growth of all for 1977–82 (a period of profit troubles in the industry also). 'Building materials' only recorded one period of above-average growth (1967–72), but its performance was not far below average from 1972–82. The 'shipbuilding, railroad and transportation equipment' industry recovered from a notably poor growth performance in 1967–72 to record a significantly above-average one in 1977–82. In growth terms, 'industrial and farm equipment' has been the most healthy of the MRI industries over the period, though 1977–82 represented its most notably below-average performance.

The LRI industries' growth performance was less consistent than that of other groups, recording well below-average performance in 1962–67 and 1972–77, marginally below average in 1967–72 and above average in 1977–82. The most consistently vulnerable LRI industry in growth terms was 'textiles, apparel and leather goods' with below-average performance from 1967 to 1982 (very substantially so in 1972–82). 'Food' had below-average growth performance over the whole period, though only marginally so from 1977 to 1982. By contrast, 'tobacco' had substantially above-average growth rates from 1967 to 1982, and 'drink' in all periods except 1972–77. 'Publishing and printing' had above-average growth performances in all periods except 1967–72, with a particularly healthy growth rate in 1977–82. 'Paper and wood products' followed above-average growth performance in 1962–72 with increasingly below-average rates from 1972 to 1982.

We have already referred to the vast growth rates in 'petroleum' sales from 1972 to 1982. These followed a below-average performance between 1962 and 1967 and slightly above average between 1967 and 1972.

Of the geographical areas and countries covered, Japan had the most notably above-average sales growth[2] throughout the 20-year period, with rates very considerably above the norm in all periods except 1972–77. Between 1962 and 1972, Japanese growth rates were well above average in all three industry groups, but in the second decade only in the HRI industries. US firms' growth rates were persistently below average from 1967 to 1982, after equalling the average between 1962 and 1967. US growth rates in HRI and MRI industry groups tended to be below the sample average for these industries, though in LRI industries their performance

---

1 The aggregate average growth rates for all industries other than 'petroleum'.
2 Once again these comparisons are made with 'petroleum'-excluded norms.

was generally closer to the norm. After a relatively poor growth performance between 1962 and 1967, European firms achieved a decade of above-average growth before falling back to a marginally below-average performance in the final quinquennium. This pattern of above-average growth performance by European firms from 1967 to 1977 was to be found in both HRI and MRI industry groups in aggregate, whilst in the LRI industries above-average rates were concentrated in 1967—72.

Tables 6.4 and 6.5 clearly show that growth rates have tended to differ substantially between firms of different nationalities. However, since very different growth rates are also observed between industries we can again speculate (as we did for profitability) on the extent to which a country's growth performance reflects the industry composition of its firms or tendencies endemic to its own economy. This, too, was tested econometrically[1] (for 1972—77) with a strong conclusion being reached that, after allowing for industrial composition of enterprises and other influences (for example, firm size), national characteristics still had a significant influence on growth rates. The opposite proposition, concerning industry growth rates, was also tested and it was found that, after taking account of the nationality composition, the industry of firms still remained important as an independent influence on growth. Thus both the industry of activity and country of origin were separately important influences on the growth rates achieved by firms.

1   Buckley, Dunning and Pearce, op. cit.

Table 6.1
Rate of return on sales and assets of rationalised samples,[1] 1962–82, by country

	Percentage rate of return on sales					Percentage rate of return on assets				
	1962	1967	1972	1977	1982	1962	1967	1972	1977	1982
USA	6.1	6.0	5.1	4.9	3.6	7.0	6.8	5.9	6.6	4.6
Europe	4.2	3.7	2.3	1.3	0.6	3.8	3.2	2.0	1.3	0.7
EEC[2]	4.1	3.6	2.1	1.4	0.6	3.7	3.2	2.0	1.4	0.7
Germany	3.1	2.3	1.2	1.2	0.6	3.6	2.7	1.4	1.4	0.8
France	2.4	2.0	1.5	0.1	−1.4	2.5	1.7	1.3	0.1	−1.5
Italy	2.0	2.4	−5.6	−3.4	−7.7	1.3	1.4	−3.2	−2.6	−9.5
Netherlands	6.6	4.4	2.8	0.3	0.7	4.7	3.3	2.5	0.3	0.9
Belgium	4.2	3.4	2.3	−1.1	0.4	2.6	2.1	1.9	−1.0	0.5
Luxembourg	4.8	2.0	0.8	−13.4	−8.7	2.8	1.1	0.5	−7.4	−5.2
UK	4.3	4.2	4.0	3.1	1.8	3.7	3.9	4.0	3.5	2.3
Denmark				2.8	4.6				2.4	5.2
Germany/Belgium		2.0	1.8				2.5	2.4		
UK/Italy			0.3					0.3		
UK/Netherlands	7.1	6.8	4.5	5.0	3.9	5.8	5.9	4.2	6.2	5.1
Other Europe	5.3	4.5	3.4	1.0	0.9	5.3	3.9	2.6	0.8	1.0
Austria	1.0	0.1	0.4	0.6	−0.4	1.1	0.1	0.3	0.6	−0.5
Finland				0.3	−0.5				0.3	−0.5
Greece					0.3					0.8
Norway				1.5	0.9				0.6	0.6
Sweden	4.5	2.9	2.5	−0.5	1.0	4.6	2.7	2.0	−0.4	1.3
Switzerland	6.1	5.6	4.2	4.0	3.0	6.1	4.9	3.5	2.8	2.7
Portugal		4.3	5.4	1.9	0.4		1.9	1.5	1.2	0.3
Spain			3.6	−1.3	−3.5			2.7	−1.2	−5.6
Turkey				0.8	4.0				0.7	5.9
Japan	4.0	3.3	2.5	1.7	1.6	3.0	2.7	1.8	1.5	1.9
Other Countries	8.0	7.1	6.5	7.2	1.6	5.8	4.8	4.7	6.4	1.4
Australia	5.6	4.3	4.2	2.6	3.2	4.0	4.2	3.8	2.5	3.2
Canada	8.0	7.3	5.6	4.8	−0.1	6.4	5.8	4.9	4.4	−0.1
New Zealand					4.8					5.6
South Africa	19.5	18.9	17.0	12.6	6.8	9.6	9.5	10.4	9.3	6.0
Netherlands Antilles	8.3	8.5	8.9	13.2	19.4	7.8	8.2	7.7	14.0	15.5
Israel				1.2	2.1				2.1	2.3
Argentina		2.0	−15.0		−82.4		1.3	−8.6		−85.7
Brazil		16.6	19.9	10.5	2.3		7.9	13.4	8.1	1.9
Chile			27.9	12.9	6.9			10.9	8.1	5.0
Colombia					−0.5					−0.7
India	7.4	−10.6	−1.1	4.1	1.5	3.9	−2.1	−0.7	3.2	1.7
Indonesia			5.1					1.3		
Kuwait				2.7	8.6				6.2	9.8
Mexico	1.7	3.4	0.4	1.6	−3.1	1.0	1.7	0.2	0.6	−2.2
Panama					16.6					15.6
Peru					0.5					0.5
Philippines				3.8	1.8				4.9	2.5
South Korea				4.1	0.8				4.4	1.1
Taiwan				1.5	1.3				3.2	4.3
Venezuela				18.9	13.5				28.8	8.1
Zambia			23.0	0.2				14.9	0.1	
TOTAL	5.5	5.3	4.1	3.6	2.3	5.8	5.4	4.1	4.0	2.7

1 Covers all firms from rationalised samples for which data needed to compile the ratios were available.
2 The listed countries are treated as having constituted the EEC throughout the period 1962–82. See comment in Part 1.

Source: *Fortune* July and August 1963; June and September 1968; May and September 1973; 8 May and 14 August 1978; 2 May and 22 August 1983.

Table 6.2
Rate of return on sales and assets of rationalised sample,[1] 1962–82, by industry

	Percentage rate of return on sales					Percentage rate of return on assets				
	1962	1967	1972	1977	1982	1962	1967	1972	1977	1982
High Research Intensity										
Aerospace	2.3	2.6	2.4	2.9	2.5	4.8	4.2	2.7	3.9	3.4
Office equipment (incl. computers)	6.5	8.2	7.6	9.0	7.8	7.1	8.7	6.7	9.0	8.2
Electronics and electrical appliances	4.2	4.1	4.2	3.9	3.3	4.5	4.5	4.5	4.2	3.9
Measurement, scientific and photographic equipment	13.3	14.8	12.0	8.7	7.5	12.7	16.3	11.6	9.0	8.0
Industrial and agricultural chemicals	7.7	5.7	3.1	3.2	1.8	6.5	4.7	2.6	3.1	2.0
Pharmaceuticals and consumer chemicals	8.3	8.7	8.2	7.4	7.7	10.3	11.2	9.7	8.4	8.9
Motor vehicles (incl. components)	6.0	4.1	4.0	3.3	0.6	8.9	5.6	5.5	5.0	0.9
Total	5.7	5.0	4.5	4.1	3.0	6.9	5.7	4.9	4.9	3.6
Medium Research Intensity										
Industrial and farm equipment	4.3	4.6	3.5	3.8	0.2	5.0	5.5	3.9	3.6	0.2
Shipbuilding, railroad and transportation equipment	3.0	3.0	1.7	0.7	1.8	4.6	3.6	1.1	0.5	1.7
Rubber	3.5	4.0	3.9	2.8	−1.2	4.8	4.9	4.3	3.4	−1.5
Building materials	6.4	4.7	4.8	3.6	1.2	6.6	4.7	4.7	3.7	1.2
Metal manufacturing and products	4.4	4.4	2.4	0.3	−2.3	3.6	3.5	1.9	0.2	−2.1
Total	4.3	4.3	2.9	1.5	−1.1	4.1	4.0	2.5	1.4	−1.1
Low Research Intensity										
Textiles, apparel and leather goods	3.7	3.8	2.4	1.2	1.9	4.3	4.2	2.7	1.4	2.5
Paper and wood products	5.7	5.4	3.3	4.5	1.6	5.6	5.1	3.2	4.7	1.6
Publishing and printing	4.7	6.0	5.0	4.9	4.6	5.6	7.3	6.0	6.5	6.2
Food	3.0	2.9	2.8	2.6	2.9	6.2	5.8	5.1	5.1	5.6
Drink	7.7	7.9	6.7	6.0	5.0	6.4	7.1	6.6	6.5	5.3
Tobacco	10.4	10.0	7.4	5.7	5.2	7.4	7.6	6.8	6.2	6.3
Total	4.3	4.3	3.6	3.4	3.2	6.0	5.8	4.7	4.8	4.5
Petroleum	8.6	8.9	5.6	4.4	2.7	6.3	6.4	4.3	5.1	3.5
Other manufacturing	3.7	3.7	3.1	5.3	4.5	3.4	3.4	2.9	5.2	4.0
TOTAL	5.5	5.3	4.1	3.6	2.3	5.8	5.4	4.1	4.0	2.7

1   Covers all firms from the rationalised samples for which data needed to compile the ratios were available.

Source: *Fortune* July and August 1963; June and September 1968; May and September 1973; 8 May and 14 August 1978; 2 May and 22 August 1983.

Table 6.3

Rate of return on sales of rationalised samples,[1] 1962–82, by industry and country

	USA					Europe (total)					EEC[2]				
	1962	1967	1972	1977	1982	1962	1967	1972	1977	1982	1962	1967	1972	1977	1982
High Research Intensity															
Aerospace	2.4	2.7	2.5	3.6	3.4	1.7	1.9	1.9	-0.2	-1.1	1.7	1.9	1.9	-0.2	-1.1
Office equipment (incl. computers)	6.7	8.4	8.0	9.8	8.7	3.8	4.6	1.4	2.4	-1.3	3.8	4.6	1.4	2.4	-1.3
Electronics and electrical appliances	4.6	4.8	4.9	5.4	4.7	3.2	2.8	3.1	2.4	1.9	3.3	2.8	3.1	2.3	2.0
Measurement, scientific and photographic equipment	13.3	14.8	12.7	9.3	9.0			1.5	1.1	0.7			1.5		0.1
Industrial and agricultural chemicals	9.6	7.0	5.9	5.9	4.6	4.8	4.2	0.4	1.1	0.1	4.7	4.2	0.2	0.9	0.2
Pharmaceuticals and consumer chemicals	8.1	8.4	9.1	8.3	8.6	9.7	10.6	6.3	5.1	5.0	7.0	7.9	4.7	5.0	5.5
Motor vehicles (incl. components)	7.2	4.7	5.1	4.6	0.4	2.4	2.2	1.9	1.5	-0.8	2.5	2.2	1.8	1.3	-0.9
Total	6.5	5.6	5.8	5.9	4.7	3.5	3.3	2.0	1.7	0.5	3.4	3.1	1.8	1.5	0.5
Medium Research Intensity															
Industrial and farm equipment	4.5	5.1	4.3	5.5	0.2	3.6	2.5	1.7	1.6	0.1	3.4	2.2	1.3	1.3	0.4
Shipbuilding, railroad and transportation equipment	3.0	3.4	1.8	3.2	2.7			2.1	-7.8	2.3			2.1	-0.1	-1.5
Rubber	3.7	4.3	4.5	2.9	1.4	3.0	3.1	2.4	3.0	-8.0	3.0	3.1	2.4	3.0	-8.0
Building materials	7.3	4.8	5.0	4.7	0.8	4.3	4.1	4.5	2.9	1.1	4.3	4.1	4.5	3.0	0.9
Metal manufacturing and products	4.9	5.9	3.2	1.8	-3.1	2.8	1.7	0.8	-2.7	-3.9	2.6	1.7	0.7	-2.7	-4.2
Total	4.7	5.2	3.7	3.3	-1.2	3.0	2.1	1.4	-1.2	-2.5	2.9	2.0	1.3	-1.1	-2.9
Low Research Intensity															
Textiles, apparel and leather goods	3.3	3.8	2.5	1.8	3.7	5.1	4.4	4.6	1.6	0.8	5.1	4.4	4.6	1.6	0.8
Paper and wood products	5.7	5.7	3.5	6.2	2.2	3.9	4.0	3.1	0.9	1.1	3.9	4.0	3.1	1.4	1.9
Publishing and printing	4.6	6.9	5.3	7.7	6.3	3.9	3.4	1.9	1.7	1.8	3.9	3.4	1.9	1.7	1.6
Food	2.7	2.8	2.7	3.1	3.5	4.0	3.4	3.2	2.3	2.7	3.6	3.2	3.1	2.0	2.4
Drink	6.5	7.7	5.4	6.2	5.6	8.5	8.1	10.1	6.6	5.3	8.5	8.1	10.1	6.6	5.3
Tobacco	10.5	9.7	8.3	7.2	8.5	10.3	10.4	6.3	4.3	2.3	10.3	10.4	6.3	4.7	2.5
Total	4.0	4.3	3.5	4.3	4.1	5.0	4.7	4.3	2.6	2.6	5.0	4.7	4.3	2.7	2.7
Petroleum	9.0	9.7	6.6	4.6	3.9	7.8	7.3	3.6	2.7	1.9	7.8	7.3	3.6	3.1	1.9
Other manufacturing	5.3	5.3	5.2	5.2	4.6	0.2	-2.5	-4.2	1.0	0.2	0.2	-2.5	-4.2	0.6	0.1
TOTAL	6.1	6.0	5.1	4.9	3.6	4.2	3.7	2.3	1.3	0.6	4.1	3.6	2.1	1.4	0.6

Table 6.3 (cont.)

	Germany					France					UK				
	1962	1967	1972	1977	1982	1962	1967	1972	1977	1982	1962	1967	1972	1977	1982
High Research Intensity															
Aerospace			0.4	-4.3	1.1	1.8	1.0	0.9	-0.8	0.8	1.7	2.1	3.6	2.8	-4.4
Office equipment (incl. computers)	3.1	2.5	1.8	2.0	3.1	2.1	1.1	1.6	3.8	-16.6			0.7	4.3	1.7
Electronics and electrical appliances			1.5		1.0				1.3	-0.3	2.1	3.4	5.7	4.5	6.1
Measurement, scientific and photographic equipment					0.1										
Industrial and agricultural chemicals	4.7	4.0	3.1	1.4	0.7	3.2	2.5	2.5	1.6	0.8	6.2	5.6	5.3	5.0	2.3
Pharmaceuticals and consumer chemicals			2.7	2.3	2.4			2.9	2.4	4.7	7.0	7.9	8.1	7.8	7.5
Motor vehicles (incl. components)	4.7	3.1	1.9	2.1	0.9	0.7	0.9	1.5	1.3	-1.8	1.6	2.0	2.8	0.6	-5.5
Total	4.3	3.3	2.3	1.7	0.9	1.7	1.3	1.7	1.3	-0.8	2.9	3.6	4.7	3.8	2.0
Medium Research Intensity															
Industrial and farm equipment	4.6	3.3	0.6	1.2	-0.9	0.5	1.0	2.0	0.3	-0.9	3.7	1.6	3.9	3.8	2.8
Shipbuilding, railroad and transportation equipment									0.9						-1.5
Rubber	4.0		2.8	0.8	0.6	4.3	4.5	5.7	3.5	-11.4	1.9	2.5	6.1	4.6	-5.2
Building materials		0.6	0.5	0.2	0.5	1.9	2.0	3.3	2.1	0.5	6.2	9.1	2.6	1.0	1.2
Metal manufacturing and products	1.7					1.5	2.1	-0.5	-7.5	-9.6	4.2	3.0			-3.0
Total	2.2	1.0	0.6	0.5	0.2	1.7	2.2	1.3	-2.3	-5.9	4.1	3.1	3.5	2.2	-0.9
Low Research Intensity															
Textiles, apparel and leather goods								-0.5	-0.9	0.3	6.2	5.4	5.8	3.8	0.9
Paper and wood products				-0.9	0.4		2.7	1.9	0.7	3.0	3.9	4.0	3.1	1.6	2.1
Publishing and printing				0.8	0.5				-0.1		5.8	4.2		4.1	3.3
Food								2.8		1.6	3.6	2.5	2.5	2.0	2.2
Drink	1.7		2.3				3.8			6.7	8.5	8.1	10.1	7.2	5.4
Tobacco				4.0	1.1				-5.3	2.2	10.3	11.4	6.9	5.4	2.9
Total	2.3		2.3	1.3	0.6	1.7	3.2	2.2	-0.5	1.6	6.3	5.5	4.9	3.6	2.9
Petroleum	1.9	1.1	-0.3	-1.5	-0.6	7.4	8.3	2.4	2.1	1.2	9.8	7.5	3.9	2.1	2.6
Other manufacturing	-4.3		-5.1	0.7	0.2		-12.1	-0.4	-2.0		0.4	0.6	-3.3	1.6	0.0
TOTAL	3.1	2.3	1.2	1.2	0.6	2.4	2.0	1.5	0.1	-1.4	4.3	4.2	4.0	3.1	1.8

Table 6.3 (cont.)

	Other Europe					Sweden					Japan				
	1962	1967	1972	1977	1982	1962	1967	1972	1977	1982	1962	1967	1972	1977	1982
High Research Intensity															
Aerospace															
Office equipment (incl. computers)	3.1	2.5	3.1	2.9	1.3	5.1	4.8	4.1	2.9	1.3	4.2	4.2	4.8	2.9	3.7
Electronics and electrical appliances				1.1	1.3				1.1	1.3			4.1	2.8	3.2
Measurement, scientific and photographic equipment	5.5	4.7	2.1	3.2	−0.3				2.6	1.8	3.9	2.6	1.8	4.3	3.8
Industrial and agricultural chemicals	11.7	12.0	9.9	5.4	4.2						6.5	7.5	4.8	0.7	0.7
Pharmaceuticals and consumer chemicals	1.8	2.3	2.4	2.3	−0.2	1.8	2.3	2.3	1.4	1.0	6.1	4.1	3.2	3.3	3.7
Motor vehicles (incl. components)														2.7	2.4
Total	5.1	5.3	3.9	3.2	0.7	3.9	3.1	2.9	2.0	1.1	4.9	4.0	3.4	2.5	2.6
Medium Research Intensity															
Industrial and farm equipment	4.6	3.1	2.5	2.1	−0.5	4.6	2.7	2.5	2.3	−0.5	6.0	7.0	3.1	2.5	1.9
Shipbuilding, railroad and transportation equipment				−16.7	5.8				−39.7	8.4	3.8	1.5	1.6	2.2	1.6
Rubber													5.6	1.8	0.9
Building materials			3.9	1.7	4.5				2.0				6.6	1.5	2.3
Metal manufacturing and products	7.4	3.1	1.9	−2.5	−1.9	11.8		1.6	−2.7	0.9	3.1	2.7	1.3	0.8	1.4
Total	5.9	3.1	2.3	−2.0	−0.5	7.0	2.7	2.1	−3.0	0.6	3.5	2.8	1.7	1.2	1.5
Low Research Intensity															
Textiles, apparel and leather goods				1.4	1.0			3.1			3.3	3.1	1.0	−0.3	0.9
Paper and wood products				0.5	0.1				0.8	1.7			1.4	0.7	0.2
Publishing and printing				1.5	2.9				1.5	2.9			3.9	3.6	3.4
Food	5.2	4.2	4.1	3.5	3.6	1.3			0.2	2.0	1.5	1.1	1.2	1.0	0.7
Drink											6.3	6.3	5.0	4.6	4.1
Tobacco				0.4	0.7										
Total	5.2	4.2	4.0	2.1	2.4	1.3	2.9	3.1	0.7	2.1	2.9	2.8	1.5	0.9	1.0
Petroleum			0.3	−0.3	1.6				−0.2	1.1	0.4	1.7	1.1	1.0	−1.8
Other manufacturing				7.6	0.4								4.5	1.1	1.1
TOTAL	5.3	4.5	3.4	1.0	0.9	4.5	2.9	2.5	−0.5	1.0	4.0	3.3	2.5	1.7	1.6

Table 6.3 (cont.)

	Other Countries					Canada					TOTAL				
	1962	1967	1972	1977	1982	1962	1967	1972	1977	1982	1962	1967	1972	1977	1982
High Research Intensity															
Aerospace											2.3	2.6	2.4	2.9	2.5
Office equipment (incl. computers)	3.2	0.7	3.8	3.2	1.9	3.2	0.7	3.8	6.7	5.2	6.5	8.2	7.6	9.0	7.8
Electronics and electrical appliances											4.2	4.1	4.2	3.9	3.3
Measurement, scientific and photographic equipment				4.7							13.3	14.8	12.0	8.7	7.5
Industrial and agricultural chemicals					1.5				2.6	-3.1	7.7	5.7	3.1	3.2	1.8
Pharmaceuticals and consumer chemicals					16.6						8.3	8.7	8.2	7.4	7.7
Motor vehicles (incl. components)											6.0	4.1	4.0	3.3	0.6
Total	3.2	0.7	3.8	3.6	2.4	3.2	0.7	3.8	5.4	0.5	5.7	5.0	4.5	4.1	3.0
Medium Research Intensity															
Industrial and farm equipment	3.0	2.9	3.4	3.7	-2.4	3.0	2.9	3.4	2.0	-20.1	4.3	4.6	3.5	3.8	0.2
Shipbuilding, railroad and transportation equipment				7.9	1.4						3.0	3.0	1.7	0.7	1.8
Rubber			2.8	3.1	1.2						3.5	4.0	3.9	2.8	-1.2
Building materials			4.0	1.6	0.3			4.0	6.0	-4.8	6.4	4.7	4.8	3.6	1.2
Metal manufacturing and products	11.3	8.4	8.2	4.8	-1.4	12.3	11.9	8.1		-2.8	4.4	4.4	2.4	0.3	-2.3
Total	9.6	7.5	7.3	4.9	-1.0	9.7	9.6	6.8	4.9	-5.5	4.3	4.3	2.9	1.5	-1.1
Low Research Intensity															
Textiles, apparel and leather goods	8.4	4.6	3.1	3.3	0.1	8.4	4.6	3.1	2.7	0.8	3.7	3.8	2.4	1.2	1.9
Paper and wood products	7.9	9.6	9.2	3.1	0.8	7.9	9.6	9.2	3.1	4.6	5.7	5.4	3.3	4.5	1.6
Publishing and printing	1.7	2.3	1.9	6.5	4.6	0.9	1.1	1.1	6.5	1.0	4.7	6.0	5.0	4.9	4.6
Food				2.3	2.4				1.2	4.7	3.0	2.9	2.8	2.6	2.9
Drink	9.8	9.2	7.5	5.3	3.1	9.8	9.2	7.5	5.7	7.2	7.7	7.9	6.7	6.0	5.0
Tobacco			5.9	4.9	5.6			5.9	4.9		10.4	10.0	7.4	5.7	5.2
Total	6.4	4.7	4.6	3.7	2.7	7.0	5.2	4.7	3.8	3.4	4.3	4.3	3.6	3.4	3.2
Petroleum	1.7	6.6	4.8	10.2	1.0				12.9	-1.3	8.6	8.9	5.6	4.4	2.7
Other manufacturing	15.4	18.1	14.8	14.6	10.4				5.3	1.5	3.7	3.7	3.1	5.3	4.5
TOTAL	8.0	7.1	6.5	7.2	1.6	8.0	7.3	5.6	4.8	-0.1	5.5	5.3	4.1	3.6	2.3

1   Covers all firms from rationalised samples for which data needed to compile the ratios was available.

2   The EEC is treated as Germany, France, Italy, Netherlands, Belgium, Luxembourg, UK, Denmark throughout the period 1962–82. See comment in Part I.

Source: *Fortune* July and August 1963; June and September 1968; May and September 1973; 8 May and 14 August 1978; 2 May and 22 August 1983.

Table 6.4
Rate of growth of sales, 1962/67, 1967/72, 1972/77, 1977/82, for constant samples of firms,[1] by country

	1962/67 1962 = 100	1967/72 1967 = 100	1972/77 1972 = 100	1977/82 1977 = 100
USA	156.3	156.9	198.7	161.3
Europe	145.5	188.4	215.6	168.5
EEC[2]	145.7	186.3	215.5	167.9
Germany	139.1	218.3	223.9	150.6
France	165.8	202.2	235.2	161.9
Italy	153.4	186.8	235.6	163.9
Netherlands	149.9	227.0	208.4	134.3
Belgium	151.9	203.3	224.0	169.2
Luxembourg	136.7	182.2		114.0
UK	146.0	163.0	186.8	189.0
Denmark				143.3
Germany/Belgium		201.1		
UK/Italy		139.8	154.2	
UK/Netherlands	137.2	164.5	242.7	192.1
Other Europe	142.4	212.5	217.0	172.3
Austria	127.8	179.6	404.2	182.7
Finland				187.8
Norway				272.3
Sweden	160.6	212.5	226.2	173.8
Switzerland	135.9	214.3	205.9	156.2
Portugal		213.2		
Spain			185.3	179.7
Turkey				191.5
Japan	217.5	241.3	201.9	189.7
Other Countries	160.1	173.4	226.2	232.4
Australia	196.7	186.6	165.7	198.5
Canada	154.4	154.3	193.0	160.4
South Africa	174.0	173.5	235.3	216.9
Netherlands Antilles	138.2	214.6	274.3	212.4
Israel				221.4
Argentina		217.3		
Brazil		302.0	541.1	206.4
Chile			196.0	134.8
India		191.0	302.2	280.5
Kuwait				889.1
Mexico	148.0	165.0	257.5	399.7
Philippines				293.1
South Korea				428.2
Taiwan				289.6
Venezuela				170.9
TOTAL	155.9	169.9	204.4	170.2

1   For each time period the sample used comprises all firms from the rationalised sample for which sales data were available for both years.
2   The listed countries are treated as having constituted the EEC throughout the period 1962–82. See comment in Part 1.

Source: *Fortune* July and August 1963; June and September 1968; May and September 1973; 8 May and 14 August 1978; 2 May and 22 August 1983.

Table 6.5

Rate of growth of sales, 1962/67, 1967/72, 1972/77, 1977/82, for constant samples of firms,[1] by industry and country

	USA				Europe			
	1962/67 1962 = 100	1967/72 1967 = 100	1972/77 1972 = 100	1977/82 1977 = 100	1962/67 1962 = 100	1967/72 1967 = 100	1972/77 1972 = 100	1977/82 1977 = 100
High Research Intensity								
Aerospace	168.4	97.4	184.9	183.9	142.5	118.8	199.4	199.2
Office equipment (incl. computers)	223.9	180.9	181.6	196.1	134.2	172.2	169.9	165.2
Electronics and electrical appliances	173.1	177.3	154.6	155.8	157.0	212.6	196.3	166.1
Measurement, scientific and photographic equipment	238.3	151.5	187.9	188.3			217.9	136.6
Industrial and agricultural chemicals	167.6	144.0	202.0	147.7	154.3	212.4	218.3	148.9
Pharmaceuticals and consumer chemicals	185.4	174.3	192.5	166.4	189.1	192.3	183.0	160.2
Motor vehicles (incl. components)	146.7	162.5	182.9	101.7	159.8	208.8	216.7	148.8
Total	167.0	155.9	180.9	146.2	157.2	205.7	208.3	155.0
Medium Research Intensity								
Industrial and farm equipment	176.0	158.4	195.5	141.1	128.9	174.0	181.5	150.7
Shipbuilding, railroad and transportation equipment	140.1	88.1	179.2	150.2			166.8	139.6
Rubber	137.0	144.2	161.2	109.0	148.7	167.4	178.9	157.3
Building materials	133.9	189.7	164.3	128.8	149.4	129.7	207.7	165.2
Metal manufacturing and products	136.5	147.8	173.4	135.1	142.2	172.2	202.2	146.9
Total	144.8	148.7	176.7	133.3	140.9	171.3	196.9	150.1
Low Research Intensity								
Textiles, apparel and leather goods	152.9	148.4	148.6	143.7	141.2	178.0	145.7	113.4
Paper and wood products	155.9	171.3	180.3	133.1	174.4	224.7	185.5	139.6
Publishing and printing	180.4	152.7	173.9	217.3	135.6	130.0	197.9	174.5
Food	138.5	154.1	179.3	154.2	133.3	173.5	180.3	157.3
Drink	177.5	190.9	195.3	198.3	155.7	139.0	141.1	175.0
Tobacco	139.5	185.0	207.8	208.0	152.9	236.1	202.9	193.3
Total	146.3	161.0	178.7	158.8	140.6	181.6	176.9	158.8
Petroleum	154.6	163.7	295.4	202.2	142.0	187.0	324.4	223.5
Other manufacturing	160.2	164.6	179.3	162.0	100.7	120.3	208.7	179.2
TOTAL	156.3	156.9	198.7	161.3	145.5	188.4	215.6	168.5

Table 6.5 (cont.)

	EEC[2]				Germany			
	1962/67 1962 = 100	1967/72 1967 = 100	1972/77 1972 = 100	1977/82 1977 = 100	1962/67 1962 = 100	1967/72 1967 = 100	1972/77 1972 = 100	1977/82 1977 = 100
High Research Intensity								
Aerospace	142.5	118.8	199.4	199.2			200.3	
Office equipment (incl. computers)	134.2	172.2	169.9	165.2			203.2	139.5
Electronics and electrical appliances	157.9	213.0	192.3	163.9	146.6	251.9	217.9	117.1
Measurement, scientific and photographic equipment			217.9	117.1			254.1	147.4
Industrial and agricultural chemicals	151.8	212.7	220.7	145.4	150.5	254.3	150.4	133.5
Pharmaceuticals and consumer chemicals	163.1	184.3	174.3	165.3				151.5
Motor vehicles (incl. components)	158.9	204.8	214.5	140.1	139.8	239.6	229.6	
Total	155.3	204.3	207.4	150.4	145.6	248.1	226.0	146.4
Medium Research Intensity								
Industrial and farm equipment	121.1	163.5	169.4	158.7	119.0	229.5	183.0	151.0
Shipbuilding, railroad and transportation equipment			166.8					
Rubber	148.7	167.4	178.9	157.3			191.8	158.9
Building materials	149.4	129.7	209.0	164.8				
Metal manufacturing and products	142.4	172.3	198.3	144.8	142.5	174.5	216.9	150.2
Total	140.7	169.9	193.7	150.2	138.8	182.8	209.7	150.5
Low Research Intensity								
Textiles, apparel and leather goods	141.2	178.0	145.7	124.8			180.0	128.5
Paper and wood products	174.4	224.7	173.7	136.4				162.1
Publishing and printing	135.6	130.0	197.9	169.8				186.1
Food	144.0	163.0	175.4	157.3				
Drink	155.7	139.0	141.1	175.0				
Tobacco	152.9	236.1	202.9	198.3			130.8	105.5
Total	147.3	176.4	172.8	162.6			150.4	154.9
Petroleum	142.0	187.0	323.5	221.9	86.4	166.6	679.0	208.7
Other manufacturing	100.7	120.3	208.7	178.8			240.0	157.1
TOTAL	145.7	186.3	215.5	167.9	139.1	218.3	223.9	150.6

125

Table 6.5 (cont.)

	France				UK			
	1962/67 1962=100	1967/72 1967=100	1972/77 1972=100	1977/82 1977=100	1962/67 1962=100	1967/72 1967=100	1972/77 1972=100	1977/82 1977=100
High Research Intensity								
Aerospace	155.5		249.5	178.8	139.9	118.8	122.9	227.3
Office equipment (incl. computers)	178.8	283.7	209.7	160.4	163.9	133.4	182.6	182.5
Electronics and electrical appliances				222.0			149.6	217.9
Measurement, scientific and photographic equipment								
Industrial and agricultural chemicals	137.1	222.3	193.5	140.2	164.1	164.1	190.3	167.6
Pharmaceuticals and consumer chemicals			243.5	171.9	163.1	184.3	187.3	190.4
Motor vehicles (incl. components)	202.7	218.8	239.0	146.1	157.1	155.1	157.3	122.4
Total	174.6	233.1	223.9	162.2	158.2	146.2	164.9	175.3
Medium Research Intensity								
Industrial and farm equipment	117.2	92.2		160.6	131.4	76.3	135.1	172.8
Shipbuilding, railroad and transportation equipment								
Rubber	153.9	250.2	216.9	156.9	142.1	129.7	158.3	221.1
Building materials	133.3		238.5	132.7	209.3		177.7	
Metal manufacturing and products	181.8	164.9	179.9	124.4	121.3	183.8		146.3
Total	156.0	167.6	205.8	137.4	130.0	158.1	168.7	165.4
Low Research Intensity								
Textiles, apparel and leather goods				112.4	164.7	177.3	136.2	130.5
Paper and wood products					174.4	224.7	173.7	131.1
Publishing and printing					116.2			219.4
Food	157.0	130.0	197.9	118.3	165.6	167.9	171.9	180.5
Drink			167.6	145.4	155.7	139.0	141.1	180.8
Tobacco				140.8	152.9	236.1	212.9	209.0
Total	157.0	130.0	175.8	138.0	160.0	187.4	170.5	179.3
Petroleum	161.8	226.3	358.1	203.0	147.9	198.2	340.8	243.6
Other manufacturing		134.0	204.4		100.7	115.9	178.5	214.7
TOTAL	165.8	202.2	235.2	161.9	146.0	163.0	186.8	189.0

126

Table 6.5 (cont.)

	Other Europe				Sweden			
	1962/67 1962 = 100	1967/72 1967 = 100	1972/77 1972 = 100	1977/82 1977 = 100	1962/67 1962 = 100	1967/72 1967 = 100	1972/77 1972 = 100	1977/82 1977 = 100
High Research Intensity								
Aerospace								
Office equipment (incl. computers)								
Electronics and electrical appliances	149.9	209.8	226.0	179.9	167.2	203.8	267.6	216.0
Measurement, scientific and photographic equipment	183.2	209.1	187.2	168.5				168.5
Industrial and agricultural chemicals	208.6	197.0	199.6	189.9				144.8
Pharmaceuticals and consumer chemicals				151.1				
Motor vehicles (incl. components)	181.0	267.6	235.2	217.0	181.0	267.6	241.3	248.8
Total	176.3	218.2	215.2	189.7	175.2	247.1	250.8	228.5
Medium Research Intensity								
Industrial and farm equipment	149.3	192.1	200.7	139.2	149.3	173.1	203.1	134.1
Shipbuilding, railroad and transportation equipment				139.6				126.2
Rubber								
Building materials			192.0	172.1				
Metal manufacturing and products	121.3	169.9	246.5	161.9			220.3	144.4
Total	144.7	185.4	219.1	149.5	149.3	173.1	210.0	134.9
Low Research Intensity								
Textiles, apparel and leather goods				86.4				116.6
Paper and wood products			207.5	143.2			207.5	208.0
Publishing and printing				208.0				122.7
Food	98.2	230.0	203.2	157.3				
Drink								
Tobacco				148.5				
Total	98.2	230.0	204.0	143.8			207.5	130.4
Petroleum			404.2	247.0				156.3
Other manufacturing				182.9				
TOTAL	142.4	212.5	217.0	172.3	160.6	212.5	226.2	173.8

127

Table 6.5 (cont.)

	Japan				Other Countries			
	1962/67 1962 = 100	1967/72 1967 = 100	1972/77 1972 = 100	1977/82 1977 = 100	1962/67 1962 = 100	1967/72 1967 = 100	1972/77 1972 = 100	1977/82 1977 = 100
High Research Intensity								
Aerospace								
Office equipment (incl. computers)	176.1	251.0	198.3	260.4				
Electronics and electrical appliances			194.0	206.3	143.5	144.5	221.5	297.4
Measurement, scientific and photographic equipment			211.9	320.6				
Industrial and agricultural chemicals	223.3	262.8	182.7	166.1				
Pharmaceuticals and consumer chemicals	228.8	195.6	210.8	158.9				
Motor vehicles (incl. components)	292.1	276.6		207.0				210.9
Total	219.1	261.5	203.2	200.2	143.5	144.5	221.5	284.3
Medium Research Intensity								
Industrial and farm equipment	177.7	285.6	191.2	159.0	153.4	140.8	235.7	191.5
Shipbuilding, railroad and transportation equipment	314.8	212.4	180.7	177.6			277.0	310.2
Rubber			229.8	164.5			153.2	230.7
Building materials			205.2	202.6				
Metal manufacturing and products	223.4	225.1	186.8	169.5	176.7	172.3	182.5	165.9
Total	227.8	227.4	189.1	169.8	171.4	166.7	192.6	184.6
Low Research Intensity								
Textiles, apparel and leather goods	196.1	193.2	154.1	152.3	146.6	168.8	178.5	122.5
Paper and wood products			182.8	177.5	186.1	162.5	237.5	156.0
Publishing and printing			233.9	205.3			191.3	144.1
Food	200.6	222.3	208.7	158.2	149.4	153.7	174.0	217.3
Drink		270.1	189.5	141.3	151.6	141.9	188.0	191.8
Tobacco								
Total	197.1	206.3	181.6	162.2	152.0	157.2	185.7	158.8
Petroleum	192.6	251.1	349.7	243.1	148.0	217.9	387.1	308.1
Other manufacturing			232.4	169.8	160.3	190.5	244.6	203.7
TOTAL	217.5	241.3	201.9	189.7	160.1	173.4	226.2	232.4

Table 6.5 (cont.)

	Canada				TOTAL			
	1962/67 1962 = 100	1967/72 1967 = 100	1972/77 1972 = 100	1977/82 1977 = 100	1962/67 1962 = 100	1967/72 1967 = 100	1972/77 1972 = 100	1977/82 1977 = 100
High Research Intensity								
Aerospace					165.2	99.7	187.1	186.0
Office equipment (incl. computers)	143.5	144.5	221.5	206.0	217.5	180.5	181.4	196.7
Electronics and electrical appliances					168.9	196.3	174.5	173.4
Measurement, scientific and photographic equipment					238.3	151.5	189.6	191.0
Industrial and agricultural chemicals					163.1	174.3	210.0	150.7
Pharmaceuticals and consumer chemicals					187.0	177.2	189.9	164.6
Motor vehicles (incl. components)					156.2	182.6	194.9	134.3
Total	143.5	144.5	221.5	206.0	167.1	174.3	190.9	157.3
Medium Research Intensity								
Industrial and farm equipment	153.4	140.8	235.7	73.4	163.8	165.2	192.8	148.8
Shipbuilding, railroad and transportation equipment					151.8	120.6	185.7	203.8
Rubber					139.8	150.1	168.6	125.5
Building materials					137.1	184.9	182.0	154.7
Metal manufacturing and products	164.2	154.6	201.5	129.1	146.3	166.6	185.9	149.1
Total	161.0	151.0	209.0	115.3	148.7	162.8	185.4	149.1
Low Research Intensity								
Textiles, apparel and leather goods	146.6	168.8	178.5	122.5	157.2	164.0	149.7	136.2
Paper and wood products	186.1	162.5	237.3	156.0	157.2	177.1	180.9	137.5
Publishing and printing	137.7	161.2	160.0	143.0	161.8	149.6	192.9	196.9
Food	151.6	141.9	174.0	217.3	138.2	161.4	181.8	155.3
Drink			188.0	191.8	168.7	179.2	178.2	190.1
Tobacco					144.5	204.9	205.0	199.7
Total	148.8	160.2	177.5	161.4	146.6	168.1	178.9	159.2
Petroleum				483.5	151.6	172.0	307.0	217.9
Other manufacturing				225.2	134.3	152.6	193.4	179.0
TOTAL	154.4	154.3	193.0	160.4	155.9	169.9	204.4	170.2

1 For each time period the sample used comprises all firms from the rationalised sample for which sales data were available for both years.
2 The EEC is treated as Germany, France, Italy, Netherlands, Belgium, Luxembourg, UK, Denmark throughout the period 1962–82. See comment in Part I.

Source: *Fortune* July and August 1963; June and September 1968; May and September 1973; 8 May and 14 August 1978; 2 May and 22 August 1983.

PART VII International operations

(a) INTRODUCTION

This part of our study explores various questions concerning the international operations of the world's leading industrial enterprises, including the extent and pattern of their foreign production and exports from their home countries. A number of sources proved of value in compiling this information:

1 special surveys carried out by the authors in 1979 and 1983;
2 company reports and accounts;
3 J. M. Stopford, *The World Directory of Multinational Enterprises 1982–83*, Macmillan, London 1983;
4 United Nations Centre on Transnational Corporations, *Trans-national Corporations in World Development – Third Survey*, United Nations, New York 1983 (Annex table 11–31); and
5 'The 50 Leading Exporters', *Fortune*, 8 August 1983.

In tables 7.1 to 7.4 the information is derived from two questions in our survey put to each of the 792 firms in the 1982 rationalised sample. These are:

1 What percentage of your worldwide production for 1982 was accounted for by your foreign affiliates or associated companies? (Foreign production should include the final value of all goods produced and sold abroad minus the value of finished goods and components imported from the parent company for resale or further processing. Goods produced overseas but sold back to the parent company should be included as foreign production.)
2 What percentage of the total sales of your domestic operations were exported in 1982? (Exports include both exports to foreign affiliates and to independent foreign customers.)

Where firms did not reply to these questions, answers to them were often found among the sources listed above.

From this information, we produce four ratios:

1 *Overseas production ratio*: the sales of overseas affiliates or associated companies (excluding goods imported from parent for resale) divided by the total worldwide sales of the group, that is, the proportion of the firm's total production carried out outside its home country.
2 *Parent export ratio*: parent company's exports divided by parent company's total sales, that is, the proportion of the parent company's production which is exported.
3 *Overseas sales ratio*: sales of overseas affiliates and associated companies (excluding goods imported from parent for resale) plus parent companies' exports divided by

worldwide sales of the group, that is, the proportion of the firm's total sales which take place outside its home country.

4 *Overseas market sourcing ratio*: sales of overseas affiliates and associated companies (excluding goods imported from parent for resale) divided by sales of overseas affiliates and associated companies plus parent company exports, that is, the proportion of the firm's total foreign sales accounted for by overseas production.

These ratios, for firms for which values were available from the listed sources, are set out in tables 7.1 to 7.4. In tables 7.5 and 7.6 we provide estimated values for the four ratios for the complete rationalised sample of 792 firms for 1982. This has involved grossing up the data in tables 7.1 to 7.4 by including estimated values for the firms not covered. In some cases we were aided in this by indications of the values from the sources listed above which were not sufficiently precise for inclusion in the main sample. In other cases, the estimated value relied on information on similar firms derived from tables 7.1 and 7.2.

Information on internal transactions is covered in Table 7.7. The survey question relating to this issue was 'what percentage of your total exports in 1982 were exported to affiliate or associate companies?'.

(b) OVERSEAS PRODUCTION RATIO (Table 7.1)

In Table 7.1 we present average overseas production ratios by industry, area and major country. This information was available for 509 firms, these accounting for 77 per cent of the sales of the 792 firms in the 1982 rationalised sample. The coverage for the USA was 88 per cent of rationalised sample sales and for Europe 75 per cent (with the UK, Finland, Sweden, Austria and Norway having coverage of over 90 per cent and France and Germany also over 75 per cent). For Japan coverage was a relatively low 61 per cent of rationalised sample sales, and for the 'other countries' only 45 per cent (with Canada 73 per cent and Australia 66 per cent). The coverage was also satisfactory for most industries, it being less than half of sales in only one industry ('shipbuilding, railroad and transportation equipment') and less than two-thirds of sales for only three more ('measurement, scientific and photographic equipment'; 'paper and wood products' and 'publishing and printing'). By industry grouping, the coverage was 82 per cent of rationalised sample sales for HRI, 75 per cent for LRI and 70 per cent for MRI. This level of coverage encourages us to believe that the overseas production ratios presented in Table 7.1 provide a good reflection of the international production behaviour of the rationalised sample as a whole.

From Table 7.1 we see:

(i) In 1982 the world's largest industrial enterprises produced almost 30 per cent of their output outside of their parent countries. The figure for the USA was marginally above this sample average. The highest overseas production ratios were revealed by several European countries, including the UK, Sweden and Switzerland.[1] The overseas production ratio for Japan was considerably below the average, as was that for most other countries outside Europe and the USA (though the ratio for Canada was marginally above the average).

(ii) The table shows fairly clear patterns of overseas production ratios by main economic activity. First, high values are recorded by a number of technologically advanced *research and innovation-based* industries. Here, overseas production of a new product is initiated soon after its first innovation in the firm's home market as a response to barriers to trade (tariffs, quotas or other forms of non-tariff barrier) or as a defensive measure to ensure a degree of dominance of overseas markets that could not be ensured by exports. 'Office equipment', 'industrial and agricultural chemicals' and 'pharmaceuticals and consumer chemicals' are the most conspicuous cases here. As we shall see later, some doubts have been expressed about the economic suitability of high levels of overseas investment in such industries.

1   The figure was also over 50 per cent for Belgian and Netherlands firms.

Secondly, high levels of overseas production ratios are to be found in several *market-oriented manufacturing* industries, where overseas production takes place as a complement to the firm's extended use of its marketing expertise and established trade marks. 'Food' and 'tobacco' are notable examples here, though both cases also involve elements of backward integration into agricultural production. A variation on this is 'pharmaceuticals and consumer chemicals', where trade marks and marketing expertise may again have a role in stimulating overseas production, along with the technological influences already mentioned. Marketing factors, along with relatively high transport costs, may also influence the high level of overseas production in 'rubber'.

Thirdly, the influence of backward integration into overseas production in basically *resource-based* industries is perhaps less prevalent now than it once was. This is clearly still relevant to the 'petroleum' industry and perhaps to some degree in 'building materials'. By contrast, the low overseas production ratio in 'metal manufacturing and products' is noteworthy, reflecting the fact that while that part of the industry concerned with extractive activity is undertaken where the resource is located, a substantial part of the secondary processing of the mined material is undertaken in the home country. In 'paper and wood products' the technology and skills needed for successful forestry operations are accessible to local firms in most timber-rich countries, so that home country operations predominate in this industry.

(iii) A prominent line of argument in recent years has been that for some countries the industrial distribution of overseas production has not been one that makes the most efficient use of the world's productive resources. The high levels of overseas production in the technologically dynamic industries, which are strong in both research and innovation, have been considered as inappropriate. Thus proponents of this mode of criticism select, in particular, the high levels of overseas production carried out by US firms near the frontiers of the technically advanced industries as a crucial misallocation of resources.[1] Specifically US overseas production in these industries is delineated as being 'trade destroying', since, it is asserted, it is in such industries that the US retains the greatest competitive strength and it should meet the demand for these products by exporting from its home factories rather than through overseas production. This is, of course, in line with the dictates of the familiar product-cycle[2] approach which also suggests that newly innovated, technically advanced, products should be most effectively manufactured in the countries of initial implementation, overseas production only becoming prominent where the technology is much more standardised, familiar and easily assimilated. This leads to the other side of the critique which argues that US overseas production should be encouraged in those activities where the USA is basically weak, including certain resource-based industries, but most notably in those sectors which use the more familiar and standardised types of technology in conjunction with large amounts of relatively unskilled labour. The relocation of productive facilities in such industries to countries with large supplies of cheap labour would, it is suggested, benefit both the host countries and the USA itself, where labour released from these relatively low-productivity industries could be re-employed in the higher-productivity advanced industries in which the USA still has a genuine comparative advantage.

The advocates of this line of argument see the evolving patterns of Japanese overseas production as exemplifying a more suitable corollary to the US pattern criticised above. The industries where overseas production is most prominent for Japanese firms, the thesis argues, are those in which Japanese enterprises have had a long-standing competitive advantage, based upon a mastery of relatively mature and standardised technology utilised in conjunction with large supplies of cheap labour. Though Japanese *firms* retain the basic elements of their competitive advantage, it is then argued, Japanese *production* has ceased to be competitive as wage rates have risen considerably. In response to this, Japanese firms have, therefore, moved their production activities overseas in search of cheap labour. This is approved as a trade-

1   See K. Kojima, *Direct Foreign Investment. A Japanese Model of Multinational Business Operations*, Croom Helm, London 1978.
2   R. Vernon, 'International Investment and International Trade in the Product Cycle', *Quarterly Journal of Economics*, vol. 80, 1966, pp. 190−207.

creating form of overseas production, keeping production located as determined by comparative advantage. Thus the host country has a potential source of competitive advantage (cheap labour) and the Japanese firms have complementary productive factors (technology and other knowledge, capital, market access, etc.) which the host country lacks. Japanese firms now continue to supply their established markets, but by exporting from their overseas subsidiary rather than from Japan.

Before evaluating elements of this thesis in the light of Table 7.1, two obvious and general qualifications should be noted. First, any systematic attempt to achieve an increased migration of labour-intensive activity out of the more industrialised countries will be looked at with extreme scepticism by policy-makers and labour leaders as long as general employment prospects remain poor. Similarly, countries in which recent experience suggests that the adjustment mechanism is not working as well as it might (that is, resources do not move smoothly and efficiently out of low-productivity industries and into high-productivity industries) would not welcome the additional stress resulting from increased overseas production in high-employment industries. Secondly, it is likely that some, at least, of the overseas production in the HRI industries has taken place in response to transport costs or trade policies of importing countries, and in such circumstances blame for the resulting distortions in trade and production cannot be placed with the firms.

Are the industrial distributions of US and Japanese overseas production as distinctively different as the thesis outlined above characterises them as being? Clearly Japanese overseas production ratios in the HRI industries are very much lower than those for the USA. Even the one industry with a relatively high ratio, 'electronics and electrical appliances', is often argued to possess labour-intensive stages of production whose overseas location could explain the higher value in line with the thesis. But, of course, Japanese overseas production ratios are *generally* much lower than those of the USA, so do the low values for HRI merely reflect this or does there remain a distinctive difference? Here our data does not permit a dogmatic answer to what is, in fact, a many-faceted question, but it does at least seem to be an arguable interpretation to suggest that, compared with firms in the USA, Japanese firms have tended to remain at home in the substantially skill- and technology-based industries and to move abroad, more notably in the labour-intensive MRI and LRI industries.

In the context of the line of argument explored above, Europe seems to represent something of a hybrid case. First, Europe shares the USA's criticised propensity for extensive overseas production in HRI industries, having higher average ratios than the USA in 'electronics and electrical appliances', 'industrial and agricultural chemicals' and 'pharmaceuticals and consumer chemicals'. Secondly, European firms tend to have extensive overseas production in the types of LRI industry approved by the thesis.

In Table 7.1 (b) we present information on the distribution of firms by their individual overseas production ratios. This reinforces the impression that high levels of overseas production are more of a European than a US or Japanese phenomenon. Thus, while European firms account for 34 per cent of the 509 firms covered, they account for 74 per cent (36) of the 49 with over 52.5 per cent of their production overseas. On the other hand, the USA accounts for 239 (47 per cent) of the 509 firms but for only 10 (20 per cent) of the 49 most overseas-production-oriented firms.

In the industry data of Table 7.1 (b) it is interesting to note, for several industries, the wide diversity of the overseas production ratios around the industry average of Table 7.1 (a). In 'petroleum', for instance, for which the average ratio in Table 7.1 (a) was 38 per cent, 11 of the 52 firms have individual ratios over 42.5 per cent but, more surprisingly, 21 have ratios of less than 2.5 per cent. Other industries where firms are quite widely spread by the extent of overseas production include 'industrial and agricultural chemicals', 'industrial and farm equipment', 'building materials' and 'food'.

Of the 68 GOFs in the 1982 rationalised sample, we were only able to obtain overseas production data for 33. Of those 33 GOFs, 14 (42 per cent) had overseas production ratios of over 12.5 per cent in 1982 compared with 36 per cent of the privately-owned enterprises covered by Table 7.1 (b). This, of course, reflects the prevalence of GOFs in the 'petroleum' sector and it is interesting to note, by contrast, that only seven of the 33 GOFs have overseas production ratios above the average for their respective industries (five of these being French).

Table 7.1 (a) has clearly revealed considerable differences in the average overseas production ratios between countries, and also between industries. We conclude this section by briefly reviewing some evidence on the causes of these differences. The reason why, for example, the UK has a larger average overseas production ratio than the USA could be that UK firms, in general, have a greater tendency to produce overseas than US firms, that is, the difference may be partly, at least, due to basic differences in the behaviour of UK firms *vis-à-vis* US firms. Table 7.1 (a) can be seen to provide plausible support for this type of assertion since the UK has notably higher overseas production ratios than the USA in the majority of industries where the comparison can be made. Similarly, the likelihood that an essential national characteristic underlies the low overall average overseas production ratio for Japan is strongly suggested in Table 7.1 (a). However, a second possibility is that different overseas production ratios between two countries might reflect differences in their industrial structures, that is, the country with the higher overall overseas production ratio might only have this high ratio because it has a greater proportion of its firms in industries which tend to have high overseas production ratios. A third factor, which may be of some influence, is that of firm size; thus, if it was the case that large firms tend systematically to have higher overseas production ratios than small firms, then a country which has a very high proportion of the very largest firms will tend to have a higher overseas production ratio than one with a lower proportion of large firms. In a similar way, the differences in average overseas production ratios between industries in Table 7.1 (a) may reflect basic differences between industries, but might also be influenced by the national composition of the industry samples or by size factors.

A recently published study,[1] using 1977 data compiled and organised as here, uses econometric techniques to isolate separately the influences of the various factors identified above. With regard to country effects, the study found that, even after allowing for the influence of industry and size, the nationality of a firm remained a significant factor influencing overseas production ratios. The UK, Sweden, Switzerland, Belgium, Canada and 'UK-Netherlands' were found to have firms with overseas production ratios significantly higher than the USA, even after allowing for industry composition and size, and Japan significantly lower overseas production ratios. In a similar way, industry factors also retained a significant influence on overseas production ratios after other likely influences were taken into account, with 'tobacco', 'chemicals',[2] 'office equipment' and 'industrial and farm equipment' revealing significantly higher values after allowing for nationality and size influences. After allowing for country and industry influences the overseas production ratio was found to be positively related to size of firm.

(c)   PARENT EXPORT RATIO (Table 7.2)

In Table 7.2 we set out the parent export ratios for 459 firms for which 1982 export data were available, these accounting for 69 per cent of the sales of the 792 firms in the 1982 rationalised sample. Though a detailed review of the specific industry and country differences revealed in Table 7.2 is not necessary here, it should be noted that the magnitude of the parent export ratio for a given industry from a given country will reflect two factors. First, whether the firms in that industry have particular and specific advantages that make them internationally competitive, and secondly, where this is the case, whether they can make the best use of this competitive advantage by exporting from the parent country or by producing overseas (usually, but by no means always, in the major markets they wish to service). So, if a parent export ratio is low, this may be because the firms in that industry are not sufficiently competitive to obtain any substantial foreign demand for their product. However, it could also reflect the fact that the firms do have overseas demand for their products, but find it more profitable to meet this demand by overseas production.

The econometric study referred to in the discussion of the overseas production ratio[3] also

1   P. J. Buckley and R. D. Pearce, 'Market Servicing by Multinational Manufacturing Firms: Exporting versus Foreign Production' in *Managerial and Decision Economics*, vol. 2, number 4, December 1981, pp. 229–247.
2   'Industrial and agricultural chemicals' and 'pharmaceuticals and consumer chemicals' were grouped as one industry in 1977. Otherwise the same industry classification was used as for this study.
3   Buckley and Pearce, op. cit.

attempted to separate out the ways in which country, industry and size factors influenced the parent export ratio. Generally, differences between industries remain a significant factor after the removal of other influences, with 'shipbuilding, railroad and transportation equipment', 'aerospace' and 'rubber' notably above average and 'food' below. Country factors too were a significant influence on parent export ratio, with the value for the USA significantly lower than that for most other countries, even after the removal of industry and size influences. This low parent export ratio for the USA obviously owes much to the large size of the US domestic market. The basic relationship between the size of a firm and parent export ratio is a positive but non-linear one, so that the positive effect of firm size on parent export ratio weakens at higher sizes.

Another likely influence on parent export ratio is the level of overseas production. Thus, it has often been asserted that overseas production meets foreign markets that would otherwise have been supplied by exports, so that a negative relationship between levels of overseas production and parent export ratio would be expected. A crucial point here is that, even if such a negative relationship were empirically established, it would not prove that higher overseas production *causes* lower exports. A frequent argument in such a case is that much overseas investment is defensive, a firm undertaking production in a foreign country to which it had previously exported extensively only when foreign production is necessary to stave off the loss of the market to local firms or other MNEs. Such defensive overseas production has often been a response to increasing trade barriers. In such a case, lower exports may occur more or less simultaneously with a rise in overseas production, but both are caused by a change in the competitive or trading environment external to the firm. Obviously the opposite case may also occur where the firm has a real choice — either to serve a market by overseas production or by exports — and it may choose overseas production, thereby replacing its own exports.

But while overseas production may well replace exports of final products from the parent country, it could at the same time stimulate additional exports in the form of components to be embodied in the output of overseas subsidiaries.

Another recent study[1] has attempted to analyse the relationship between parent export ratio and overseas production ratio. Once again we need to take account of the other factors which we have seen influence parent export ratio, that is, industry, country and size. Once this is done, the study showed that as overseas production ratio rises the parent export ratio at first rises also but, after a threshold value, the relationship becomes negative so that the parent export ratio then falls as the overseas production ratio rises.

(d) OVERSEAS SALES RATIO (Table 7.3)

In Table 7.3, we present average overseas sales ratios for the 483 firms for which this information was available, these covering 72 per cent of the sales of the 792 firms in the rationalised sample. The coverage here is larger than that for exports in Table 7.2 because a number of firms, notably Japanese and Scandinavian, report *total* overseas sales without providing a breakdown into overseas production and exports (such firms are also not covered in Table 7.1 (a)).

The table shows that the overseas sales ratio is consistently above the average for European firms, both across countries and industries. Leading influences on this are the increasing ease of, and experience with, intra-European trade and investment, and the greater propensity of smaller countries to engage in international commerce than larger ones. The average overseas sales ratio is highest for European firms in the HRI industries, the figure (65 per cent) being well in excess of the sample average for those industries (47 per cent). For each of the five HRI industries for which a figure is available the European overseas sales ratio is over 60 per cent and at least 15 per cent above the sample average for that industry. Similarly, European firms also have overseas sales ratios at least 10 per cent above the sample average in all four MRI industries for which figures are given, so that the overall average for these industries

1   Robert D. Pearce, 'Overseas Production and Exporting Performance: An Empirical Note', University of Reading *Discussion Papers in International Investment and Business Studies*, No. 64, September 1982.

(57 per cent) was well in excess of the sample average (42 per cent). In the LRI industries the European overseas sales ratio is again well above the sample average (55 per cent compared with 37 per cent), and this is again true for all industries, by 20 per cent or more in 'textiles, apparel and leather goods', 'paper and wood products' and 'food'.

The lowest overseas sales ratios for the US firms tend to be concentrated amongst the LRI industries. Thus, of the eight industries covered with overseas sales ratios of less than 30 per cent, the LRI industries account for six. Overall the HRI group is again the highest (37 per cent), followed by MRI (29 per cent) and LRI (24 per cent). Similarly, the highest overseas sales ratios for Japanese firms are spread amongst the HRI and MRI groups, both of which have overall ratios of 36 per cent. LRI industries have substantially the lowest overseas sales ratios for Japanese firms, though the ratio is almost up to the sample average value for 'textiles, apparel and leather goods'.

The econometric analysis of the overseas sales ratio showed that differences between industries remained significant (after the removal of country and size influences) as did differences between countries (after the removal of industry and size influences). As was the case with the parent export ratio, the overseas sales ratio rises with size but in a non-linear way (that is, less steeply as size increased).

(e) OVERSEAS MARKET SOURCING RATIO (Table 7.4)

The overseas market sourcing ratio analyses the extent to which a firm meets its overseas demand by overseas production rather than exports. Table 7.3 has shown those industries and countries from which firms have been able to establish a strong orientation towards the serving of overseas markets. Here we are concerned with the factors which influence a firm's decision as to whether its overseas markets are best met by exports from plants located in its home country, or whether overseas production will make better use of its competitive advantages. Overseas production will be used, for example, if exports are ruled out by high transport costs or tariffs and other artificial trade barriers. Clearly some resource-based industries will involve substantial overseas production if the greatest knowledge and skill in mining and processing is possessed by firms from countries which do not possess such resources. Again, a firm will undertake overseas production if factors of production complementary to its own strength (for example, cheap reliable labour, energy supplies) are more readily available in a foreign rather than a home location. A 'push' rather than 'pull' motive for some overseas production exists where firms undertake it to spread risks or escape from unfavourable circumstances at home — for example, high taxation and government intervention and/or an unsatisfactory labour relations environment.

In Table 7.4 we observe that the USA has an overseas market sourcing ratio of 84 per cent, that is, overseas production accounts for 84 per cent of the overseas sales of US firms.[1] The ratio exceeds 90 per cent in seven industries and 70 per cent in seven more. Only in 'aerospace' do exports exceed overseas production, and in only two more industries ('measurement, scientific and photographic equipment' and 'paper and wood products') do they account for over one-third of overseas sales.[2]

The most extreme contrast with the USA is Japan, where overseas production only accounts for 20 per cent of overseas sales. Relatively high ratios are found in several industries which are, to a greater or lesser degree, resource oriented, including 'petroleum', 'building materials' and 'food', and two where overseas production in response to lower-cost labour will be an influence, that is, 'electronics and electrical appliances' and 'textiles, apparel and leather goods'. Less in line with familiar reasoning on the motivations for overseas production by Japanese firms is the high overseas market sourcing ratio in 'pharmaceuticals and consumer chemicals', though marketing factors may be relevant in what is one of the more mass-market-oriented of the HRI industries.

1   Including sales of overseas subsidiaries back to the USA.
2   Intuitively we would expect the overseas market sourcing ratio to also be low for the 'shipbuilding, railroad and transportation equipment' industry, not covered in Table 7.4

Once again, the influence on the overseas market sourcing ratio of differences between industries and countries remain significant when other influences are removed. But here the influence of size is not relevant, at least to the extent that it was for the other ratios discussed earlier.

In the above discussion, we have considered two routes of servicing foreign markets available to firms which possess particular advantages which enable them to compete effectively in those markets. There is a third route for securing overseas income from such advantages, namely the direct marketing of the advantage itself. Thus, instead of producing in foreign markets the firm might attempt to isolate its advantages in communicable form and sell or rent the rights to these to local firms in these markets. Thus firms often conclude contracts with foreign firms for the transfer of technology (for example, by licensing or technical service agreements), management skills (for example, by management contracts), and trade marks or marketing skills (for example, by franchise arrangements). Such contracts represent the *externalised* route for transferring competitive advantages, since, at least as far as the foreign markets involved are concerned, the productive use of the advantages originally created by the firm is made by enterprises outside its influence.[1] On the other hand, overseas production by the advantage-owning firm represents the *internal* route, since the foreign market is supplied by operations which allow the firm to keep full control over the exploitation of its advantage (that is, it remains internalised). The literature[2] suggests that the choice between the two routes will depend on the extent to which the market, that is, the externalised route, can fully compensate the firm possessing the advantages for the income it could obtain by exploiting them itself in its own productive activity. *Inter alia* the greater the market failure involved in the markets for these advantages (that is, the more difficult it is for such markets to determine unique prices which satisfy both buyers and sellers) and the more the kind of advantages possessed by the firms are those which can only be exploited by themselves, for example, those associated with joint production and with operating geographically and industrially diversified activities, the more likely they are to internalise by extending the scope of their own operations.

Unfortunately, we do not know the extent to which the firms in our sample earned income from the external marketing of productive advantages, and indeed aggregate published data have not yet facilitated systematic tests of firms' choices between the internalised and externalised modes of utilisation of these forms of competitive strength. However, the rather fragmentary published data on licenses and intra-firm transactions do provide some hints. These suggest that:

(i)   Firms in high technology industries generally derive a larger proportion of their foreign income (from the exploitation of their ownership specific advantages) from their own producing affiliates than from non-affiliated firms.

(ii)   After allowing for any host-government constraints or controls on their ability to do so, firms engaged in transferring resources to LDCs generally do so more through the (internalised) medium of foreign direct investment than through (externalised) contractual ventures. This is often because there is an inappropriate or inadequate technological, communications or commercial infrastructure to make the latter mode of transaction economically viable.

(iii)   MNEs primarily engaged in resource-based, export-platform and rationalised foreign investment (that is, outward-looking activities with limited interest in the host-country market), derive more of their income from transactions with their own affiliates, and engage in more intra-group trade [see section (g) below], than those primarily engaged in import-substituting industries oriented to the servicing of the local market.

---

1   Though some LDCs, for example, have asserted that the contracts used to transfer advantages in this way are so worded that the purchasing enterprise is *not* entirely free of the influence of the selling firm.
2   See especially M. Casson, *Alternatives to the Multinational Enterprise*, London, Macmillan 1979, and M. C. Casson (ed.), *The Growth of International Business*, London, Allen and Unwin 1983.

These conclusions tend to suggest that the overseas production ratio in HRI industries would be higher than those in MRI and LRI industries because the incentives of firms to internalise their advantages in these industries are higher. Moreover, it is in these industries where the economies of rationalisation and joint production are likely to be the greatest, these being of a type which cannot be externalised but may require an extension of the firms' scope for full realisation. Several LRI industries, on the other hand, are of the import-substituting kind, with comparatively little intra-group trade between parent or affiliate companies or between individual affiliates. The gains from internalisation are, therefore, unlikely to be as great in these sectors, whilst the sale of the productive assets to local firms may produce a healthy income.

(f)   ESTIMATED VALUES OF INTERNATIONAL RATIOS FOR THE 1982 RATIONALISED SAMPLE (tables 7.5 and 7.6)

In tables 7.5 and 7.6 we present our estimates of the values of the various ratios for the complete 1982 rationalised sample of 792 firms, obtained as described at the start of this part. We can now see that the overseas production plus parent exports of the 792 largest firms in 1982 accounted for approximately 42 per cent of their total sales, and that overseas production accounted for approximately two-thirds of this total. Thus, the 792 largest industrial enterprises in 1982 carried out approximately 28 per cent of their total production outside their parent countries and exported approximately 20 per cent of their parent country output.

By referring to the data from which tables 7.5 and 7.6 were derived, we can make some other aggregate-level observations. Thus, of the $3204 billion sales of the 792 firms in 1982, overseas production accounted for approximately $900 billion and parent country exports for approximately $450 billion. Of the $900 billion overseas production we estimate that US firms accounted for $452 billion or 50 per cent.[1] European firms accounted for approximately $395 billion (44 per cent) of the overseas production, with the UK having the greatest amount $108 billion (12 per cent), followed by France $47 billion (5 per cent), Germany $44 billion (5 per cent) and Switzerland $33 billion (4 per cent). Japan accounted for overseas production of $23 billion (3 per cent of the estimated sample total) and Canada for $20 billion (2 per cent).

As far as the parent country exports of the world's largest enterprises are concerned, the pattern differs somewhat from that for overseas production. Here Japan has the largest share, viz $95 billion out of the total of $450 billion, this representing 21 per cent compared with its 3 per cent share of overseas production. The USA ranks a close second with an estimated parents exports of $90 billion, though its 20 per cent share of estimated sample exports is a clear contrast with its 50 per cent share of overseas production. Overall, European exports of $200 billion were 44 per cent of the sample total, Germany clearly leading with $70 billion (16 per cent), twice that of France, $35 billion (8 per cent), and the UK's $30 billion (7 per cent).

On an industry basis, 'petroleum' dominates overseas production with $360 billion or 40 per cent of the estimated rationalised sample total. Next come 'motor vehicles' and 'food', each with 8 per cent of the total followed by 'electronics and electrical appliances' and 'industrial and agricultural chemicals' with 7 per cent each. In reflection of this, HRI industries have 32 per cent of the estimated overseas production ($285 billion), well in excess of LRI industries with 15 per cent ($135 billion) and MRI 12 per cent ($110 billion).

(g)   INTERNAL EXPORTS (Table 7.7)

Using survey results discussed in the introduction to this part, Table 7.7 provides information

---

1   It is this high aggregate value of overseas production (rather than the overseas production ratio) which led, at least until recent years, to the treatment of international production as predominantly a US phenomenon.

on the internal export ratio for 172 firms in 1982. This suggests that these firms sent about one-third of their parent country exports to their subsidiaries overseas. The ratio for the USA was significantly above the average at 43 per cent, whilst that for Europe overall equalled the average, with the UK notably below at 25 per cent.

The table also suggests that internal exports are quite strongly related to research intensity, with the average internal export ratio for the HRI group (43 per cent) well in excess of that for MRI (23 per cent) and LRI (13 per cent). The four industries where internal exports account for over half of parent exports ('measurement, scientific and photographic equipment'; 'office equipment'; 'pharmaceuticals and consumer chemicals'; and 'motor vehicles') are all amongst the HRI group.

The results in Table 7.7 are in line with some of our earlier speculations on the circumstances in which firms would be likely to internalise the use of productive advantages through overseas production rather than market them through contractual agreements. Thus, firms in HRI industries see their continued competitive strength as being dependent on the ability to retain full control over their current technology and its evolution. This leads to a strong preference for overseas production so that their technological advantages are transferred across national boundaries but within the firm, often embodied in the physical form of parts and components supplied by the parent to its overseas subsidiaries, that is, internal exports. This is a distinctive manifestation of a particular form of international activity indulged in by HRI industries especially, namely rationalised operations. Thus many products in these industries involve a large number of components and it is often the case that optimum production efficiency dictates that separate parts should be produced in different countries. This may be desirable to make full use of economies of scale, and so that components whose production requires differing factor proportions shall be manufactured in the lowest-cost environment. When this occurs considerable intra-group trading will occur, including that from parents to subsidiaries reflected in Table 7.7.

(h)   CHANGES IN THE RATIOS BETWEEN 1977 AND 1982 (tables 7.8 to 7.10)

In tables 7.8 and 7.9 we present data on samples of firms for which our four main ratios [that is, those discussed in section (b) to (e) above] were available for both 1977 and 1982.[1] The general picture revealed by these samples is of an increasing internationalisation of activity by the world's largest enterprises, which during the five years covered was rather more oriented to rising overseas production than to higher export ratios. Thus the share of their total production carried out overseas by these firms rose from 31.2 per cent to 33.6 per cent, whilst the increase in the proportion of their domestic output exported was rather less notable, from 19.5 per cent to 19.9 per cent. In reflection of this, the proportion of overseas markets met by overseas production (that is, the sourcing ratio) rose from 69.2 per cent in 1977 to 71.5 per cent in 1982. Indeed, of the total increase in sales between 1977 and 1982 of the 232 firms for which both overseas production and export data were available for both years, overseas production accounted for 38 per cent, parent exports for 13 per cent and domestic market sales by parent companies for 49 per cent. This indicates the possibility that the increase in the overseas sales ratio for some countries may reflect more the stagnation of domestic demand than a particularly dynamic growth of overseas production or exports. Overall, the overseas sales ratio rose from 44.0 per cent in 1977 to 46.7 per cent in 1982.

Table 7.8 shows that the changes in the ratios for the USA are quite similar to those outlined for the overall sample above, with a rise in overseas production ratio accounting for most of the rise in overseas sales and this being reflected in a rise in the overseas market sourcing ratio. The general tendency for European firms is for rises in both overseas production ratios and parent export ratios, though the net result is a rise in the sourcing ratio. Germany has substantial rises in both overseas production ratio and parent export ratio.

---

1   It should be noted that the number of firms covered varies between the different ratios included in tables 7.8 to 7.10. This was allowed in order to provide the fullest available coverage of each ratio. It seems unlikely that this variable coverage is likely significantly to distort the overall picture revealed by these tables.

France also has had increases in both ratios though only that in exports is pronounced, so that France alone has a conspicuous fall in the overseas market sourcing ratio. The UK and Sweden have substantial rises in the overseas production ratio without comparable changes in the parent export ratio. Japan also records a substantial rise in the overseas sales ratio and, though exporting remains notably the preferred means of serving these overseas markets, there is a pronounced rise in the overseas production ratio. Canada records the only notable fall in overseas production ratio amongst the countries covered.

In terms of industry, Table 7.9 shows that the most prevalent pattern of change from 1977 to 1982 has been to record rises in both the overseas production ratio and the parent export ratio. Quite significant rises for both ratios are recorded by seven industries, of which four are from the HRI industry group (most extensively in the case of 'motor vehicles'). Only two industries (including 'petroleum') recorded declines in both the overseas production ratio and the parent export ratio. There are also two cases (interestingly including 'office equipment') in which the overseas production ratio falls but the parent export ratio rises, and three in which the overseas production ratio rises and the parent export ratio falls. Industries which have most substantially moved towards overseas production, away from exports, as a means of serving international markets are 'measurement, scientific and photographic equipment', 'motor vehicles', 'metals', 'textiles, apparel and leather goods' and 'publishing and printing'. The opposite change, towards an increased use of the export route, is most strongly seen in 'office equipment', 'paper and wood products' and 'tobacco'.

Finally in this section, Table 7.10 covers the four main internationalisation ratios for those firms for which information was available for 1972 as well as 1977 and 1982. In fact, as the coverage here is relatively small it would be dangerous to draw any detailed conclusions. Two broad impressions may, however, be gained from Table 7.10. Firstly, it seems that the rising internationalisation of the activity of the largest firms seen in the two previous tables was a rather more muted continuation of a more substantial increase between 1972 and 1977. Secondly, whilst increases in overseas production prevailed over rises in exports in 1977–82, the opposite had been so in 1972–77, (especially for Japan and Europe).

(i) SURVEY EVIDENCE ON ACTUAL AND EXPECTED CHANGES IN OVERSEAS PRODUCTION (tables 7.11 to 7.16)

In our survey, firms were asked if the production of their overseas affiliates accounted, in 1982, for a higher, the same or a lower percentage of total worldwide sales than in 1977. Using these replies to augment the information in tables 7.8 and 7.9 provided answers to this question for 389 firms. This permits an alternative perspective on the evolving international productive activity of our largest firms.

There were 189 firms (49 per cent) found to have a higher overseas production ratio in 1982 than in 1977 and 23 per cent lower. The USA showed a slightly less-than-average move towards overseas production with a below-average 45 per cent of its firms having a higher ratio in 1982 and an above-average 26 per cent having a lower one. Overall Europe showed modest signs of an above-average tendency towards increased overseas production, with 53 per cent of its firms having a higher ratio and 23 per cent lower. The strongest signs of moves towards increased emphasis on overseas production were shown, amongst European countries, by Germany, France and Finland. UK firms produced above-average numbers of firms with both higher ratios (53 per cent) and lower ratios (32 per cent). As might have been expected, Japanese firms are oriented to increased overseas production, with 18 of 28 (64 per cent) of their firms covered having higher ratios in 1982, though two recorded falls since 1977. Canada was the only country covered in Table 7.11 to have a higher number of firms with lower ratios in 1982 than higher ones.

Amongst industry groups, those for which Table 7.12 shows the strongest indication of moves towards increasing overseas production[1] were 'pharmaceuticals and consumer chemicals' and 'motor vehicles' (in the HRI industries) and 'textiles, apparel and leather

---

1   We only comment here on those industries covered by reasonably large numbers of firms.

goods'; 'food' and 'drink' (in the LRI). Weaker tendencies towards overseas production manifested by either a notably below-average proportion of higher ratios and/or above-average proportion of lower ratios) were suggested for two HRI industries ('aerospace' and 'office equipment'), one MRI industry ('industrial and farm equipment'), two LRI industries ('paper and wood products' and 'publishing and printing') and also 'petroleum'.

For 248 of the firms covered by tables 7.11 and 7.12, similar information was also available for changes between 1972 and 1977. This enables us to compare the move towards inter-nationalisation of production in the two five-year periods, and also to note the tendency of firms to alter, or persist in, the direction of change. Thus, Table 7.13 shows that of the 116 firms which increased their overseas production ratio between 1977 and 1982, 84 had also increased their ratio in the previous five years, while for 12 the rise in 1977–82 represented a reversal of a decline between 1972 and 1977. Similarly, of the 64 firms whose overseas production ratio fell during the second quinquennium, 47 had had rises in the previous period, whilst for 10 it was a repeat of an earlier fall.

Generally, Table 7.13 supports our earlier view (from Table 7.10) that, though the tendency in 1977–82 was still towards increased overseas production, this propensity was much less pronounced than it had been in the earlier five years. Thus, in 1972–77, 157 of the 248 firms had rises in the overseas production ratio, this number falling to 116 in 1977–82. Similarly, 64 firms had falls in the ratio in 1977–82 compared with only 29 in the earlier period. This decline was very noticeable for US firms. Thus between 1972 to 1977, 88 US firms (out of 130) had rises in ratio and only 17 had falls, while the comparable numbers for 1977–82 were 56 and 39. The pattern for Europe is similar but rather less pronounced. There is little difference to be noted between the industries as grouped by research intensity, all tending to reflect the slowing rise in the internationalisation of production. Of interest, though, is the pattern for 'petroleum', where only three of the 17 firms increased the ratio between 1977 and 1982 compared with nine in 1972–77, whilst eight recorded falls in the latter period compared with two in the first quinquennium. Thus, only one of the nine 'petroleum' firms which increased the ratio in 1972–77 did so again in 1977–82, with six of the nine reversing the trend to record a fall in ratio.

In our earlier survey, firms were asked whether they expected their overseas production ratio to rise, fall or remain unchanged between 1977 and 1982. In Table 7.14 we compare the response of 123 firms to this question with their actual change over this period. Of the 123 firms the expectation was for 77 rises (63 per cent), 35 unchanged (28 per cent) and 11 lower (9 per cent). The actual changes were 58 rises (47 per cent), 36 unchanged (29 per cent) and 29 lower (24 per cent). Thus, 46 of the 77 firms which had predicted increases in the ratio achieved them, and 17 of them suffered declines, whilst of the 58 firms which achieved higher ratios 46 had expected to do so. By contrast, only 11 of the 29 firms whose overseas production ratio fell had expected that outcome. This indicates that the slowing in the growth in the overseas production ratio detected for 1977–82 compared to 1972–77 was not fully expected or desired by the firms. Table 7.14 also indicates that firms from HRI industries achieved their optimistic expectations more effectively than other groups, as did European firms as compared to US.

Our 1983 survey also asked firms about the changes expected in the overseas production ratio between 1982 and 1987. There were 136 replies to this question — a somewhat lower response rate than that to the same question in the earlier survey. This fact, of course, may itself reflect increasing uncertainty by firms concerning the evolution of their approach to internationalised operations. Nevertheless, of the 136 respondents 79 (58 per cent) expected a rise in the overseas production ratio in 1982–87, 41 (30 per cent) predicted no change and 16 (12 per cent) expected a fall.

By industry groups, the expectation of increased internationalisation of production was greatest in LRI industries and lowest in MRI industries. European and Japanese firms showed much greater orientation to an expansion of overseas activity than did those from the USA.

Finally, in Table 7.16, we relate, for 126 of the respondents, the expected changes for 1982–87 to the actual changes in the ratio for 1977–82. Sixty-five firms expect to repeat the change of 1977–82 in 1982–87; these being 48 cases of further rises, three of further falls and 14 where the ratio is predicted to again remain unchanged. That the mood of the world's largest enterprises does still remain oriented towards expanding overseas production where possible seems to be indicated by the fact that of the 72 firms in the 126 which actually had rises in the overseas production ratio in 1977—82, 48 (67 per cent) expect further changes in that direction, and only nine a reversal with falls in 1982—87. Further, of the 22 firms whose overseas production ratio actually fell in 1977—82, 13 (59 per cent) expect to reverse this with rises from 1982 to 1987 and only three predicted further falls. This latter result also reinforces our impression that between 1977 and 1982 a number of firms suffered unexpected setbacks in their programmes for the increased internationalisation of production, which they now still seek to persist with and see implemented when possible.

Table 7.1 (a)

Average overseas production ratios[1] of sample firms[2] by industry, area and major country, 1982

All figures are expressed in percentages

	USA	Europe (total)	Germany	France	UK	Sweden	Switzerland	Japan	Other Countries (total)	Canada	TOTAL
Aerospace	9.4	3.5		NAS	NAS	NAS	NAS	NAS	NAS	NAS	8.4
Office equipment (incl. computers)	33.6	NAS		NAS	NAS			10.7			33.3
Electronics and electrical appliances	24.9	38.5	24.3		34.4						25.7
Measurement, scientific and photographic equipment	26.8	NAS				NAS	NAS				25.5
Industrial and agricultural chemicals	24.2	40.4	39.1	31.8	39.9	NAS	NAS	2.9			29.7
Pharmaceuticals and consumer chemicals	37.7	58.4	50.8	NAS	58.2	NAS	NAS	4.6			40.3
Motor vehicles (incl. components)	27.4	28.8	22.3	28.1	29.6	NAS		2.8			26.2
Total High Research Intensity	26.2	35.7	29.9	21.7	34.6	49.7	68.8	7.5	19.1	NAS	27.2
Industrial and farm equipment	24.5	33.0	3.3		38.9	46.5	NAS	11.4	NAS	NAS	27.3
Shipbuilding, railroad and transportation equipment	NAS	NAS									4.7
Rubber	34.8	51.6	NAS	NAS	NAS	NAS	NAS	5.4	34.6	NAS	31.9
Building materials	24.7	48.2		13.4	44.2	22.9		6.9	9.2	18.5	36.5
Metal manufacturing and products	18.0	22.0	10.4		40.6			3.1			15.2
Total Medium Research Intensity	22.0	29.9	9.1	32.0	42.7	39.3	64.7	4.6	21.1	37.3	21.2
Textiles, apparel and leather goods	11.8	46.5	NAS		49.0	NAS		9.3	20.8	20.8	17.8
Paper and wood products	15.1	26.0	NAS		26.9	NAS		0.4	NAS	NAS	17.6
Publishing and printing	5.3	36.2		27.0	NAS		NAS	NAS	NAS	NAS	23.4
Food	25.1	57.6			33.8			4.8	60.6	60.6	36.1
Drink	24.2	22.4			22.4				NAS	NAS	26.2
Tobacco	22.4	66.8			66.8						44.3
Total Low Research Intensity	21.3	50.5	36.2	27.0	41.3	44.9	NAS	6.6	35.4	38.4	31.4
Petroleum	44.9	39.1	NAS	NAS	NAS	NAS	NAS	1.1	0.0	0.3	38.4
Other manufacturing	17.5	5.3	NAS		NAS				NAS	NAS	13.8
TOTAL	31.6	37.1	23.0	30.9	41.2	44.3	77.5	5.5	14.1	32.0	29.9

NAS – results not given for reasons of confidentiality and disclosure. The information is, however, included in the appropriate aggregates.

1 Sales of overseas affiliates and associate companies (excluding goods imported from parent for resale) divided by total worldwide sales of group. Expressed as a percentage.

2 Covers the 509 firms from 1982 rationalised sample for which information on overseas production was available from the sources described in the text. The 509 firms covered accounted for 77 per cent of the sales of the 792 firms in the 1982 rationalised sample.

Source: Sales data *Fortune* 2 May and 22 August 1983, organised as described in Part I. Ratios obtained from authors survey and other sources listed in Part VII.

Table 7.1 (b)

Distribution of firms by overseas production ratio,[1] by industry and country[2]

Number of firms

	Overseas production ratio[1]						
	0 to 2.5 per cent	2.5 per cent to 12.5 per cent	12.5 per cent to 22.5 per cent	22.5 per cent to 32.5 per cent	32.5 per cent to 42.5 per cent	42.5 per cent to 52.5 per cent	Over 52.5 per cent
[A] By Area and Country							
USA	27	45	66	43	36	12	10
Europe (total)	20	21	25	28	17	27	36
UK	4	8	6	11	12	14	16
Germany	6	6	6	5	1	5	1
France	3	2	3	5	2	5	2
Sweden	1	3	1	2	1	3	6
Japan	27	30	5	1	1		
Other Countries	11	4	5	3	4	2	3
Canada	4	1	4	3	3	2	3
Total	85	100	101	75	58	41	49
[B] By Industry							
Aerospace	6	8	2				
Office equipment (incl. computers)		1	4		2	2	2
Electronics and electrical appliances	3	8	13	4	9	4	5
Industrial and agricultural chemicals	7	12	10	3	7	2	
Pharmaceuticals and consumer chemicals	1	2		4	9	8	7
Motor vehicles (incl. components)	2	5	9	8	2	1	1
Total High Research Intensity	19	36	38	28	29	18	15
Industrial and farm equipment	1	6	10	8	6	2	7
Rubber	1	2	2	1	2		1
Building materials		5	4	1	2	7	3
Metal manufacturing and products	19	11	15	12	3	3	3
Total Medium Research Intensity	22	27	32	22	13	12	14
Textiles, apparel and leather goods	5	7	1	2	2	1	1
Paper and wood products	6	5	6	2	4		1
Food	5	8	7	9	8	5	4
Drink	2	3	2	4		2	1
Total Low Research Intensity	21	27	19	19	14	9	11
Petroleum	21	8	6	5	1	2	9
TOTAL	85	100	101	75	58	41	49

1 Definition as in Table 7.1.
2 Coverage same as Table 7.1.

Table 7.2
Average parent export ratios[1] of sample firms[2] by industry, area and major country, 1982

	USA	Europe (total)	Germany	France	UK	Sweden	Switz-erland	Japan	Other Countries (total)	Canada	TOTAL
Aerospace	24.2	60.3		NAS	NAS			NAS	NAS		30.0
Office equipment (incl. computers)	14.1	NAS		NAS	NAS			31.8	NAS		15.4
Electronics and electrical appliances	14.1	38.6	38.1		27.2	NAS	NAS			NAS	28.5
Measurement, scientific and photographic equipment	20.8	NAS		39.3	37.7	NAS	NAS	13.8	NAS	NAS	20.8
Industrial and agricultural chemicals	13.6	48.9	49.8	NAS	35.3	NAS	NAS	7.0			29.7
Pharmaceuticals and consumer chemicals	6.5	42.4	44.3	44.3	30.3	NAS	NAS	28.9	12.8	41.6	11.4
Motor vehicles (incl. components)	12.3	48.7	54.2			NAS			25.2	37.2	28.2
Total High Research Intensity	14.6	46.3	49.0	42.4	35.0	50.5	90.0	26.3	34.2		26.4
Industrial and farm equipment	20.7	42.8	47.9		30.9	43.0	NAS	39.7			31.9
Shipbuilding, railroad and transportation equipment		NAS				NAS		NAS	NAS	NAS	55.6
Rubber	3.0	NAS	NAS	NAS	7.4		NAS	31.3	12.8		14.4
Building materials	3.3	15.7	NAS	39.2	22.3	72.7		5.4	25.2	41.6	10.4
Metal manufacturing and products	4.5	42.0	40.4					31.0			25.1
Total Medium Research Intensity	9.0	38.6	41.6	33.7	20.6	48.2	54.1	32.4	22.2	37.2	25.5
Textiles, apparel and leather goods	3.4	27.8	NAS		28.7	NAS		19.6	47.7	47.7	13.6
Paper and wood products	7.8	40.2	NAS		8.8	NAS		5.0	NAS	NAS	19.3
Publishing and printing	0.6	8.2		9.5	NAS		NAS	NAS	NAS	NAS	2.9
Food	3.3	9.9			2.9			0.6	5.0	5.0	5.1
Drink	1.2	10.8			10.4					NAS	5.8
Tobacco	8.2	5.5			5.5						7.2
Total Low Research Intensity	4.2	14.4	5.8	9.5	8.4	44.0	NAS	11.4	23.4	26.0	8.5
Petroleum	3.2	14.1	NAS	NAS	NAS	NAS		1.9	36.5	6.4	9.7
Other manufacturing	7.2	NAS			NAS				NAS	NAS	11.6
TOTAL	9.1	33.4	43.6	34.6	19.7	47.7	77.3	22.9	31.6	24.9	19.5

NAS – results not given for reasons of confidentiality and disclosure. The information is, however, included in the appropriate aggregates.

1 Parent companies' exports divided by parent companies' total sales. Expressed as a percentage.

2 Covers the 458 firms from 1982 rationalised sample for which information on parents' exports was available. The 458 firms covered accounted for 69 per cent of the sales of the 792 firms in the 1982 rationalised sample.

Source: Sales data *Fortune* 2 May and 22 August 1983, organised as described in Part I. Ratios obtained from authors' survey and other sources listed in Part VII.

Table 7.3

Average overseas sales ratios[1] of sample firms,[2] by industry, area and major country, 1982

	USA	Europe (total)	Germany	France	UK	Sweden	Switzerland	Japan	Other Countries (total)	Canada	TOTAL
Aerospace	31.5	61.9		NAS	NAS			NAS			36.1
Office equipment (incl. computers)	43.1	NAS		NAS	NAS						42.7
Electronics and electrical appliances	34.7	62.1	53.1		52.2			38.5			46.3
Measurement, scientific and photographic equipment	42.0	NAS	NAS		NAS			NAS			47.0
Industrial and agricultural chemicals	36.6	68.2	68.8	58.6	62.6	NAS	NAS	16.3	NAS	NAS	50.5
Pharmaceuticals and consumer chemicals	41.5	78.7	72.6	NAS	72.9	NAS	NAS	11.2			48.6
Motor vehicles (incl. components)	36.4	63.5	64.4	59.9	50.9	NAS		45.2			47.8
Total High Research Intensity	37.3	65.2	63.9	55.2	57.5	74.5	96.2	36.4	46.8	NAS	46.6
Industrial and farm equipment	38.3	59.7	50.9	50.4	57.8	69.5	NAS	46.6	NAS	NAS	49.6
Shipbuilding, railroad and transportation equipment		NAS	NAS		NAS			NAS			
Rubber	42.8	62.9	NAS	NAS		NAS		35.1	NAS		57.8
Building materials	31.2	56.3	47.1		48.3			11.9	40.9		43.1
Metal manufacturing and products	21.3	55.0		47.4	53.9	78.9		33.1	33.0	52.3	44.6
Total Medium Research Intensity	28.7	56.6	47.6	53.9	54.5	68.5	86.8	35.5	39.0	65.3	37.9
Textiles, apparel and leather goods	10.6	61.4	NAS		63.7	NAS		27.1	NAS	NAS	27.9
Paper and wood products	19.7	56.4	NAS		43.4			5.4	58.6	58.6	34.2
Publishing and printing	5.9	41.4			NAS			NAS			33.8
Food	27.8	62.2		33.0	38.8		NAS	2.8	NAS	NAS	42.3
Drink	25.1	32.5		NAS	30.5				24.9	24.9	28.7
Tobacco	28.7	40.1			40.1					NAS	30.7
Total Low Research Intensity	23.9	54.5	39.9	31.5	39.3	69.1	NAS	16.9	52.9	56.8	36.5
Petroleum	48.9	45.5	NAS	NAS	NAS	NAS		3.0	36.5	6.7	44.2
Other manufacturing	23.7		NAS		NAS					NAS	25.3
TOTAL	38.0	57.3	56.4	51.4	50.9	70.6	94.9	30.2	41.3	50.7	43.4

NAS – results not given for reasons of confidentiality and disclosure. The information is, however, included in the appropriate aggregates.

1 Sales of overseas affiliates plus parent exports divided by total worldwide sales of group. Expressed as a percentage.

2 Covers the 483 firms from 1982 rationalised sample for which information on overseas sales was available from the sources described in the text. The 483 firms covered accounted for 72 per cent of the sales of the 792 firms in the 1982 rationalised sample.

Source: Sales data Fortune 2 May and 22 August 1983, organised as described in Part I. Ratios obtained from authors' survey and other sources listed in Part VII.

Table 7.4

Average overseas market sourcing ratios[1] of sample firms,[2] by industry, area and major country, 1982

	USA	Europe (total)	Germany	France	UK	Sweden	Switz-erland	Japan	Other Countries (total)	Canada	TOTAL
Aerospace	30.8	6.2		NAS	NAS			NAS			24.4
Office equipment (incl. computers)	78.6	NAS		NAS	NAS			26.2			76.9
Electronics and electrical appliances	69.0	61.9	45.8		65.9	NAS	NAS		NAS	NAS	53.9
Measurement, scientific and photographic equipment	63.8	NAS									59.9
Industrial and agricultural chemicals	72.7	55.9	56.3	54.3	63.8	NAS	NAS	17.9	NAS	NAS	58.7
Pharmaceuticals and consumer chemicals	90.2	76.8	69.9	NAS	79.7	NAS	NAS	40.8			85.5
Motor vehicles (incl. components)	75.6	45.4	34.5	46.8	58.0	NAS		9.0			55.8
Total High Research Intensity	71.3	53.9	46.6	40.2	60.2	66.2	71.1	22.8	40.8	NAS	58.3
Industrial and farm equipment	59.7	53.4	6.6		67.3	66.9		24.6		NAS	53.7
Shipbuilding, railroad and transportation equipment		NAS				NAS			NAS		8.6
Rubber	95.9	NAS	NAS	NAS	91.5		NAS	NAS	78.9	NAS	77.8
Building materials	92.5	85.6				29.0		57.7			85.6
Metal manufacturing and products	82.5	40.2	22.3	28.4	75.4			9.3	31.6	44.5	41.2
Total Medium Research Intensity	75.5	52.5	19.5	58.3	78.3	57.3	77.2	12.9	55.4	68.5	51.2
Textiles, apparel and leather goods	70.1	75.7	NAS		77.0	NAS		34.3	35.5	35.5	59.3
Paper and wood products	65.3	46.6	NAS		80.6	NAS		7.3	NAS	NAS	50.5
Publishing and printing	90.7	87.4			94.4		NAS	NAS	NAS	NAS	91.2
Food	91.1	93.4		78.7	73.4			77.4	NAS	NAS	92.5
Drink	96.5	72.8			91.4				84.3	84.3	84.0
Tobacco	77.8	91.4									82.4
Total Low Research Intensity	85.9	85.9	90.8	78.7	84.2	65.0	NAS	36.9	62.5	63.1	83.0
Petroleum	96.4	80.3	NAS	NAS	NAS	NAS		36.7	0.1	4.9	86.2
Other manufacturing	74.8	NAS		NAS	NAS				NAS	NAS	60.5
TOTAL	83.5	62.5	42.3	50.5	76.2	62.6	83.7	19.8	31.4	63.9	67.9

NAS – results not given for reasons of confidentiality and disclosure. The information is, however, included in the appropriate aggregates.

1 Sales of overseas affiliates divided by sales of overseas affiliates plus parent country exports. Expressed as a percentage.

2 Covers the 458 firms from the 1982 rationalised sample for which information on overseas production and parents exports was available from the sources described in the text. The 458 firms covered accounted for 69 per cent of the sales of the 792 firms in the 1982 rationalised sample.

Source: Sales data Fortune 2 May and 22 August 1983, organised as described in Part I. Ratios obtained from authors' survey and other sources listed in Part VII.

Table 7.5

Estimated ratios for rationalised sample of 792[1] firms 1982, by country and industry group

	Overseas Production Ratio[2]				Parents Export Ratio[3]				Overseas Sales Ratio[4]				Overseas Market Sourcing Ratio[5]			
	HRI	MRI	LRI	Total	HRI	MRI	LRI	Total	HRI	MRI	LRI	Total	HRI	MRI	LRI	Total
USA	25.5	20.7	19.6	29.5	14.0	8.5	3.6	8.2	35.9	27.4	22.5	35.3	70.9	75.4	87.3	83.6
Europe (total)	33.7	26.9	47.1	38.8	44.1	39.6	16.0	31.8	62.9	55.9	55.6	58.2	53.6	48.2	84.7	66.6
Germany	28.4	10.2	30.2	20.6	47.9	42.7	11.1	41.3	62.7	48.6	37.9	53.4	45.4	21.0	79.6	38.6
France	21.5	29.0	23.3	29.1	39.8	36.3	14.3	30.7	52.7	54.8	34.3	50.9	40.8	52.9	68.1	57.3
UK	34.6	41.0	41.8	41.1	35.0	21.3	9.1	19.3	57.5	53.5	47.1	52.5	60.2	76.5	88.7	78.3
Italy	22.5	0.0	NAS	18.2	35.9	30.9	NAS	24.2	50.3	30.9	NAS	38.0	44.6	0.0	NAS	47.9
Netherlands	59.3	NAS	41.3	53.6	61.6	NAS	33.0	57.8	84.4	NAS	60.7	80.4	70.3	NAS	68.1	66.6
Finland		17.9	14.8	NAS		53.0	68.7	NAS		61.4	73.3	NAS		29.2	20.2	NAS
Sweden	48.9	37.8	43.5	43.2	50.1	50.9	41.2	48.1	74.5	69.5	66.8	70.5	65.7	54.4	65.1	61.3
Switzerland	70.7	59.7	NAS	76.3	87.1	64.1	NAS	65.8	96.2	85.5	NAS	91.9	73.4	69.8	NAS	83.0
Japan	7.5	4.3	4.9	5.6	31.8	29.9	7.2	24.4	36.9	32.9	11.8	28.6	20.2	13.1	41.7	19.4
Other Countries (total)	17.8	15.3	31.4	12.6	33.8	23.3	28.1	32.1	45.6	35.0	50.7	40.7	39.2	43.8	61.9	30.9
Canada	NAS	42.7	43.7	33.4	NAS	37.9	28.7	24.4	NAS	64.4	59.8	49.7	NAS	66.3	73.0	67.2
TOTAL	24.8	19.5	27.9	28.1	26.7	25.1	8.5	19.5	44.9	39.7	34.1	42.2	55.2	49.1	82.0	66.8

NAS – results not given for reasons of confidentiality and disclosure. The information is, however, included in the appropriate aggregates.

1 For each ratio the data cover the firms for which values of the ratio were available (see tables 7.1 (a) to 7.4) plus estimated values for the remaining firms from the 1982 rationalised sample.
2 For definition see Table 7.1 (a).
3 For definition see Table 7.2.
4 For definition see Table 7.3.
5 For definition see Table 7.4.

Source: Sales data *Fortune* 2 May and 22 August 1983. Ratios obtained from authors' survey and other sources listed in Part VII plus authors' estimates for firms not covered by tables 7.1 (a)–7.4.

Table 7.6

Estimated ratios for rationalised sample of 792[1] firms, 1982, by industry and area

	Overseas Production Ratio[2]					Parent Exports Ratio[3]				
	USA	Europe	Japan	Other Countries	Total	USA	Europe	Japan	Other Countries	Total
Aerospace	9.0	3.5			8.0	24.7	57.0			31.0
Office equipment (incl. computers)	34.1	36.7	3.2		32.6	13.9	24.5	23.9		15.3
Electronics and electrical appliances	21.6	37.5	10.3	8.2	23.3	12.3	38.8	31.0	34.0	26.0
Measurement, scientific and photographic equipment	27.2	NAS	11.4		23.5	19.7	NAS	61.8		30.5
Industrial and agricultural chemicals	23.7	38.3	2.6	24.6	27.9	11.4	44.8	13.0	33.4	26.1
Pharmaceuticals and consumer chemicals	37.9	61.8	3.8	99.0	41.3	6.5	44.3	5.5	0.0	11.5
Motor vehicles (incl. components)	27.0	26.6	7.0		21.8	12.3	45.4	40.2		32.0
Total High Research Intensity	25.5	33.7	7.5	17.8	24.8	14.0	44.1	31.8	33.8	26.7
Industrial and farm equipment	22.4	29.0	9.0	NAS	22.8	18.2	43.1	41.3	NAS	29.9
Shipbuilding, railroad and transportation equipment	3.9	6.0	NAS	0.0	2.3	9.6	40.3	NAS		25.0
Rubber	32.2	51.6	5.2	NAS	35.0	3.4	42.2	31.5	6.8	18.2
Building materials	23.0	48.2	4.8	NAS	32.0	4.1	15.7	4.6	NAS	8.7
Metal manufacturing and products	17.4	20.1	2.9	14.1	15.2	4.3	41.2	28.2	30.3	26.2
Total Medium Research Intensity	20.7	26.9	4.3	15.3	19.5	8.5	39.6	29.9	23.3	25.1
Textiles, apparel and leather goods	11.5	31.3	8.7	0.0	15.9	3.1	30.5	20.2	50.0	17.8
Paper and wood products	12.1	27.7	2.7	20.8	14.6	5.5	38.9	3.8	47.7	13.7
Publishing and printing	4.2	34.1	2.9	92.4	23.1	2.0	8.5	3.5	35.4	4.1
Food	22.6	55.6	4.4	7.5	31.9	2.8	10.7	2.9	18.9	5.2
Drink	23.6	23.6	NAS	40.3	25.2	1.1	11.6	NAS	25.4	8.2
Tobacco	28.8	60.4		NAS	44.0	7.7	9.1		NAS	7.9
Total Low Research Intensity	19.6	47.1	4.9	31.4	27.9	3.6	16.0	7.2	28.1	8.5
Petroleum	42.5	53.1	1.1	0.1	38.1	2.9	12.2	1.9	36.4	11.5
Other manufacturing	17.1	4.8	0.0	46.0	20.4	7.5	13.6	19.0	31.7	15.5
TOTAL	29.5	38.8	5.6	12.6	28.1	8.2	31.8	24.4	32.1	19.5

149

Table 7.6 (cont.)

	Overseas Sales Ratio[4]					Overseas Market Sourcing Ratio[5]				
	USA	Europe	Japan	Other Countries	Total	USA	Europe	Japan	Other Countries	Total
Aerospace	31.5	58.2			36.4	28.6	6.0	12.1		22.0
Office equipment (incl. computers)	43.2	52.2	26.4		42.9	78.8	70.3	27.0		76.0
Electronics and electrical appliances	31.3	61.7	38.1	39.4	43.3	69.0	60.7		20.9	53.9
Measurement, scientific and photographic equipment	41.5	NAS	66.1		46.8	65.4	NAS	17.2		50.1
Industrial and agricultural chemicals	32.4	65.9	15.3	49.8	46.7	73.2	58.1	17.3	49.5	59.8
Pharmaceuticals and consumer chemicals	41.9	78.7	9.0	99.0	48.1	90.4	78.5	41.9	100.0	85.9
Motor vehicles (incl. components)	35.9	60.0	44.4		46.8	75.1	44.4	15.8		46.5
Total High Research Intensity	35.9	62.9	36.9	45.6	44.9	70.9	53.6	20.2	39.2	55.2
Industrial and farm equipment	36.5	59.6	46.6	NAS	46.0	61.4	48.6	19.2	NAS	49.8
Shipbuilding, railroad and transportation equipment	13.1	43.9	NAS	6.8	26.6	29.9	13.6	NAS	0.0	8.5
Rubber	34.5	72.1	35.0	NAS	46.8	93.3	71.6	14.7	NAS	74.7
Building materials	26.1	56.3	9.1	NAS	38.1	88.0	85.6	52.2	NAS	84.4
Metal manufacturing and products	21.0	53.0	30.3	40.1	37.4	83.0	37.9	9.7	35.1	40.7
Total Medium Research Intensity	27.4	55.9	32.9	35.0	39.7	75.4	48.2	13.1	43.8	49.1
Textiles, apparel and leather goods	14.2	52.3	27.1	50.0	30.9	80.9	59.9	32.2	0.0	51.6
Paper and wood products	16.9	55.8	6.4	58.6	26.4	71.5	49.6	42.5	35.5	55.5
Publishing and printing	6.1	39.7	6.4	95.1	26.2	68.8	85.8	46.0	97.2	88.1
Food	24.7	60.4	7.1	25.0	35.5	91.3	92.2	61.6	30.1	90.0
Drink	24.5	32.5	NAS	55.4	31.3	96.5	72.6	NAS	72.6	80.5
Tobacco	34.3	64.0		NAS	48.4	83.9	94.4		NAS	90.8
Total Low Research Intensity	22.5	55.6	11.8	50.7	34.1	87.3	84.7	41.7	61.9	82.0
Petroleum	44.2	58.8	2.9	36.5	45.2	96.2	90.3	36.6	0.1	84.3
Other manufacturing	23.3	17.7	19.0	63.1	32.7	73.2	27.0	0.0	72.9	62.2
TOTAL	35.3	58.2	28.6	40.7	42.2	83.6	66.6	19.4	30.9	66.8

NAS – results not given for reasons of confidentiality and disclosure. The information is, however, included in the appropriate aggregates.

1 For each year the data cover the firms for which values of the ratios were available (see tables 7.1 (a) to 7.4) plus estimated values for the remaining firms from the 1982 rationalised sample.
2 For definition see Table 7.1 (a).
3 For definition see Table 7.2.
4 For definition see Table 7.3.
5 For definition see Table 7.4.

Source: Sales data *Fortune* 2 May and 22 August 1983. Ratios obtained from authors' survey and other sources listed in Part VII plus authors' estimates for firms not covered by tables 7.1 (a) to 7.4.

150

Table 7.7
Internal exports ratio[1] for sample firms[2] by area and industry, 1982

	USA	Europe	UK	Other incl. Japan	TOTAL
Aerospace	0.5	9.5	NAS		3.2
Office equipment (incl. computers)	75.5	75.1		NAS	71.9
Electronics and electrical appliances	18.5	32.1	18.3	35.1	28.1
Measurement, scientific and photographic equipment	78.3	NAS			78.1
Industrial and agricultural chemicals	31.6	26.9	48.9	14.6	27.7
Pharmaceuticals and consumer chemicals	80.2	50.4	45.2	36.8	60.2
Motor vehicles (incl. components)	94.9	62.5	NAS	5.2	60.5
Total High Research Intensity	47.1	44.2	40.4	17.1	42.6
Industrial and farm equipment	66.3	42.0	25.2	23.4	46.1
Building materials	30.1	4.5	7.6	6.3	7.9
Metal manufacturing and products	10.3	18.2	19.6	77.4	20.7
Total Medium Research Intensity	40.6	18.9	18.2	23.9	23.1
Textiles, apparel and leather goods	0	17.8	17.3	2.2	7.9
Paper and wood products	0.8	2.9		0	1.7
Publishing and printing	14.9	28.0			21.6
Food	12.5	35.6	19.2	8.0	30.3
Drink		13.7	11.3		13.7
Total Low Research Intensity	4.9	19.3	13.9	2.7	13.2
Petroleum	35.3	4.8	NAS	0	17.4
Other manufacturing	10.0	NAS	NAS	11.0	5.8
TOTAL	43.1	33.2	24.8	15.5	34.0

NAS – results not given for reasons of confidentiality and disclosure. The information is, however, included in the appropriate aggregates.

1   Proportion of parents total exports accounted for by exports of parts and components etc. to overseas affiliates.
2   Covers the 172 firms for which information of 'internal exports' was available.

Source: Sales data *Fortune* 2 May and 22 August 1983. Ratio from authors' survey.

Table 7.8
Overseas ratios for 1977 and 1982 for a constant sample of firms, by country

	Overseas production ratio[1] per cent		Parents export ratio[2] per cent		Overseas sales ratio[3] per cent		Overseas market sourcing ratio[4] per cent	
	1977	1982	1977	1982	1977	1982	1977	1982
USA	31.3	33.4	9.5	9.7	38.0	40.9	82.8	84.5
Europe (total)	34.2	38.2	35.9	38.1	56.5	60.2	56.7	59.2
Germany	19.5	24.1	41.6	46.6	52.1	58.7	38.2	42.1
France	33.4	34.5	31.3	36.8	51.2	51.4	55.4	45.1
UK	35.4	40.0	20.5	20.5	43.9	47.6	66.6	71.3
Sweden	40.2	49.5	53.9	53.1	64.7	71.5	55.5	64.9
Switzerland	79.0	81.4	75.7	77.0	94.3	95.2	83.3	85.0
Japan	4.1	7.1	24.7	25.2	30.7	36.7	15.4	23.4
Other Countries (total)	39.5	34.6	38.3	37.6	62.4	55.8	65.3	58.2
Canada	39.5	34.6	38.3	37.6	64.2	59.1	65.3	58.2
TOTAL	31.2	33.6	19.5	19.9	44.0	46.7	69.2	71.5

1   For definition, see Table 7.1 (a). Covers 308 firms for which overseas production ratio was available for both 1977 and 1982. The 1982 sales of these 308 firms accounted for 54 per cent of the sales of the 792 firms in the 1982 rationalised sample.

2   For definition, see Table 7.2. Covers 232 firms for which parent export ratio was available for both 1977 and 1982. The 1982 sales of these 232 firms accounted for 42 per cent of the sales of the 792 firms in the 1982 rationalised sample.

3   For definition, see Table 7.3. Covers 272 firms for which overseas sales ratio was available for both 1977 and 1982. The 1982 sales of these 272 firms accounted for 47 per cent of the sales of the 792 firms in the 1982 rationalised sample.

4   For definition, see Table 7.4. Covers 232 firms for which sourcing ratio was available for both 1977 and 1982. The 1982 sales of these 232 firms accounted for 42 per cent of the sales of the 792 firms in the 1982 rationalised sample.

Source: Sales data *Fortune* 8 May and 14 August 1978, 2 May and 22 August 1983. Ratios obtained from authors' survey and other sources listed in Part VII.

Table 7.9
Overseas ratios for 1977 and 1982 for a constant sample of firms, by industry

	Overseas[1] production ratio per cent		Parents export[2] ratio per cent		Overseas sales[3] ratio per cent		Overseas market[4] sourcing ratio per cent	
	1977	1982	1977	1982	1977	1982	1977	1982
Aerospace	10.1	10.5	26.3	28.3	34.0	36.0	30.5	29.8
Office equipment (incl. computers)	38.3	35.6	10.0	11.7	44.3	42.2	87.2	82.9
Electronics and electrical appliances	21.4	23.9	26.0	28.0	39.2	43.2	51.1	52.8
Measurement, scientific and photographic equipment	25.2	26.9	30.8	22.7	49.8	48.4	52.2	61.9
Industrial and agricultural chemicals	30.6	32.9	30.7	33.9	51.5	55.9	58.6	59.6
Pharmaceuticals and consumer chemicals	42.6	45.4	12.4	13.2	49.0	50.7	86.2	86.5
Motor vehicles (incl. components)	21.0	27.0	23.0	29.2	37.7	48.3	48.6	53.7
Total High Research Intensity	25.4	28.4	25.0	27.9	42.6	47.3	56.2	57.7
Industrial and farm equipment	26.6	26.8	26.1	30.9	47.0	50.3	57.7	53.6
Rubber	33.8	35.3						
Building materials	36.1	40.7	10.5	12.4	43.4	49.7	84.6	85.7
Metal manufacturing and products	15.3	18.6	26.7	28.7	37.5	42.5	35.2	40.8
Total Medium Research Intensity	22.4	24.8	24.6	27.5	41.8	46.1	51.7	53.0
Textiles, apparel and leather goods	24.1	27.3	22.1	20.3	40.1	41.3	57.6	63.8
Paper and wood products	19.1	17.3	23.8	25.7	39.2	38.8	51.5	45.5
Publishing and printing	30.9	29.3	4.2	3.6	24.7	28.2	83.8	88.1
Food	37.2	38.3	7.5	6.3	50.7	50.4	90.6	93.3
Drink	27.6	29.1	2.1	2.2	43.0	39.5	96.5	96.1
Tobacco	44.2	46.0	4.8	7.6	26.6	31.8	86.2	82.4
Total Low Research Intensity	33.5	35.1	12.0	11.1	44.0	43.7	81.3	83.5
Petroleum	48.0	45.8	4.0	3.4	51.2	49.4	96.1	96.3
Other manufacturing	8.9	9.0	4.9	7.1	16.7	17.8	69.6	58.7
TOTAL	31.2	33.6	19.5	19.9	44.0	46.7	69.2	71.5

1 For definition, see Table 7.1 (a). For coverage see Table 7.8.
2 For definition, see Table 7.2. For coverage see Table 7.8.
3 For definition, see Table 7.3. For coverage see Table 7.8.
4 For definition, see Table 7.4. For coverage see Table 7.8.

Source: Sales data *Fortune* 8 May and 14 August 1978; 2 May and 22 August 1983. Ratios obtained from authors' survey and other sources listed in Part VII.

Table 7.10
Overseas ratios for 1972, 1977, 1982 for a constant sample of firms

	Overseas production ratio[1] per cent			Parents exports ratio[2] per cent			Overseas sales ratio[3] per cent			Overseas market sourcing ratio[4] per cent		
	1972	1977	1982	1972	1977	1982	1972	1977	1982	1972	1977	1982
[A] *By Area and Country*												
USA	22.3	25.9	25.8	10.8	11.8	12.4	28.1	31.8	33.3	68.9	70.6	71.8
Europe (total)	31.7	34.1	37.0	30.8	37.5	40.0	51.4	57.2	61.3	59.5	57.5	60.1
Germany	15.9	19.8	24.3	37.1	42.8	48.4	45.7	52.7	59.1	35.1	38.1	41.7
France	27.7	30.4	24.3	29.2	34.4	39.8	45.5	51.1	53.2	54.3	55.1	45.8
UK	26.3	30.5	33.5	18.0	22.0	21.1	38.8	44.9	48.1	65.4	65.6	71.2
Sweden	45.2	48.5	56.1	56.7	58.5	52.7	60.9	62.4	71.0	46.3	54.2	68.6
Japan	1.3	1.7	3.0	17.3	27.2	30.3	22.6	32.0	39.4	7.9	7.2	11.8
TOTAL	25.4	28.3	29.0	21.0	25.3	25.7	39.7	45.1	47.4	61.5	60.3	62.4

Table 7.10 (cont.)

[B] By Industry	Overseas production ratio[1] per cent			Parents exports ratio[2] per cent			Overseas sales ratio[3] per cent			Overseas market sourcing ratio[4] per cent		
	1972	1977	1982	1972	1977	1982	1972	1977	1982	1972	1977	1982
Aerospace	5.7	11.8	11.5	25.8	26.8	28.6	29.9	35.4	37.1	18.3	33.4	31.9
Office equipment (incl. computers)	29.1	28.7	26.8	10.0	10.0	11.0	40.7	47.8	44.8	83.7	87.9	84.8
Electronics and electrical appliances	22.0	25.2	26.3	21.2	27.4	28.0	34.0	40.6	43.4	57.1	54.5	55.8
Industrial and agricultural chemicals	31.1	34.0	37.8	28.7	32.2	34.8	50.3	54.8	58.9	60.2	60.8	62.8
Pharmaceuticals and consumer chemicals	37.3	43.5	45.7	10.6	11.0	10.9	40.2	44.9	46.4	85.6	88.2	88.9
Motor vehicles (incl. components)	19.4	23.2	28.6	36.5	40.2	45.4	43.6	48.9	58.0	31.7	33.1	43.2
Total High Research Intensity	24.2	27.6	30.4	27.0	31.2	33.2	41.3	47.0	50.9	52.7	53.5	55.8
Industrial and farm equipment	25.1	27.2	25.0	23.3	29.5	35.6	41.3	46.1	48.7	53.4	51.0	41.8
Building materials	36.9	44.6	43.0	15.6	16.9	19.6	46.7	54.0	54.2	78.9	82.7	79.3
Metal manufacturing and products	16.1	17.8	19.8	23.6	32.4	36.5	34.6	43.1	47.6	37.5	31.9	33.4
Total Medium Research Intensity	24.2	25.3	25.6	22.7	29.8	34.4	38.2	45.3	48.7	50.8	47.8	43.9
Paper and wood products	19.9	22.4	19.9	6.6	5.8	6.4	26.3	27.9	25.2	80.1	84.0	79.8
Food	39.8	41.3	41.1	6.2	8.0	6.0	52.9	57.4	57.1	93.6	91.9	95.2
Drink	23.5	26.6	27.5	0.4	0.3	0.4	31.1	35.9	33.5	99.1	99.4	99.2
Total Low Research Intensity	32.8	34.8	34.3	6.2	7.4	6.2	42.0	45.7	44.4	90.4	89.2	91.6
Petroleum	23.4	28.5	24.5	5.3	7.4	6.3	18.7	23.1	28.9	75.5	73.5	83.4
TOTAL	25.4	28.3	29.0	21.0	25.3	25.7	39.7	45.1	47.4	61.5	60.3	62.4

1   For definition see Table 7.1 (a). Covers 163 firms for which overseas production ratio was available for all 3 years.
2   For definition see Table 7.2. Covers 110 firms for which parent export ratio was available for all 3 years.
3   For definition see Table 7.3. Covers 131 firms for which overseas sales ratio was available for all 3 years.
4   For definition see Table 7.4. Covers 110 firms for which sourcing ratio was available for all 3 years.

Source: Sales data *Fortune* May and September 1973; 8 May and 14 August 1978; 2 May and 22 August 1983. Ratios obtained from authors' survey and sources listed in Part VII.

Table 7.11
Changes in overseas production ratio of sample firms 1977—82, by country

Number of firms

	Higher	Same	Lower
USA	86	56	51
Europe (total)	79	36	34
Germany	15	7	1
France	10	4	2
UK	35	10	21
Netherlands	3	1	2
Finland	5	1	1
Sweden	5	5	4
Switzerland	1	4	
Japan	18	8	2
Other Countries (total)	6	9	4
Canada	3	7	4
TOTAL	189	109	91

Source: Authors' survey plus sources listed in text.

156

Table 7.12
Changes in overseas production ratio of sample firms, 1977–82, by industry

Number of firms

	Higher	Same	Lower
High Research Intensity			
Aerospace	3	7	3
Office equipment (incl. computers)	2	2	6
Electronics and electrical appliances	16	10	6
Measurement, scientific and photographic equipment	2	1	
Industrial and agricultural chemicals	20	12	8
Pharmaceuticals and consumer chemicals	14	5	3
Motor vehicles (incl. components)	17	3	3
Total	74	40	29
Medium Research Intensity			
Industrial and farm equipment	13	10	7
Shipbuilding, railroad and transportation equipment	1	3	
Rubber	3		2
Building materials	11	7	3
Metal manufacturing and products	23	12	11
Total	51	32	23
Low Research Intensity			
Textiles, apparel and leather goods	8	2	1
Paper and wood products	5	11	5
Publishing and printing	2	3	2
Food	26	8	10
Drink	8	1	2
Tobacco	3		3
Total	52	25	23
Petroleum	9	10	14
Other manufacturing	3	2	2
TOTAL	189	109	91

Source: Authors' survey plus sources listed in text.

Table 7.13

Changes in overseas production ratio of sample firms, 1977–82, by industry, country and by change in overseas production ratio, 1972–77

	Number of firms	Change in overseas production ratio								
		Higher 1977–82			Same 1977–82			Lower 1977–82		
	Higher 1972–77	Higher 1972–77	Same 1972–77	Lower 1972–77	Higher 1972–77	Same 1972–77	Lower 1972–77	Higher 1972–77	Same 1972–77	Lower 1972–77
[A] By Industry										
Electronics and electrical appliances	7		1		4	2	2	3	2	
Industrial and agricultural chemicals	12		4	2	2	2	1	4		2
Pharmaceuticals and consumer chemicals	7		1		3	1		1		
Motor vehicles (incl. components)	9		1	1	1	1		2		
Total High Research Intensity	39	8		4	11	8	3	14	3	4
Industrial and farm equipment	7	1		1	1	3	2	5		2
Metal manufacturing and products	7	3		1	2	8		5	2	2
Total Medium Research Intensity	21	5		2	5	11	2	12	2	2
Paper and wood products	14	2		3	4	3	2	3		
Food	22	3			3	5		6	2	2
Total Low Research Intensity	22	5		3	8	11	2	13	2	2
Petroleum	1	2			2	4		6		2
TOTAL	84	20		12	26	35	7	47	7	10
[B] By Country										
USA	42	6		8	18	14	3	28	5	6
Europe	37	12		4	8	13	3	16	2	3
UK	17	7		3	5	2		11	2	2
Germany	9	1			2	4		1	1	
Japan	4	1				4		1		
Other	1	1			2	4	1	2		1
TOTAL	84	20		12	26	35	7	47	7	10

Source: Authors' surveys (1979 and 1983) plus other sources listed in text.

Table 7.14

Expected and actual changes in overseas production ratio of sample firms, 1977–82, by industry group and country

Number of firms

Change in overseas production ratio

	Higher (expected)			Same (expected)			Lower (expected)		
	Higher (actual)	Same (actual)	Lower (actual)	Higher (actual)	Same (actual)	Lower (actual)	Higher (actual)	Same (actual)	Lower (actual)
[A] *By Industry Group*									
High Research Intensity	19	6	2	5	6	3	2	2	1
Medium Research Intensity	12	4	7	4	5	2	1	2	2
Low Research Intensity	13	3	7		6	2			
TOTAL	46	14	17	9	18	8	3	4	4
[B] *By Country*									
USA	17	7	8	6	7	6	2	3	3
Europe	24	7	6	3	5	2	1	1	1
Japan	3				3				
Other Countries	2		3						
TOTAL	46	14	17	9	18	8	3	4	4

Source: Authors' surveys (1979 and 1983) plus other sources listed in text.

Table 7.15
Expected changes in overseas production ratio of sample firms 1982–87

Number of firms

	Higher	Same	Lower
[A] *By Industry Group*			
High Research Intensity	29	17	5
Medium Research Intensity	19	17	4
Low Research Intensity	26	7	4
TOTAL	79	41	16
[B] *By Country*			
USA	14	15	7
Europe (total)	47	22	7
UK	15	9	4
Germany	7	4	1
Japan	11	3	
Other Countries (total)	7	1	2
TOTAL	79	41	16

Source: Authors' survey.

160

Table 7.16

Expected changes in overseas production ratio 1982–87 of sample firms by actual change in overseas production ratio 1977–82

Number of firms

	Change in overseas production ratio								
	Expected higher 1982–87			Expected same 1982–87			Expected lower 1982–87		
	Actual higher 1977–82	Actual same 1977–82	Actual lower 1977–82	Actual higher 1977–82	Actual same 1977–82	Actual lower 1977–82	Actual higher 1977–82	Actual same 1977–82	Actual lower 1977–82
[A] *By Industry Group*									
High Research Intensity	18	6	4	5	6	3	3	1	1
Medium Research Intensity	9	4	4	9	4	2	4		
Low Research Intensity	19	5	3	1	4	1	1	1	
TOTAL	48	16	13	15	14	6	9	2	3
[B] *By Country*									
USA	7	2	5	4	5	2	4		2
Europe (total)	28	10	7	10	6	4	5		1
Japan	9	2	1	1	2			2	
Other Countries (total)	4	2			1				
TOTAL	48	16	13	15	14	6	9	2	3

Source: Authors' survey plus sources listed in text.

PART VIII Research and development expenditures of the world's largest enterprises

As we have seen in various earlier parts of this volume, one characteristic of firms which has a frequently decisive influence on both their behaviour and performance is their level of technological intensity. The competitive performance of a firm at a point in time is likely to be, in most industries at least, strongly related to its level of technology *vis-à-vis* its leading competitors. Unfortunately, measures of existing *stocks* of technology are not easy to obtain at an enterprise level and, it will be recalled, in Part VI we used R and D expenditure as an indicator of levels of technology. In terms of several important aspects of firms' behaviour (for example, their means of servicing overseas markets – see Part VII), levels of technology are likely to be again of importance, but here the nature of a firm's *dynamic* commitment to technological improvement is also of crucial relevance. Thus levels of commitment to R and D, and subsequent product and process innovation, strongly affect firms' behaviour.

We now have quite substantial knowledge of R and D performance of the world's leading firms, and this is reviewed in this part. The main sources used are:

1 an authors' survey in 1983;
2 company reports and accounts;
3 J. M. Stopford, *The World Directory of Multinational Enterprises 1982–83*, Macmillan, London 1983; and
4 R and D Scoreboard – 1982, in *International Business Week*, 20 June 1983, pp.56–72.

Certain problems of definition may exist for R and D data of this type. For example, in some resource-based industries it may sometimes be difficult to distinguish clearly between exploration expenditure oriented to the discovery of new sources of raw materials and R and D expenditures oriented to extracting the greatest value from known sources. Similarly, in research-intensive, mass-market oriented, industries (for example, 'pharmaceuticals' or 'motor vehicles') it may not always be clear where expenditures are intended merely to improve the marketability of basically established products and where they are truly aimed at the creation and innovation of essentially new products. Nevertheless, in this case firms are usually required to report expenditures in two clearly delineated budgets (R and D and advertising), so that any distortions are likely to be more marginal than systematically misleading.

Perhaps more intractable as a definitional problem is the case of those industries where customer-funded R and D is prominent. Thus, leading firms in some technologically advanced industries undertake programmes for the development of specific products commissioned by individual customers, with the R and D budget for these products substantially underwritten by the customers. The obvious example is various governments' defence and/or space contracting to the 'aerospace' industry, but similar projects also occur in the 'office equipment (including computers)' industry. In such industries, the data reported in our tables is that for company-funded R and D only, that is, the companies' own budgets aimed at developing their underlying technological potential and the products aimed at the open market. The main reason for this choice is that this is the best reported of the levels of expenditure in these industries, but also it seems the more indicative measure of the firms' basic technical strength

162

given the product-specific nature of the customer-funded R and D. Nevertheless, it should be remembered that in such industries the use of company-funded R and D will probably, to some degree, understate the technological dynamism of these firms since some of the customer-funded R and D is likely to spill over into improving the wider technical capability of the commissioned enterprises.

Table 8.1 provides R and D information on 427 of the 792 rationalised sample firms, presented in the frequently used form of R and D expenditure as a percentage of sales. Bearing in mind the qualifications discussed above, the results conform very much to intuitive expectations. Those industries where persistent innovation of essentially new products is a major plank of competition report the higher ratios, whereas those where both products and production processes are accepted as being standardised and unlikely to be amenable to radical change, so that advertising and other marketing ploys represent the staple means of competition, have the lower R and D ratios. Table 8.1 also suggests that there is no general tendency for the USA, Japan or Europe to be persistently the most R and D-oriented area. Thus, each of them has the highest R and D ratio in at least two industries.

Table 8.2 presents the R and D expenditure as a percentage of sales ratio for 1982 and 1977 for the 239 firms for which information was available. A very general tendency towards a rise in the ratio is discernible, notably in several of the already more R and D-intensive industries. In many cases this surely does represent an increased commitment to R and D as a competitive reaction to the difficult markets faced during a recessionary period. However, there may be an alternative explanation. It may well be that firms do project R and D programmes on the basis of budgets determined on an historically established percentage of expected sales, but during the period 1977–82 fulfilled these programmes and the predetermined levels of expenditure, despite the fact that, in the face of lower than anticipated sales, this represented a rise in the R and D/sales ratio above conventionally established levels.[1]

The extensive R and D efforts of the world's largest firms, and the suggestion that this strength underlies much of their success in overseas markets, especially as overseas producers, has been a source of considerable controversy. Many of the countries which are predominantly hosts to, rather than parents of, MNEs fear that these companies use technology almost exclusively created in their home countries and that this has detrimental effects on the host economies. In the short term the current use of technology, essentially created elsewhere, may mean it is inappropriate to the host country and neither serves the local mass market with suitable goods nor produces output in ways that make the best use of the local country's available productive factors. Further, in the longer term, it is feared that if firms using predominantly imported technology play a leading role in the vital industrial sectors of the economy this will greatly retard the creation of the distinctive indigenous technology needed to establish the uniquely local advantages required as a basis for a competitive and independent industrialisation. It has, therefore, often been advocated that MNEs could mitigate some of these concerns by diffusing their R and D activity more extensively into the range of countries in which they operate.

Table 8.3 provides evidence on overseas R and D for 122 of our rationalised sample firms. The sources used were:

1 an authors' survey in 1983;
2 company reports and accounts; and
3 J. M. Stopford, *The World Directory of Multinational Enterprises 1982–83*, Macmillan, London 1983.

The table derived the R and D expenditure as a percentage of sales measure separately for home country and overseas operations. The results show that the belief that R and D efforts are relatively concentrated in the MNEs home countries is substantially confirmed. Nevertheless, quite significant R and D activity overseas is to be found in a number of HRI and LRI

---

1 The opposite of this argument may explain, to some degree, the low levels of R and D in 'petroleum' in tables 8.1 and 8.2. Thus the ratio in this industry may have been historically higher but, during the first half of the 1970s, firms in the industry may not have found it necessary or feasible to increase R and D expenditure in line with sales rises, so that the ratio fell.

industries. What we cannot tell from Table 8.3 is how relevant the geographical dispersion of the overseas R and D operations is in terms of solving the more distinctively different problems which emerge in various foreign locations. Similarly, we do not know the nature of the overseas R and D activities, whether they are set up to solve problems defined locally or merely play a closely delineated role in the wider R and D efforts of the firms.

Table 8.1
Research and development expenditure as a percentage of sales, 1982,
by industry and area[1]

	USA	Europe	Japan	Other	TOTAL
Aerospace	4.4	10.7			5.3
Office equipment (incl. computers)	6.4	5.5	NAS		6.5
Electronics and electrical appliances	3.4	6.7	4.6	NAS	4.8
Measurement, scientific and photographic equipment	6.5	NAS	NAS		5.9
Industrial and agricultural chemicals	3.2	3.8	2.4	NAS	3.4
Pharmaceuticals and consumer chemicals	4.8	7.6	9.4		5.5
Motor vehicles (incl. components)	3.7	3.2	3.7		3.5
Industrial and farm equipment	2.7	3.2	1.9	NAS	2.6
Shipbuilding, railroad and transportation equipment			2.0		2.0
Rubber	2.4	2.4			2.4
Building materials	1.8	1.7		NAS	1.6
Metal manufacturing and products	0.8	1.1	0.9	0.7	0.9
Textiles, apparel and leather goods	0.2	0.7	2.0		0.9
Paper and wood products	0.8	0.8	0.4		0.8
Publishing and printing	0.1			NAS	0.4
Food	0.7	1.1	2.5	0.2	0.8
Drink	0.9	0.1		NAS	0.2
Tobacco	0.5	0.3		NAS	0.4
Petroleum	0.7	0.6	1.0	0.4	0.6
Other manufacturing	2.2	1.2		NAS	1.6

NAS – results not given for reasons of confidentiality and disclosure. The information is, however, included in the appropriate aggregates.

1   Sample covers 427 firms from the 1982 rationalised sample. These 427 accounted for 70 per cent of the sales of the 792 rationalised sample firms.

Source: Sales data *Fortune* 2 May and 22 August 1983. R and D data from authors' survey and other sources listed in text.

Table 8.2

Research and development expenditure as a percentage of sales for a constant sample of firms,[1] 1982 and 1977, by industry and area

	USA 1982	USA 1977	Europe 1982	Europe 1977	Japan 1982	Japan 1977	Other 1982	Other 1977	TOTAL 1982	TOTAL 1977
Aerospace	4.4	3.2	8.8	8.9	NAS	NAS	NAS	NAS	4.7	3.5
Office equipment (incl. computers)	6.4	5.5	4.2	2.6	4.4	3.5			6.4	5.5
Electronics and electrical appliances	3.3	2.4	7.3	7.2	NAS	NAS			4.9	4.3
Measurement, scientific and photographic equipment	6.5	6.0	NAS	NAS	3.1	2.6			6.1	5.6
Industrial and agricultural chemicals	3.2	2.5	4.1	4.0					3.7	3.3
Pharmaceuticals and consumer chemicals	4.9	3.8	8.4	8.8			NAS	NAS	5.5	4.7
Motor vehicles (incl. components)	3.7	2.6	4.1	3.7	2.2	2.4			3.8	2.8
Industrial and farm equipment	3.3	2.7	2.5	2.7					3.1	2.6
Rubber	2.4	1.7	1.9	1.3					2.4	1.7
Building materials	1.6	1.3	0.8	0.9					1.7	1.3
Metal manufacturing and products	0.8	0.9			0.9	1.0	1.1	1.2	0.9	0.9
Textiles, apparel and leather goods	0.2	0.2			2.0	1.9			1.1	0.9
Paper and wood products	0.9	0.8	1.4	1.2			0.4	0.4	0.9	0.8
Food	0.8	0.6	0.3	0.2					0.9	0.7
Tobacco									0.3	0.2
Petroleum	0.7	0.5	0.6	0.5			0.4	0.2	0.6	0.5
Other manufacturing	2.1	1.9	1.5	1.6			NAS	NAS	2.3	2.0

NAS — results not given for reasons of confidentiality and disclosure. The information is, however, included in the appropriate aggregates.

1 Sample covers 239 firms, from the rationalised samples, for which data on R and D were available for both 1982 and 1977. These 239 firms accounted for 54 per cent of the sales of the 792 rationalised sample firms in 1982.

Source: Sales data *Fortune* 8 May and 14 August 1978; 2 May and 22 August 1983. R and D data from authors' survey and other sources listed in text.

Table 8.3
Research and development expenditure as a percentage of sales, 1982,
for parent country and overseas operations[1]

	USA		Europe		TOTAL[4]	
	Home Country[2]	Overseas[3]	Home Country[2]	Overseas[3]	Home Country[2]	Overseas[3]
Aerospace	4.9	0	10.7	0	5.9	0
Office equipment (incl. computers)	9.0	2.3	12.4	3.6	9.2	2.4
Electronics and electrical appliances	1.8	0.8	9.3	4.4	8.1	3.9
Industrial and agricultural chemicals	4.6	2.6	5.0	3.2	4.6	3.0
Pharmaceuticals and consumer chemicals	5.9	3.6	13.4	4.2	8.9	4.3
Motor vehicles (incl. components)	4.8	3.2	3.8	1.2	4.1	2.2
Total High Research Intensity	5.4	2.9	5.9	3.2	5.6	3.0
Industrial and farm equipment	5.2	1.5	5.2	1.1	4.7	1.4
Building materials	3.9	0.7	1.8	0.8	1.7	0.8
Metal manufacturing and products	1.6	0.7	1.4	0.4	1.5	0.5
Total Medium Research Intensity	3.2	1.2	1.9	0.6	2.4	0.9
Paper and wood products	1.2	0.1	0.6	0.1	1.0	0.1
Food	0.9	0.6	2.0	0.9	1.2	0.8
Total Low Research Intensity	1.0	0.5	1.1	0.8	1.0	0.7
Petroleum	1.3	0.1	0.6	0.4	1.1	0.2
TOTAL	3.1	0.8	3.6	1.8	3.3	1.2

1   Sample covers 122 firms from the 1982 rationalised sample for which information on overseas R and D was available. These 122 firms accounted for 22 per cent of the sales of the 792 firms in the rationalised sample.
2   R and D expenditure in parent country divided by parent country production (percentage).
3   R and D expenditure overseas divided by overseas production (percentage).
4   Includes Japan and Other Countries.

Source: Sales data *Fortune* 2 May and 22 August 1983. R and D data from authors' survey and other sources listed in text. Overseas production data as listed in Part VII.

APPENDIX 1

The industrial classification

Below we seek to provide an indication of the coverage of the industries used in our study. We do not seek to provide a comprehensive list of all the products in each industry, but rather to suggest the nature of the coverage.

Aerospace

Aircraft; missiles; space vehicles and satellites; electrical and other components for aircraft, space and defence (for example, radar and surveillance) applications.

Office equipment (including computers)

Office equipment, for example, typewriters, word processors, photocopiers; computers and other electronic data storage and processing equipment; cash registers.

Electronics and electrical appliances

Radios, TVs; electric cookers, refrigerators and household appliances; lamps, bulbs and other lighting equipment; electrical musical instruments; telegraph, telephone and other telecommunications equipment; electrical instruments and control systems; electrical switchgear and control systems; electrical alarms and signalling systems; batteries; composite insulated wires and cables for electricity transfer; electronic components, for example, semiconductors, electrical subassemblies etc; blank audio and video tapes.

Measurement, scientific and photographic equipment

Measuring, checking and precision instruments and apparatus; medical, surgical, dental and veterinary equipment; optical precision instruments; photographic and cinematographic equipment; clocks and watches.

Industrial and agricultural chemicals

Basic industrial chemicals (organic and inorganic); industrial gases; fertilisers; synthetic resins and plastic materials and their products; dye stuffs and pigments; paints, varnishes and printing ink; explosives; pesticides; adhesive film and foil; photographic materials and chemicals.

168

Pharmaceuticals and consumer chemicals

Pharmaceutical products; soap and toilet preparations; synthetic detergents; perfumes, cosmetics.

Motor vehicles (including components)

On-road motor vehicles (passenger and commercial) including components (for example, electrical equipment, engines, body shells); motor-cycles and parts.

Industrial and farm equipment

Agricultural, construction and forestry machinery, including off-road vehicles (for example, tractors, harvesters, bulldozers, earth-moving equipment), machinery, plant and tools for manufacturing industry; furnaces and gas and water treatment plant; mining machinery; lifting and hauling equipment; conveyors, hoists and handling plant; cranes, lifts and elevators; ball-bearings and roller-bearings; industrial internal-combustion engines; compressors; pneumatic control equipment; pumps, industrial valves; electricity generating equipment; oilfield equipment (but not basic offshore platforms etc.), industrial engineering services when linked to equipment production.

Shipbuilding, railroad and transportation equipment

Shipbuilding and ship repair; basic offshore oilfield platforms etc.; marine engines for ocean-going ships etc. (excludes outboard motors); yachts and pleasure craft; locomotives and parts; railway and tramway rolling stock; armoured vehicles, for example, tanks.

Rubber

Natural and synthetic rubber; rubber tyres and inner tubes; rubber hose, tubing and belts.

Building materials

Mining and quarrying of slate, stone etc; clay extraction; manufacture of cement, lime and plaster; ready-mixed concrete; building products of cement, lime and concrete; asbestos products; manufacture of basic glass and construction glass (other glass products, for example, bottles, ornaments, domestic glassware allocated to 'other industries'; glass-based scientific instruments to 'measurement, scientific and photographic equipment'); earthenware tiles; ceramic sanitary ware; plumbing fixtures and fittings; prefabricated homes.

Metal manufacture and products

Extraction of metal ores; refining of iron and steel; aluminium, copper, brass alloys; other non-ferrous metals; precious metals; operation of ferrous and non-ferrous metal foundaries; metal products, for example, steel tubes, basic steel wires; forging, pressing and stamping of metal parts; bolts, nuts, screws etc; metal hand tools and instruments; razor blades; metal containers and packaging products; constructional steelwork; metal furniture; includes metal trading only where integrated to productive activities.

Textiles, apparel and leather goods

Synthetic and natural fibres and production of fabrics from them; garments, including sports-wear; carpets and rugs; tanning and dressing of leather and production of leather products, including footwear; other footwear; soft furnishings and household textiles.

Paper and wood products

Forestry; preservation and treatment of wood; wooden containers; domestic wood furniture; wood used in building, except where combined with minerals into composite building materials; pulp; newsprint; other writing and printing papers; paper-based wrapping and packaging products; paper wall covering; stationery and notepaper.

Publishing and printing

Publishing and printing of newspapers, periodicals and books; security printing (for example, cheque books); other printing, for example, office forms.

Food

Fish and meat products; dairy products; fruit and vegetable products; grain milling; bread, biscuits etc; sugar; chocolate, cocoa etc; confectionery; tea and coffee; breakfast cereals; animal feeding stuffs, including pet food. The management of restaurants is included only when linked to a wider interest in food production.

Drink

Spirits, wine; beer; mineral water and soft drinks; fruit and vegetable juices. The management of pubs and licensed premises is included only when linked to beverage production.

Tobacco

Tobacco processing; cigarettes; cigars; pipe tobacco.

Petroleum

Crude oil extraction; oil refining; petroleum production; petroleum marketing where linked to petroleum production; natural gas extraction, transfer systems (for example, pipelines) and marketing.

Other manufacturing

Coal; uranium and nuclear fuel; electricity generation; records and prerecorded tapes; outboard motors; garden equipment; jewellery; precious stones; non-electrical musical instruments; toys and games; sports equipment (other than clothing and footwear); manufacture of glass and composite containers.

APPENDIX 2

The world's largest industrial enterprises 1962, 1972, 1983 (rationalised samples)

(Government-owned enterprises are indicated by the symbol *.)

1962

1. General Motors (US)
2. Standard Oil (US)
3. Ford Motor (US)
4. Royal Dutch Shell (Netherlands/UK)
5. General Electric (US)
6. Unilever (Netherlands/UK)
7. Socony Mobil Oil (US)
8. US Steel (US)
9. Texaco (US)
10. Gulf Oil (US)
11. Western Electric (US)
12. Swift (US)
13. National Coal Board (UK)*
14. Du Pont (US)
15. Chrysler (US)
16. Standard Oil of California (US)
17. Standard Oil (Indiana) (US)
18. Bethlehem Steel (US)
19. British Petroleum (UK)
20. Westinghouse Electric (US)
21. IBM (US)
22. General Dynamics (US)
23. Armour (US)
24. International Harvester (US)
25. Nestlé (Switzerland)
26. National Dairy Products (US)
27. Boeing (US)
28. Lockheed Aircraft (US)
29. RCA (US)
30. North American Aviation (US)
31. Union Carbide (US)
32. ICI (UK)
33. Procter and Gamble (US)
34. Volkswagenwerk (Germany)
35. Goodyear Tyre and Rubber (US)
36. Philips (Netherlands)
37. Siemens (Germany)
38. General Telephone and Electronics (US)
39. Firestone Tyre and Rubber (US)
40. Fiat (Italy)
41. Philips Petroleum (US)
42. Martin Marietta (US)
43. General Foods (US)

1972

1. General Motors (US)
2. Exxon (US)
3. Ford Motor (US)
4. Royal Dutch Shell Group (Netherlands/UK)
5. General Electric (US)
6. Chrysler (US)
7. IBM (US)
8. Mobil Oil (US)
9. Unilever (UK/Netherlands)
10. Texaco (US)
11. ITT (US)
12. Western Electric (US)
13. Gulf Oil (US)
14. Philips (Netherlands)
15. Standard Oil of California (US)
16. British Petroleum (UK)
17. US Steel (US)
18. Nippon Steel (Japan)
19. Westinghouse Electric (US)
20. Volkswagenwerk (Germany)
21. Siemens (Germany)
22. Standard Oil (Indiana) (US)
23. Du Pont (US)
24. Hitachi (Japan)
25. ICI (UK)
26. Toyota Motor (Japan)
27. Daimler-Benz (Germany)
28. Nestlé (Switzerland)
29. Farbwerke Hoechst (Germany)
30. Goodyear Tyre and Rubber (US)
31. Mitsubishi Heavy Industries (Japan)
32. Nissan Motor (Japan)
33. RCA (US)
34. BASF (Germany)
35. Fiat (Italy)
36. British Steel (UK)*
37. Montedison (Italy)
38. Renault (France)*
39. Procter and Gamble (US)
40. LTV (US)
41. International Harvester (US)
42. Eastman Kodak (US)
43. Matsushita Electric Industrial (Japan)

1983

1. Exxon (US)
2. Royal Dutch Shell Group (Netherlands/UK)
3. General Motors (US)
4. Mobil (US)
5. British Petroleum (UK)
6. Ford Motor (US)
7. International Business Machines (US)
8. Texaco (US)
9. El du Pont de Nemours (US)
10. Standard Oil (Indiana) (US)
11. Standard Oil of California (US)
12. General Electric (US)
13. Gulf Oil (US)
14. Atlantic Richfield (US)
15. ENI (Italy)*
16. Unilever (UK/Netherlands)
17. Toyota Motor (Japan)
18. Occidental Petroleum (US)
19. Francaise des Petroles (France)
20. Elf-Aquitaine (France)*
21. US Steel (US)
22. Matsushita Electric Industrial (Japan)
23. Petrobras (Brazil)*
24. Philips (Netherlands)
25. Pemex (Mexico)*
26. Hitachi (Japan)
27. Siemens (Germany)
28. Nissan Motor (Japan)
29. Volkswagenwerk (Germany)
30. Daimler-Benz (Germany)
31. Philips Petroleum (US)
32. Sun (US)
33. United Technologies (US)
34. Bayer (Germany)
35. Hoechst (Germany)
36. Renault (France)*
37. Fiat (Italy)
38. Tenneco (US)
39. ITT (US)
40. Nestlé (Switzerland)
41. BASF (Germany)
42. Chrysler (US)
43. Volvo (Sweden)

1962	1972	1983
44 Sinclair Oil (US)	44 Continental Oil (US)	44 Idemitsu Kosan (Japan)
45 Continental Can (US)	45 Atlantic Richfield (US)	45 Imperial Chemical Industries (UK)
46 Sperry Rand (US)	46 Bayer (Germany)	46 Procter and Gamble (US)
47 American Can (US)	47 August Thyssen-Hutte (Germany)	47 BAT Industries (UK)
48 Daimler-Benz (Germany)	48 Tenneco (US)	48 R.J. Reynolds Industries (US)
49 United Aircraft (US)	49 Union Carbide (US)	49 Mitsubishi Heavy Industries (Japan)
50 Farbenfabriken Bayer (Germany)	50 British Leyland Motors (UK)	50 Nippon Steel (Japan)
51 International Paper (US)	51 Swift (US)	51 Getty Oil (US)
52 ITT (US)	52 Kraftco (US)	52 Thyssen (Germany)
53 Cities Service (US)	53 AEG-Telefunken (Germany)	53 Peugeot (France)
54 Monsanto Chemical (US)	54 Bethlehem Steel (US)	54 AT and T Technologies (US)
55 American Motors (US)	55 Tokyo Shibaura Electric (Japan)	55 Boeing (US)
56 Eastman Kodak (US)	56 Greyhound (US)	56 Dow Chemical (US)
57 Republic Steel (US)	57 Cie Française des Pétroles (France)	57 Kuwait Petroleum (Kuwait)*
58 Borden (US)	58 ENI (Italy)*	58 Canadian Pacific (Canada)
59 Fried Krupp (Germany)	59 Dunlop Pirelli Union (UK/Italy)	59 Allied (US)
60 August Thyssen-Hutte (Germany)	60 McDonnell Douglas (US)	60 Eastman Kodak (US)
61 Burlington Industries (US)	61 Firestone Tyre and Rubber (US)	61 Unocal (US)
62 US Rubber (US)	62 Pechiney Ugine Kuhlmann (France)	62 Goodyear Tyre and Rubber (US)
63 Rhône-Poulenc (France)	63 Nippon Kokan (Japan)	63 Dart and Kraft (US)
64 General Tyre and Rubber (US)	64 Caterpillar Tractor (US)	64 Westinghouse Electric (US)
65 Hitachi (Japan)	65 Saint-Gobain-Pont-à-Mousson (France)	65 Toshiba (Japan)
66 Aluminium Co of America (US)	66 British-American Tobacco (UK)	66 Philip Morris (US)
67 Dow Chemical (US)	67 Akzo (Netherlands)	67 Hyundai Group (South Korea)
68 Armco Steel (US)	68 Litton Industries (US)	68 Beatrice Foods (US)
69 Hawker Siddeley (UK)	69 National Coal Board (UK)*	69 Indian Oil (India)*
70 Mannesmann (Germany)	70 General Electric (UK)	70 Union Carbide (US)
71 Reynolds (RJ) Tobacco (US)	71 Philips Petroleum (US)	71 Honda Motor (Japan)
72 British-American Tobacco (UK)	72 Occidental Petroleum (US)	72 Petrofina (Belgium)
73 Continental Oil (US)	73 Rhône-Poulenc (France)	73 Xerox (US)
74 British Motor (UK)	74 Lockheed Aircraft (US)	74 Amerada Hess (US)
75 Allied Chemical (US)	75 General Foods (US)	75 Union Pacific (US)
76 Farbwerke Hoechst (Germany)	76 Xerox (US)	76 General Foods (US)
77 Finsider (Italy)	77 Dow Chemical (US)	77 National Coal Board (UK)*
78 Gütehoffnungshutte (Germany)	78 ELF Group (France)*	78 Cie Générale d'Electricité (France)*
79 Cie Française des Pétroles (France)	79 Beatrice Foods (US)	79 McDonnell Douglas (US)
80 Gelsenkirchener Bergswerks (Germany)	80 Boeing (US)	80 Rockwell International (US)
81 Caterpillar Tractor (US)	81 North American Rockwell (US)	81 Pepsi Co (US)
82 Goodrich (BF) (US)	82 Gütehoffnungshutte (Germany)	82 Ashland Oil (US)
83 Rheinische Stahlwerke (Germany)	83 W.R. Grace (US)	83 General Electric Co (UK)
84 Corn Products (US)	84 Monsanto (US)	84 Saint-Gobain (France)*
85 Tokyo Shibaura Electric (Japan)	85 Singer (US)	85 Veba Oil (Germany)
86 Bendix (US)	86 Borden (US)	86 Rio Tinto Zinc (UK)
87 Sun Oil (US)	87 Continental Can (US)	87 Ruhrkohle (Germany)
88 Jones and Laughlin Steel (US)	88 Cie Générale d'Electricité (France)	88 Samsung Group (South Korea)
89 AEG (Germany)	89 Imperial Tobacco Group (UK)	89 Lucky Group (South Korea)
90 Tube Investments (UK)	90 Peugeot (France)	90 General Dynamics (US)
91 Inland Steel (US)	91 Honeywell (US)	91 Minnesota Mining and Manufacturing (US)
92 Dunlop (UK)	92 Minnesota Mining and Manufacturing (US)	92 Ciba-Geigy (Switzerland)
93 Renault (France)*	93 Ciba Geigy (Switzerland)	93 Montedison (Italy)
94 Douglas Aircraft (US)	94 Krupp-Konzern (Germany)	94 Coca-Cola (US)
95 National Steel (US)	95 Union Oil of California (US)	95 DSM (Netherlands)*

172

1962

96	Olin Mathieson Chemical (US)
97	BASF (Germany)
98	Wilson (US)
99	ARBED (Luxembourg)
100	Anaconda (US)
101	Minnesota Mining and Manufacturing (US)
102	GKN (UK)
103	Yawata Iron and Steel (Japan)
104	Ralston Purina (US)
105	Colgate-Palmolive (US)
106	Borg Warner (US)
107	Saint-Gobain (France)
108	Pittsburgh Plate Glass (US)
109	Tidewater Oil (US)
110	American Tobacco (US)
111	American Cyanamid (US)
112	American Metal Climax (US)
113	Singer (US)
114	Owens-Illinois Glass (US)
115	Matsushita Electrical Industries (Japan)
116	Minneapolis-Honeywell Regulator (US)
117	Campbell Soup (US)
118	Youngstown Sheet and Tube (US)
119	Crown Zellerbach (US)
120	AEI (UK)
121	Phoenix Rheinrohr (Germany)
122	Brown Boveri (Switzerland)
123	Stevens (JP) (US)
124	Pirelli (Italy)
125	Raytheon (US)
126	Atlantic Refining (US)
127	St Regis Paper (US)
128	Grace (WR) (US)
129	ENI (Italy)*
130	Morrell (John) (US)
131	National Lead (US)
132	Pure Oil (US)
133	Coca-Cola (US)
134	Salzgitter (Germany)*
135	National Cash Register (US)
136	English Electric (UK)
137	Citroen (France)
138	KF (Sweden)
139	AKU (Netherlands)
140	Massey Ferguson (Canada)
141	Montecatini (Italy)
142	Textron (US)
143	General Mills (US)
144	Weyerhaeuser (US)
145	Deere (US)
146	Pemex (Mexico)*

1972

96	International Paper (US)
97	Citroen (France)
98	R.J. Reynolds Industries (US)
99	Ruhrkohle (Germany)
100	Sumitomo Metal Industries (Japan)
101	Mannesmann (Germany)
102	Rapid American (US)
103	United Aircraft (US)
104	American Can (US)
105	Estel (Netherlands)
106	BHP (Australia)
107	Georgia Pacific (US)
108	Sun Oil (US)
109	Armco Steel (US)
110	Courtaulds (UK)
111	Kobe Steel (Japan)
112	Coca-Cola (US)
113	Champion International (US)
114	Cities Service (US)
115	Ralston Purina (US)
116	Sperry Rand (US)
117	Burlington Industries (US)
118	Robert Bosch (Germany)
119	Colgate-Palmolive (US)
120	Consolidated Foods (US)
121	Uniroyal (US)
122	Flick Group (Germany)
123	Associated British Foods (UK)
124	Ashland Oil (US)
125	Bendix (US)
126	Brown, Boveri (Switzerland)
127	Aluminium Co. of America (US)
128	ARBED (Luxembourg)
129	American Brands (US)
130	Boise Cascade (US)
131	TRW (US)
132	Kawasaki Steel (Japan)
133	Textron (US)
134	Weyerhaeuser (US)
135	Gulf and Western Industries (US)
136	United Brands (US)
137	National Steel (US)
138	Rheinstahl (Germany)
139	Owens-Illinois (US)
140	Michelin (France)
141	Mitsubishi Electric (Japan)
142	CPC International (US)
143	Republic Steel (US)
144	American Home Products (US)
145	US Industries (US)
146	Ishikawajima Harima Heavy Industry (Japan)

1983

96	YPF (Argentina)*
97	Fried Krupp (Germany)
98	Barlow Rand (South Africa)
99	Maruzen Oil (Japan)
100	Voest-Alpine (Austria)*
101	Consolidated Foods (US)
102	Thomson (France)*
103	Lockheed (US)
104	Georgia-Pacific (US)
105	Daewoo Industrial (South Korea)
106	Kobe Steel (Japan)
107	Monsanto (US)
108	Nippon Kokan (Japan)
109	W.R. Grace (US)
110	Sunkyong (South Korea)
111	Signal Companies (US)
112	Mitsubishi Electric (Japan)
113	Zoyo Kogyo (Japan)
114	Grand Metropolitan (UK)
115	Anheuser-Busch (US)
116	Petroleos de Venezuela (Venezuela)*
117	Nabisco Brands (US)
118	Johnson and Johnson (US)
119	Coastal (US)
120	Raytheon (US)
121	NEC (Japan)
122	Honeywell (US)
123	Rhone-Poulenc (France)*
124	George Weston Holdings (UK)
125	Robert Bosch (Germany)
126	Nippon Mining (Japan)
127	Charter (US)
128	General Mills (US)
129	Schlumberger (Netherlands Antilles)
130	Mannesmann (Germany)
131	TRW (US)
132	Sumitomo Metal Industries (Japan)
133	Caterpillar Tractor (US)
134	British Steel (UK)*
135	Michelin (France)
136	Chinese Petroleum (Taiwan)*
137	Akzo Group (Netherlands)
138	Aluminium Co of America (US)
139	Toa Nenryo Kogyo (Japan)
140	BL (UK)*
141	Sperry (US)
142	Brown Boveri (Switzerland)
143	Gulf and Western Industries (US)
144	Daikyo Oil (Japan)
145	Gütehoffnungshütte (Germany)
146	Continental Group (US)

1962

147 Beatrice Foods (US)
148 Mitsubishi Electrical Manufacturers (Japan)
149 Reynolds Metals (US)
150 Petrofina (Belgium)
151 Metallgesellschaft (Germany)
152 National Biscuit (US)
153 Bergwerksgesellschaft Hibernia (Germany)*
154 Standard Brands (US)
155 Courtaulds (UK)
156 Aluminium (Canada)
157 Canada Packers (Canada)
158 Allis-Chalmers (US)
159 Kimberly Clark (US)
160 Schneider et Cie (France)
161 Associated British Foods (UK)
162 Robert Bosch (Germany)
163 Kennecott Copper (US)
164 FMC (US)
165 Pechiney (France)
166 American Home Products (US)
167 United Merchants and Manufacturers (US)
168 American Radiator & Standard Sanitary (US)
169 Distillers (UK)
170 American Smelting and Refining (US)
171 Fuji Iron and Steel (Japan)
172 National Distillers and Chemical (US)
173 SKF (Sweden)
174 Sunray DX Oil (US)
175 Union Oil of California (US)
176 Whirlpool (US)
177 Toyota Motor (Japan)
178 Nippon Kokan (Japan)
179 Thompson Ramo Wooldridge (US)
180 Hygrade Food Products (US)
181 Hercules Powder (US)
182 Continental Baking (US)
183 International Nickel (Canada)
184 Hoesch (Germany)
185 White Motor (US)
186 Kaiser Aluminium and Chemical (US)
187 Peugeot (France)
188 Carnation (US)
189 Mead (US)
190 Coats, Paton, Baldwins (UK)
191 Vickers (UK)
192 Standard Oil (Ohio) (US)
193 Klockner-Werke (Germany)
194 Foremost Dairies (US)
195 BICC (UK)
196 Michelin (France)
197 Burroughs (US)
198 Bowater Paper (UK)

1972

147 Petrofina (Belgium)
148 GKN (UK)
149 National Cash Register (US)
150 Volvo (Sweden)
151 General Dynamics (US)
152 Taiyo Fishery (Japan)
153 Petroleo Brasileiro (Brazil)*
154 Thomson-Brandt (France)
155 Alcan Aluminium (Canada)
156 BF Goodrich (US)
157 Idemitsu Kosan (Japan)
158 Allied Chemical (US)
159 Deere (US)
160 FMC (US)
161 Wendel-Sidelor (France)
162 Bowater (UK)
163 Warner Lambert (US)
164 Rio Tinto Zinc (UK)
165 Inland Steel (US)
166 Reed International (UK)
167 Standard Oil (Ohio) (US)
168 Raytheon (US)
169 Signal Companies (US)
170 Mitsubishi Chemical Industries (Japan)
171 Whirlpool (US)
172 Salzgitter (Germany)*
173 Philip Morris (US)
174 Genesco (US)
175 Getty Oil (US)
176 American Motors (US)
177 CBS (US)
178 Pepsi Cola (US)
179 PPG Industries (US)
180 American Cyanamid (US)
181 Metallgesellschaft (Germany)
182 Amerada Hess (US)
183 American Standard (US)
184 Johnson and Johnson (US)
185 Pemex (Mexico)*
186 General Mills (US)
187 Iowa Beef Processors (US)
188 Borg-Warner (US)
189 Marathon Oil (US)
190 Hoffmann-la-Roche (Switzerland)
191 Olin (US)
192 Carnation (US)
193 Usinor (France)
194 Italsider (Italy)*
195 Henkel (Germany)
196 Eaton (US)
197 Teledyne (US)

1983

147 Mitsubishi Oil (Japan)
148 Bethlehem Steel (US)
149 Weyerhaeuser (US)
150 Ralston Purina (US)
151 Colgate-Palmolive (US)
152 American Home Products (US)
153 Sanyo Electric (Japan)
154 Litton Industries (US)
155 Hewlett-Packard (US)
156 Kawasaki Steel (Japan)
157 BMW (Germany)
158 Dalgety (UK)
159 Control Data (US)
160 Texas Instruments (US)
161 LTV (US)
162 Sony (Japan)
163 Thorn EMI (UK)
164 AEG-Telefunken (Germany)
165 American Brands (US)
166 Degussa (Germany)
167 Enpetrol (Spain)*
168 International Paper (US)
169 Motorola (US)
170 Burroughs (US)
171 Taiyo Fishery (Japan)
172 Archer-Daniels-Midland (US)
173 Broken Hill Proprietary (Australia)
174 Sacilor (France)*
175 Mitsubishi Chemical Industry (Japan)
176 Digital Equipment (US)
177 Borden (US)
178 Neste (Finland)*
179 Champion International (US)
180 Usinor (France)*
181 Alcan Aluminium (Canada)
182 Electrolux (Sweden)
183 Armco (US)
184 Norsk Hydro (Norway)*
185 Esmark (US)
186 Diamond Shamrock (US)
187 CPC International (US)
188 Time Inc (US)
189 Deere (US)
190 ASEA (Sweden)
191 Bristol-Myers (US)
192 Metallgesellschaft (Germany)
193 Martin Marietta (US)
194 Flick Group (Germany)
195 Solvay (Belgium)
196 Showa Oil (Japan)
197 Firestone Tire and Rubber (US)
198 IC Industries (US)

1962

199 Leyland Motor (UK)
200 Marathon Oil (US)
201 American Machine and Foundry (US)
202 Avco (US)
203 BHP (Australia)
204 Rank Hovis McDougall (UK)
205 Stewarts and Lloyds (UK)
206 Olivetti (Italy)
207 Cie Générale d'Electricité (France)
208 Genesco (US)
209 Pullman (US)
210 Pillsbury (US)
211 Litton Industries (US)
212 Johns-Manville (US)
213 Imperial Tobacco (UK)
214 Turner and Newall (UK)
215 Dortmund-Horder Huttenunion (Germany)
216 Nissan Motor (Japan)
217 McDonnell Aircraft (US)
218 American Sugar (US)
219 Shin Mitsubishi Heavy Industry (Japan)
220 Hormel (Geo A) (US)
221 Toyo Rayon (Japan)
222 Pfizer (Chas) (US)
223 California Packing (US)
224 General Electric (UK)
225 Steel Co of Wales (UK)
226 Heinz (HJ) (US)
227 Sumitomo Metal Industries (Japan)
228 Hunt Foods and Industries (US)
229 Simca Autos (France)
230 Kobe Steel Works (Japan)
231 Studebaker (US)
232 Quaker Oats (US)
233 Tate and Lyle (US)
234 Volvo (Sweden)
235 Philip Morris (US)
236 Champion Papers (US)
237 Brunswick (US)
238 Grumman Aircraft Engineering (US)
239 Deutsche Erdol (Germany)
240 Scott Paper (US)
241 Johnson and Johnson (US)
242 McGraw-Edison (US)
243 Joseph Lucas (UK)
244 International Packers (US)
245 Northrop (US)
246 Motorola (US)
247 Feldmuhle Dynamit Nobel (Germany)
248 CSR (Australia)
249 Snia Viscosa (Italy)
250 Container Corp of America (US)

1972

199 Nabisco (US)
200 Bristol-Myers (US)
201 Kawasaki Heavy Industries (Japan)
202 Massey-Ferguson (Canada)
203 Honda Motor (Japan)
204 Solvay (Belgium)
205 Combustion Engineering (US)
206 Charbonnages de France (France)*
207 Standard Brands (US)
208 Hawker Siddeley Group (UK)
209 Motorola (US)
210 Nippon Electric (Japan)
211 Reynolds Metals (US)
212 H J Heinz (US)
213 BICC (UK)
214 Canada Packers (Canada)
215 Kennecott Copper (US)
216 Toyo Kogyo (Japan)
217 Asahi Chemical Industry (Japan)
218 Mead (US)
219 Rank Hovis McDougall (UK)
220 Boussois Souchon Neuvesel (France)
221 Crown Zellerbach (US)
222 Norton Simon (US)
223 Toray Industries (Japan)
224 General Tyre and Rubber (US)
225 Pfizer (US)
226 Campbell Soup (US)
227 Ogden (US)
228 Associated Milk Producers (US)
229 Gelsenberg (Germany)
230 Tate and Lyle (UK)
231 DSM (Netherlands)*
232 SKF (Sweden)
233 Martin Marietta (US)
234 ASEA (Sweden)
235 Burroughs (US)
236 Thorn Electrical Industries (UK)
237 NL Industries (US)
238 St Regis Paper (US)
239 Anaconda (US)
240 Cockerill (Belgium)
241 Kimberly-Clark (US)
242 Avon Products (US)
243 Maruzen Oil (Japan)
244 Rolls-Royce (UK)*
245 Kanebo (Japan)
246 Lykes-Youngstown (US)
247 Unigate (UK)
248 Kaiser Aluminium and Chemical (US)
249 Interco (US)
250 Anheuser-Busch (US)

1983

199 Imperial Group (UK)
200 Turkiye Petrolleri (Turkey)*
201 Fujitsu (Japan)
202 Pechiney (France)*
203 Sazgitter (Germany)*
204 Agway (US)
205 Pfizer (US)
206 H J Heinz (US)
207 Ishikawajima-Harima Hvy. Ind (Japan)
208 NCR (US)
209 Pirelli (Switzerland)
210 Allied-Lyons (UK)
211 Pillsbury (US)
212 PPG Industries (US)
213 Statoil (Norway)*
214 International Harvester (US)
215 American Motors (US)
216 Roche/Sapac (Switzerland)
217 Borg-Warner (US)
218 American Cyanamid (US)
219 Kerr-McGee (US)
220 Italsider (Italy)*
221 Asahi Chemical Industry (Japan)
222 United Brands (US)
223 FMC (US)
224 British Aerospace (UK)
225 Emerson Electric (US)
226 Dresser Industries (US)
227 Boise Cascade (US)
228 ALUSUISSE (Switzerland)
229 Sharp (Japan)
230 Warner Communications (US)
231 Owens-Illinois (US)
232 Carnation (US)
233 LM Ericson Telephone (Sweden)
234 American Can (US)
235 Reynolds Metals (US)
236 Campbell Soup (US)
237 Kimberly-Clark (US)
238 BSN (France)
239 Land O'Lakes (US)
240 Celanese (US)
241 Northrop (US)
242 Ssangyong Cement Industrial (South Korea)
243 Kawasaki Heavy Industries (Japan)
244 Merck (US)
245 Aérospatiale (France)*
246 Petro-Canada (Canada)*
247 Bridgestone Tire (Japan)
248 B. F. Goodrich (US)
249 Courtaulds (UK)
250 Komatsu (Japan)

	1962	1972	1983
251	Taiyo Fishery (Japan)	MacMillan Bloedel (Canada)	Smith Kline Beckman (US)
252	Hoffmann-la-Roche (Switzerland)	Nippon Mining (Japan)	Inland Steel (US)
253	Klockner Humboldt Deutz (Germany)	Illinois Central Industries (US)	Ultramar (UK)
254	Distillers Corp Seagrams (Canada)	Allis-Chalmers (US)	Sandoz (Switzerland)
255	ASEA (Sweden)	Merck (US)	Canada Development Corp (Canada)
256	United Steel (US)	J.P. Stevens (US)	Warner-Lambert (US)
257	Crane (US)	Babcock and Wilcox (US)	NOVA, AN ALBERTA CORP (Canada)
258	Babcock and Wilcox (US)	Saab-Scania (Sweden)	Combustion Engineering (US)
259	Kawasaki Steel (Japan)	Sumitomo Chemical (Japan)	Snow Brand Milk Products (Japan)*
260	Anheuser-Busch (US)	Texas Instruments (US)	Cockerill Sambre (Belgium)*
261	Time Inc (US)	White Motor (US)	Isuzu Motors (Japan)
262	Idemitsu Kosan (Japan)	Olivetti (Italy)	Sumitomo Chemical (Japan)
263	Ling-Temco-Vought (US)	Evans Products (US)	CEPSA (Spain)
264	Georgia-Pacific (US)	Statsforetag Group (Sweden)*	Eli Lilly (US)
265	Central Soya (US)	Hercules (US)	Reed International (UK)
266	Brown Shoe (US)	Squibb (US)	Avon Products (US)
267	Armstrong Cork (US)	AMF (US)	Guest Keen and Nettlefolds (UK)
268	CIBA (Switzerland)	SCM (US)	National Intergroup (US)
269	Dominion Tar and Chemical (Canada)	YPF (Argentina)*	Burlington Industries (US)
270	Ashland Oil and Refining (US)	Central Soya (US)	BTR (UK)
271	Phelps Dodge (US)	Komatsu (Japan)	Textron (US)
272	Celanese (US)	Dresser Industries (US)	Teledyne (US)
273	Signal Oil and Gas (US)	L.M. Ericsson Telephone (Sweden)	Nippondenso (Japan)
274	International Publishing (UK)	International Nickel (Canada)	Norton Simon (US)
275	Cudahy Packing (US)	Clark Equipment (US)	Koc Holding (Turkey)
276	Kaiser Industries (US)	Kubota (Japan)	Abbott Laboratories (US)
277	Budd (US)	Sandoz (Switzerland)	Steel Authority of India (India)*
278	De Wendel (France)	Dart Industries (US)	Eaton (US)
279	Rootes Motors (UK)	KHD (Germany)	Koor Industries (Israel)
280	Steel Co. of Canada (Canada)	Jim Walter (US)	Toray Industries (Japan)
281	Rolls-Royce (UK)	Toyoba (Japan)	BICC (UK)
282	Warner Lambert Pharmaceuticals (US)	Studebaker-Worthington (US)	Dana (US)
283	Metal Box (UK)	Allied Breweries (UK)	Kaiser Aluminium and Chemical (US)
284	MacMillan Bloedel & Powell River (Canada)	Coats Patons (UK)	Beecham Group (UK)
285	International Shoe (US)	Cadbury Schweppes (UK)	Deutsche Babcock (Germany)
286	US Plywood (US)	Ingersoll-Rand (US)	Asahi Glass (Japan)
287	Koppers (US)	Burmah Oil (UK)	EFIM (Italy)*
288	Sears Holdings (UK)	Gillette (US)	Unigate (UK)
289	Lorillard (P) (US)	American Broadcasting (US)	St Regis (US)
290	Republic Aviation (US)	American Metal Climax (US)	Canon (Japan)
291	Richfield Oil (US)	Joseph Lucas (Industries) (UK)	Owens-Corning Fiberglas (US)
292	Rockwell-Standard (US)	De Beers Consolidated Mines (South Africa)	Levi Strauss (US)
293	Spillers (UK)	Sanyo Electric (Japan)	Crown Zellerbach (US)
294	Merritt-Chapman and Scott (US)	Crane (US)	Saab-Scania (Sweden)
295	Zenith Radio (US)	Tube Investments (UK)	Republic Steel (US)
296	Kellogg (US)	Otis Elevator (US)	Quaker Oats (US)
297	US Gypsum (US)	CSR (Australia)	Northern Telecom (Canada)
298	Liggett and Myers Tobacco (US)	Walter Kidde (US)	Whirlpool (US)
299	Sherwin-Williams (US)	Dana (US)	BOC Group (UK)
300	Air Reduction (US)	Del Monte (US)	Hercules (US)
301	Eaton Manufacturing (US)	Eli Lilly (US)	OMV (Austria)*
302	Teijin (Japan)	Union International (UK)	Mead (US)

1962

353 Texas Instruments (US)
354 Merck (US)
355 Mergenthaler Linotype (US)
356 American Viscose (US)
357 Huttenwerk Oberhausen (Germany)
358 Crucible Steel (US)
359 Sterling Drug (US)
360 Plessey (UK)
361 John Summers (UK)
362 Glidden (US)
363 Pet Milk (US)
364 Lorraine-Escaut (France)
365 Ishikawajima Harima Heavy Ind. (Japan)
366 Revere Copper and Brass (US)
367 Stauffer Chemical (US)
368 Saarbergwerke (Germany)*
369 Toyo Kogyo (Japan)
370 Reckitt and Colman (UK)
371 Union Bag – Camp Paper (US)
372 Kaiser Steel (US)
373 Land O'Lakes Creameries (US)
374 Libbey-Owens-Ford Glass (US)
375 Isuzu Motors (Japan)
376 Cannon Mills (US)
377 EMI (UK)
378 National Gypsum (US)
379 Cie Française Thomson-Houston (France)
380 Ingersoll-Rand (US)
381 Curtiss-Wright (US)
382 Colorado Fuel and Iron (US)
383 Continental Gummi-Werke (Germany)
384 Wheeling Steel (US)
385 DEMAG (Germany)
386 Voest (Austria)*
387 General Precision Equipment (US)
388 Canadian Breweries (Canada)
389 Grinnell (US)
390 Cone Mills (US)
391 Otis Elevator (US)
392 Emerson Electric Manufacturing (US)
393 Gallaher (UK)
394 ACF Industries (US)
395 Lilly (Eli) (US)
396 Cerro (US)
397 Avon Products (US)
398 Campbell Taggart Associate Bakeries (US)
399 Buderus'sche Eisenwerke (Germany)
400 Collins Radio (US)
401 Asahi Chemical Industry (Japan)
402 Garrett (US)
403 Clark Equipment (US)
404 McLouth Steel (US)

1972

353 Essex International (US)
354 Teijin (Japan)
355 Spillers (UK)
356 Magnavox (US)
357 Mitsubishi Oil (Japan)
358 Bass Charrington (UK)
359 Grumman (US)
360 Vallourec (France)
361 Metal Box (UK)
362 Kerr-McGee (US)
363 Bridgestone Tyre (Japan)
364 Archer Daniels Midland (US)
365 Budd (US)
366 Brooke Bond Liebig (UK)
367 Ciments Lafarge (France)
368 Northwest Industries (US)
369 Whittaker (US)
370 Control Data (US)
371 Heublein (US)
372 Ready Mixed Concrete (UK)
373 Reemtsma Cigarettenfabriken (Germany)
374 Sherwin-Williams (US)
375 Snow Brand Milk Products (Japan)
376 US Gypsum (US)
377 Amstar (US)
378 Granges (Sweden)
379 Alco Standard (US)
380 British Oxygen (UK)
381 Beecham Group (UK)
382 EMI (UK)
383 J. Lyons (UK)
384 Rhine-Schelde-Verolme (Netherlands)
385 Brunswick (US)
386 Ethyl (US)
387 Le Nickel (France)
388 Codelco (Chile)*
389 Cerro (US)
390 Oji Paper (Japan)
391 Rohm and Haas (US)
392 Diamond Shamrock (US)
393 Time Inc. (US)
394 Owens-Corning Fiberglas (US)
395 Mitsui Iron and Smelting (Japan)
396 Degussa (Germany)
397 Klockner-Werke (Germany)
398 Koppers (US)
399 Jos Schlitz Brewing (US)
400 Anderson, Clayton (US)
401 Saarbergwerke (Germany)*
402 Wheeling-Pittsburgh Steel (US)
403 Avco (US)

1983

353 Matsushita Electric Works (Japan)
354 L'Air Liquide (France)
355 Hitachi Zosen (Japan)
356 Grumman (US)
357 Hawker Siddeley Group (UK)
358 Sumitomo Electric Industries (Japan)
359 PETROGAL (Portugal)*
360 General Tire and Rubber (US)
361 Gillette (US)
362 American Standard (US)
363 Wilson Foods (US)
364 Jacobs Suchard (Switzerland)
365 Williams Companies (US)
366 Schneider (France)
367 United Biscuits (Holdings) (UK)
368 Ube Industries (Japan)
369 Chiyoda Chem. Eng and Constr. (Japan)
370 Iscor (South Africa)*
371 Fruehauf (US)
372 Furukawa Electric (Japan)
373 SKF (Sweden)
374 Hoogovens Group (Netherlands)
375 Nippon Suisan (Japan)
376 Hyosung Group (South Korea)
377 Dome Petroleum (Canada)
378 Engelhard (US)
379 McGraw-Edison (US)
380 Klockner-Werke (Germany)
381 Mapco (US)
382 Toyobo (Japan)
383 White Consolidated Industries (US)
384 Northern Foods (UK)
385 Avco (US)
386 Uniroyal (US)
387 Zambia Industrial and Mining (Zambia)*
388 KUKJE (South Korea)
389 Jim Walter (US)
390 Teijin (Japan)
391 Chemische Werke Huls (Germany)
392 Kirin Brewery (Japan)
393 Rolls-Royce (UK)*
394 Métallurgie Hoboken-Overpelt (Belgium)
395 Upjohn (US)
396 Sulzer Brothers (Switzerland)
397 Tokeda Chemical (Japan)
398 Northwest Industries (US)
399 Sherwin-Williams (US)
400 Kanebo (Japan)
401 Yamaha Motor (Japan)
402 Oji Paper (Japan)
403 Lucas Industries (UK)
404 Union International (UK)

	1962		1972		1983
405	Consumers Co-operative Association (US)	405	General Host (US)	405	Olin (US)
406	Magnavox (US)	406	Times Mirror (US)	406	Toyo Seikan (Japan)
407	Mitsubishi Shipbuilding and Engineering (Japan)	407	Alfa Romeo (Italy)*	407	IMETAL (France)
408	Thomas Tilling (UK)	408	Diamond International (US)	408	J. P. Stevens (US)
409	Norton (US)	409	Preussag (Germany)	409	Ogden (US)
410	Sunshine Biscuits (US)	410	Union Camp (US)	410	Oerlikon-Buhrle (Switzerland)
411	Bristol-Myers (US)	411	L'Air Liquide (France)	411	Sterling Drug (US)
412	Toyo Spinning (Japan)	412	Pertamina (Indonesia)	412	Ajinomoto (Japan)
413	Union Minière (Belgium)	413	CUF Group (Portugal)	413	Rohm & Haas (US)
414	Westinghouse Air Brake (US)	414	Liggett and Myers (US)	414	Daihatsu Motor (Japan)
415	Springs Cotton Mills (US)	415	Mitsui Shipbuilding and Engineering (Japan)	415	Vallourec (France)
416	Reemtsma (Germany)	416	Paccar (US)	416	Empresa Colombiana de Petrol (Colombia)*
417	Stokely-Van Camp (US)	417	Libbey-Owens-Ford (US)	417	Cooper Industries (US)
418	Co-operative Grange League Fed Exch. (US)	418	Eltra (US)	418	Baxter Travenol Laboratories (US)
419	Hiram Walker Gooderham & Worts (Canada)	419	Noranda Mines (Canada)	419	Baker International (US)
420	American Brake Shoe (US)	420	Librairie Hachette (France)	420	Avions Marcel Dassault-Breguét (France)*
421	Trefimetaux (France)	421	Alusuisse (Switzerland)	421	British Shipbuilders (UK)*
422	Pepsi-Cola (US)	422	Castle and Cooke (US)	422	Britoil (UK)
423	Lear Siegler (US)	423	Williams Companies (US)	423	Moore (Canada)
424	Staatsmijnen in Limburg (Netherlands)*	424	Svenska Tandsticks (Sweden)	424	SCM (US)
425	British Oxygen (UK)	425	Northrop (US)	425	Schering Plough (US)
426	Crown Cork and Seal (US)	426	Allegheny Ludlum Steel (US)	426	L'Oréal (France)
427	CSF (France)	427	Entreprise Minière et Chimique (France)	427	Mitsui Toatsu Chemicals (Japan)
428	Kelsey-Hayes (US)	428	Brown Group (US)	428	Plessey (UK)
429	Kanegafuchi Spinning (Japan)	429	Loews (US)	429	Alfa Romeo (Italy)*
430	Philadelphia and Reading (US)	430	Domtar (Canada)	430	Australian Consolidated Ind (Australia)
431	Nippon Electric (Japan)	431	Centrale Roussel Nobel (France)	431	CODELCO-CHILE (Chile)*
432	Worthington (US)	432	Polaroid (US)	432	Squibb (US)
433	Schlitz (Jos) Brewing (US)	433	Container Corp. of America (US)	433	Fuji Electric (Japan)
434	Tecumseh Products (US)	434	Nisshin Steel (Japan)	434	Superior Oil (US)
435	Preussag (Germany)	435	Snia Viscosa (Italy)	435	Tarmac (UK)
436	General Cable (US)	436	Lear Siegler (US)	436	Tabacalera (Spain)*
437	Admiral (US)	437	Schneider (France)	437	Fletcher Challenge (New Zealand)
438	Hershey Chocolate (US)	438	Fruehauf (US)	438	Johnson Matthey (UK)
439	Sandoz (Switzerland)	439	Nippon Suisan Kaisha (Japan)	439	Hino Motors (Japan)
440	Parke, Davis (US)	440	Lonrho (UK)	440	Ethyl (US)
441	Smith Kline & French Laboratories (US)	441	Cluett, Peabody (US)	441	Henkel (Germany)
442	Blaw Knox (US)	442	VIAG (Germany)*	442	Gould (US)
443	General Aniline and Film (US)	443	Johnson Matthey (UK)	443	Manville (US)
444	Kubota Iron and Machinery (Japan)	444	Demag (Germany)	444	Central Soya (US)
445	Hooker Chemical (US)	445	Stauffer Chemical (US)	445	Harris (US)
446	Ethyl (US)	446	Mitsui Toatsu Chemicals (Japan)	446	Imasco (Canada)
447	Stahlwerke Sudwestfalen (Germany)	447	Chromalloy American (US)	447	Pilkington Brothers (UK)
448	Boise Cascade (US)	448	Asahi Glass (Japan)	448	Hershey Foods (US)
449	ES and A Robinson Holdings (UK)	449	Northern Electric (Canada)	449	Garrett (US)
450	Addressograph-Multigraph (US)	450	Scoville Manufacturing (US)	450	Sanyo-Kokusaku Pulp (Japan)
451	Staley (AE) Manufacturing (US)	451	Reckitt and Colman (UK)	451	Mitsubishi Petrochemical (Japan)
452	Dan River Mills (US)	452	SEAT (Spain)	452	Charbonnages de France (France)*
453	Upjohn (US)	453	Abbott Laboratories (US)	453	Union Camp (US)
454	ISCOR (South Africa)*	454	Deutsche Babcock and Wilcox (Germany)	454	Emhart (US)
455	West Point Manufacturing (US)	455	Fuji Electric (Japan)	455	Chesebrough-Pond's (US)

1962

456 Tata Iron and Steel (India)
457 CREPS (France)*
458 Kuhlman (France)
459 Donnelley (RR) and Sons (US)
460 Continental Motors (US)
461 Separator (Sweden)
462 Foster Wheeler (US)
463 Wiggins, Teape (UK)
464 Cluett, Peabody (US)
465 Fairmont Foods (US)
466 Honda Motor (Japan)
467 General Baking (US)
468 Cummins Engine (US)
469 Midland Ross (US)
470 Sanyo Electric (Japan)
471 Kerr-McGee Oil Industries (US)
472 Colvilles (UK)
473 Consolidated Electronics Industries (US)
474 Revlon (US)
475 Antar (France)
476 Algoma Steel (Canada)
477 Moore (Canada)
478 Scovill Manufacturing (US)
479 Anaconda Wire and Cable (US)
480 Simca (France)
481 Ex-Cell-O (US)
482 LKAB (Sweden)*
483 Bemis Bro Bag (US)
484 Chemische Werke Huls (Germany)
485 Richardson-Merrell (US)
486 Sunbeam (US)
487 Associated Portland Cement (UK)
488 Takeda Chemical Industry (Japan)
489 Beech-Nut Life Savers (US)
490 Sumitomo Chemical Industry (Japan)
491 Automobile M Berliet (France)
492 Rio Tinto Zinc (UK)
493 Diamond Alkali (US)
494 Beecham Group (UK)
495 Link-Belt (US)
496 Stora Kopparbergs (Sweden)
497 Grundig-Werke (Germany)

1972

456 Hindustan Steel (India)*
457 Suzuki Motor (Japan)
458 Electrolux (Sweden)
459 Cummins Engine (US)
460 National Gypsum (US)
461 Kayser-Roth (US)
462 Nchanga Consol. Copper Mines (Zambia)*
463 Dai Nippon Printing (Japan)
464 Voest (Austria)*
465 American Beef Packers (US)
466 Upjohn (US)
467 Schering-Plough (US)
468 Levi Strauss (US)
469 Veba-Chemie (Germany)
470 Warner Communications (US)
471 Moore (Canada)
472 Universal Leaf Tobacco (US)
473 Hino Motors (Japan)
474 Delta Metal (UK)
475 Rank Organisation (UK)
476 A.O. Smith (US)
477 Foster Wheeler (US)
478 International Minerals and Chemicals (US)
479 Ajinomoto (Japan)
480 ISCOR (South Africa)*
481 Crown Cork and Seal (US)
482 Tarmac (UK)
483 Sharp (Japan)
484 Grundig (Germany)
485 Hewlett-Packard (US)
486 National Can (US)
487 Mitsubishi Metal (Japan)
488 Universal Oil Products (US)
489 Westvaco (US)
490 Gould (US)
491 Timken (US)
492 Chemische Werke Huls (Germany)
493 M. Lowenstein and Sons (US)
494 Admiral (US)
495 Sumitomo Shipbuilding & Machinery (Japan)
496 Morinaga Milk Industry (Japan)
497 USM (US)
498 Fuji Heavy Industries (Japan)
499 Meiji Milk Products (Japan)
500 Lone Star Industries (US)
501 Consolidated Gold Fields (UK)
502 Metallurgie Hoboken-Overpelt (Belgium)
503 Kuraray (Japan)
504 Glaxo Group (UK)
505 Di Giorgio (US)
506 Hoover (US)
507 Varta (Germany)

1983

456 A.E. Staley Manufacturing (US)
457 Nissan Shatai (Japan)
458 Schering (Germany)
459 Preussag (Germany)
460 Dainippon Ink and Chemicals (Japan)
461 Crown Central Petroleum (US)
462 Showa Denko (Japan)
463 Glaxo Holdings (UK)
464 MacMillan Bloedel (Canada)
465 James River Corp. of Virginia (US)
466 Stelco (Canada)
467 National Can (US)
468 Pitney Bowes (US)
469 Vale do Rio Doce (Brazil)*
470 Air Products and Chemicals (US)
471 Hammermill Paper (US)
472 US Gypsum (US)
473 Cummins Engine (US)
474 De Beers Consolidated Mines (South Africa)
475 RMC Group (UK)
476 Corning Glass Works (US)
477 Tribune (US)
478 Colt Industries (US)
479 General Signal (US)
480 Koppers (US)
481 Great Northern Nekoosa (US)
482 Ricoh (Japan)
483 Jujo Paper (Japan)
484 KHD (Germany)
485 Cabot (US)
486 John Labbatt (Canada)
487 Pacific Resources (US)
488 Mitsubishi Metal (Japan)
489 R.R. Donnelley and Sons (US)
490 Babcock International (UK)
491 Wang Laboratories (US)
492 Béghin-Say (France)
493 Bull (France)*
494 Nisshin Steel (Japan)
495 Ent. Minière et Chimique (France)*
496 AMP (US)
497 Asarco (US)
498 Alumax (US)
499 Morton Thiokol (US)
500 Nippon Gakki (Japan)
501 Consolidated Gold Fields (UK)
502 Westvaco (US)
503 Union Laitière Normande (France)
504 Fuji Kosan (Japan)
505 Reckitt and Colman (UK)
506 Mitsui Mining (Japan)
507 Genstar (Canada)

1962

1972

508	International Multifoods (US)
509	Gold Kist (US)
510	English Calico (UK)
511	Kelsey-Hayes (US)
512	Thyssen-Bornemisza Group (Netherlands)
513	Sunbeam (US)
514	National Industries (US)
515	Dassault (France)
516	Dominion Foundries & Steel (Canada)
517	Kaiser Steel (US)
518	Gervais Danone Group (France)
519	Richardson-Merrell (US)
520	Pennwalt (US)
521	Revlon (US)
522	Flintkote (US)
523	Continental Gummi-Werke (Germany)
524	Burns Food (Canada)
525	Associated Portland Cement Manufacturers (UK)
526	Freudenberg (Germany)
527	Addressograph Multigraph (US)
528	Pilkington Bros (US)
529	Vickers (UK)
530	Fuqua Industries (US)
531	Jujo Paper Manufacturing (Japan)
532	Mohasco Industries (US)
533	Fuji Photo Film (Japan)
534	McGraw-Hill (US)
535	Bemis (US)
536	'Holderbank' Financière Glaris (Switzerland)
537	Whitbread (US)
538	Molson Industries (Canada)
539	Stora Kopparbergs Berglags (Sweden)
540	Kane-Miller (US)
541	Rowntree-Mackintosh (UK)
542	Hart Schaffner and Marx (US)
543	Schering (Germany)
544	Arthur Guinness (UK)
545	FMC (UK)
546	Stahlwerke Rochling-Burbach (Germany)
547	Nippon Denso (Japan)
548	Hershey Foods (US)
549	Dainippon Ink and Chemicals (Japan)
550	Ward Foods (US)
551	Cyclops (US)
552	Great Northern Nekoosa (US)
553	Tecumseh Products (US)
554	Dunlop Australia (Australia)
555	West Point-Pepperell (US)
556	Shiseido (Japan)

1983

508	Statsforetag Group (Sweden)*
509	Domtar (Canada)
510	Brooke Bond Group (UK)
511	Knight-Ridder Newspapers (US)
512	Nippon Light Metal (Japan)
513	Shiseido (Japan)
514	Marmon Group (US)
515	Lear Siegler (US)
516	International Minerals and Chemical (US)
517	Gold Kist (US)
518	TDK (Japan)
519	AECI (South Africa)
520	NL Industries (US)
521	Rowntree Mackintosh (UK)
522	Armstrong World Industries (US)
523	Nisshin Flour Milling (Japan)
524	Thyssen-Bornermisza (Netherlands)
525	Geo A Hormel (US)
526	PACCAR (US)
527	News Corporation (Australia)
528	Farmers Union Central Exchange (US)
529	Sekisui Chemical (Japan)
530	Daido Steel (Japan)
531	Meiji Milk Products (Japan)
532	Nippon Meat Packers (Japan)
533	Standard Telephones and Cables (UK)
534	Unitika (Japan)
535	Anderson Clayton (US)
536	Empresa Nacional del Petroleo (Chile)*
537	Sumitomo Heavy Industries (Japan)
538	TI Group (UK)
539	Witco Chemical (US)
540	Blue Circle Industries (UK)
541	Distillers (UK)
542	Onoda Cement (Japan)
543	Tokyo Sanyo Electric (Japan)
544	Zenith Radio (US)
545	SSAB (Sweden)*
546	Mid-America Dairymen (US)
547	Sasol (South Africa)
548	Abitibi-Price (Canada)
549	Coats Patons (UK)
550	Sankyo (Japan)
551	Mattel (US)
552	Matra (France)*
553	Stauffer Chemical (US)
554	Mitsui Engineering and Shipbuilding (Japan)
555	PETRONOR (Spain)
556	Redland (UK)

1962

1972

557 Toppan Printing (Japan)
558 Dickinson Robinson Group (UK)
559 VMF (Netherlands)
560 L'Oreal (France)
561 Daishowa Paper Manufacturing (Japan)
562 Smith Kline & French Laboratories (US)
563 Nisshin Flour Milling (Japan)
564 Alfa-Laval (Sweden)
565 Stanley Works (US)
566 Springs Mills (US)
567 Missouri Beef Packers (US)
568 Hammermill Paper (US)
569 Outboard Marine (US)
570 Boehringer Ingelheim (Germany)
571 Macmillan (US)
572 Perrier Group (France)
573 National Service Industries (US)
574 International Computers (Holdings) (UK)
575 Revere Copper and Brass (US)
576 Stahlwerke Sudwestfalen (Germany)
577 Atlas Copco (Sweden)
578 Carrington Viyella (UK)
579 Interlake (US)
580 Agache-Willot (France)
581 Hiram Walker Gooderham & Worts (Canada)
582 ACI (Australia)
583 British Aircraft (UK)
584 Imasco (Canada)
585 A-T-O (US)
586 VFW-Fokker Group (Germany)
587 I-T-E Imperial (US)
588 OMV (Austria)
589 Potlatch Forests (US)
590 Norton (US)
591 US Shoe (US)
592 Campbell Taggart (US)
593 Harris-Intertype (US)
594 Hygrade Food Products (US)
595 General Cable (US)
596 Spencer Foods (US)
597 Morton-Norwich Products (US)
598 Champion Spark Plug (US)
599 Dan River (US)
600 Sandvik Group (Sweden)
601 DAF (Netherlands)
602 Messerschmitt-Bolkow-Blohm (Germany)
603 Bell and Howell (US)
604 Purex (US)
605 Allied Mills (US)
606 Rexnord (US)

1983

557 Daishowa Paper (Japan)
558 Continental Gummi-Werke (Germany)
559 Monfort of Colorado (US)
560 Johnson Controls (US)
561 Northern Engineering Industries (UK)
562 ICL (UK)
563 Fed. Volksbeleggings Beperk (South Africa)
564 Sandvik Group (Sweden)
565 Union Explosivos Rio Tinto (Spain)
566 Holderbank Financière Glaris (Switzerland)
567 Dofasco (Canada)
568 Allis-Chalmers (US)
569 Crown Cork and Seal (US)
570 McGraw Hill (US)
571 Whitbread (UK)
572 Kao Soap (Japan)
573 Racal Electronics (UK)
574 Svenska Cellulosa (Sweden)
575 Pioneer Electronic (Japan)
576 Dunlop Olympic (Australia)
577 PETROPERU (Peru)*
578 Aisin Seiki (Japan)
579 Koninklijke Wessanen (Netherlands)
580 Polaroid (US)
581 Heineken (Netherlands)
582 Grundig (Germany)
583 Nokia (Finland)
584 Louisiana Land and Exploration (US)
585 Mitsui Petrochemical (Japan)
586 SWEDYARDS (Sweden)*
587 Blue Bell (US)
588 Hachette (France)
589 Konishiroku Photo Industry (Japan)
590 Alfa-Laval (Sweden)
591 SNECMA (France)*
592 Mack Trucks (US)
593 Brunswick (US)
594 Bosch-Siemens Hausgerate (Germany)
595 National Semiconductor (US)
596 Massey-Ferguson (Canada)
597 West Point-Pepperell (US)
598 Vaal Reefs Exploration and Mining (South Africa)
599 Valeo (France)
600 Rheinische Braunkohlenwerke (Germany)
601 Morinaga Milk Industry (Japan)
602 Arla (Sweden)
603 Tektronix (US)
604 Amstar (US)
605 Molson (Canada)
606 Zanussi Group (Italy)

182

1962

1972

607	John Labatt (Canada)
608	Turner and Newall (UK)
609	Sumitomo Metal Mining (Japan)
610	Genstar (Canada)
611	Yamaha Motor (Japan)
612	Altos Hornos de Vizcaya (Spain)
613	Dairylea Co-operative (US)
614	Avnet (US)
615	Inmont (US)
616	Sybron (US)
617	Mitsubishi Petrochemical (Japan)
618	Chicago Bridge and Iron (US)
619	Sekisui Chemical (Japan)
620	R.R. Donnelley and Sons (US)
621	Cannon Mills (US)
622	Fairmont Foods (US)
623	Rothmans of Pall Mall Canada (Canada)
624	Harsco (US)
625	Consolidated-Bathhurst (Canada)
626	UV Industries (US)
627	Air Products and Chemicals (US)
628	Chesebrough-Ponds (US)
629	Carl-Zeiss Stiftung (Germany)
630	Nippon Gakki (Japan)
631	Société Indus Belge des Pétroles (Belgium)
632	MCA (US)
633	SNECMA (France)
634	General Signal (US)
635	Black and Decker Manufacturing (US)
636	Norddeutsche Raffinerie (Germany)

1983

607	Black and Decker Manufacturing (US)
608	Libbey-Owens-Ford (US)
609	Meiji Seika (Japan)
610	Hughes Tools (US)
611	Amatil (Australia)
612	G. Heileman Brewing (US)
613	Square D (US)
614	Mitsui Mining and Smelting (Japan)
615	National Gypsum (US)
616	Consolidated-Bathurst (Canada)
617	Norton (US)
618	Siderurgica Nacional (Brazil)*
619	Kyowa Hakko Kogyo (Japan)
620	Oljekonsumenternas Forbund (Sweden)
621	SNIA BPD (Italy)
622	Intel (US)
623	Oki Electric Industry (Japan)
624	Kuraray (Japan)
625	Becton Dickinson (US)
626	Sumitomo Metal Mining (Japan)
627	International Multifoods (US)
628	Honshu Paper (Japan)
629	Federal Co (US)
630	Nichiro Gyogyo (Japan)
631	Richardson-Vicks (US)
632	Miles Laboratories (US)
633	Burns Philp (Australia)
634	Adolph Coors (US)
635	S. Pearson and Son (UK)
636	Louisiana-Pacific (US)
637	Swedish Match (Sweden)
638	VF (US)
639	New York Times (US)
640	Yokohama Rubber (Japan)
641	John Brown (UK)
642	US Industries (US)
643	Trane (US)
644	Anomina Petroli Italiana (Italy)
645	Ito Ham Provisions (Japan)
646	Nissan Diesel Motor (Japan)
647	Wellcome Foundation (UK)
648	Nixdorf Computer (Germany)
649	Masco (US)
650	Rauma-Repola (Finland)
651	Atlas Copco (Sweden)
652	W.C. Heraeus (Germany)
653	Lion (Japan)
654	Yoshida Kogyo (Japan)
655	Mitsubishi Gas Chemical (Japan)
656	Rutgerswerke (Germany)
657	Willamette Industries (US)
658	Linde (Germany)

	1962	1972	1983

659 Zahnradfabrik Friedrichshafen (Germany)
660 Parker Hannifin (US)
661 Driefontein Consolidated (South Africa)
662 Boehringer Ingelheim (Germany)
663 Esselte (Sweden)
664 Dalmine (Italy)*
665 Mitsubishi Rayon (Japan)
666 Enso-Gutzeit (Finland)
667 Freudenberg (Germany)
668 IMI (UK)
669 Cyclops (US)
670 PWA (Germany)
671 Norddeutsche Affinerie (Germany)
672 Perkin-Elmer (US)
673 ENSIDESA (Spain)*
674 Dover (US)
675 Lesieur (France)
676 Grupo Industrial Alfa (Mexico)
677 Crane (US)
678 NVF (US)
679 Hispanoil (Spain)*
680 G. D. Searle (US)
681 Chromalloy American (US)
682 Vickers (UK)
683 Stanley Works (US)
684 Apple Computer (US)
685 Seagram (Canada)
686 Phelps Dodge (US)
687 Pennwalt (US)
688 General Instrument (US)
689 Wartsila (Finland)
690 SEAT (Spain)*
691 Toyota Auto Body (Japan)
692 AMF (US)
693 Jefferson Smurfit Group (Ireland)
694 Nihon Cement (Japan)
695 Hartmarx (US)
696 Mitchell Energy and Development (US)
697 Tyler (US)
698 Prouvost (France)
699 Cameron Iron Works (US)
700 Ex-Cell-O (US)
701 Inco (Canada)
702 Sumitomo Rubber (Japan)
703 FAG Kugelfischer Georg Schafer (Germany)
704 ARBED (Luxembourg)
705 Timken (US)
706 National Service Industries (US)
707 Kanto Auto Works (Japan)
708 Denki Kagaku Kogyo (Japan)
709 MTU (Germany)
710 General Cinema (US)

184

1962

1972

1983

711 Axel Springer (Germany)
712 Shionogi (Japan)
713 Motor Oil (Hellas) Corinth Ref (Greece)
714 Lone Star Industries (US)
715 Carl-Zeiss-Stiftung (Germany)
716 Clorox (US)
717 Citizen Watch (Japan)
718 ARBED Saarstahl (Germany)
719 Ball (US)
720 Sundstrand (US)
721 Arthur Guinness (UK)
722 Potlatch (US)
723 EBARA (Japan)
724 EG and G (US)
725 Douwe Egberts (Netherlands)
726 Quaker State Oil Refining (US)
727 Toyo Soda Manufacturing (Japan)
728 Springs Industries (US)
729 Fairchild Industries (US)
730 Reemtsma Cigarettenfabriken (Germany)
731 Storage Technology (US)
732 SAGEM (France)
733 Valmet (Finland)*
734 ISAB (Italy)
735 Washington Post (US)
736 Nippon Seiko (Japan)
737 Chemie Linz (Austria)
738 Rengo (Japan)
739 Cluett Peabody (US)
740 Dow Jones (US)
741 Pakistan State Oil (Pakistan)
742 Royal Pkg. Ind. Von Leer (Netherlands)
743 NTN Toyo Bearings (Japan)
744 Clark Equipment (US)
745 CF Industries (US)
746 Schindler Holding (Switzerland)
747 Porsche (Germany)
748 Fleetwood Enterprises (US)
749 Toyoda Automatic Loom Works (Japan)
750 AO Smith (US)
751 Butano (Spain)*
752 Elkem (Norway)
753 Niigata Engineering (Japan)
754 China Steel (Taiwan)
755 Steyr-Daimler-Puch (Austria)
756 Thomas Borthwick and Sons (UK)
757 Harsco (US)
758 Interlake (US)
759 Kymmene-Stromberg (Finland)
760 Dean Foods (US)
761 Tecumseh Products (US)
762 Petroliber (Spain)*

1962	1972	1983

763		Data General (US)
764		Brockway (US)
765		CBI Industries (US)
766		E-Systems (US)
767		DRG (UK)
768		SEITA (France)*
769		Vulcan Materials (US)
770		Fujisawa Pharmaceutical (Japan)
771		Prima Meat Packers (Japan)
772		Merlin Gerin (France)
773		Household Manufacturing (US)
774		Avery International (US)
775		Rexnord (US)
776		United Breweries (Denmark)
777		C and J Clark (UK)
778		Yamazaki Baking (Japan)
779		Showa Sangyo (Japan)
780		Toyo Rubber Industry (Japan)
781		Lubrizol (US)
782		USIMINAS (Brazil)*
783		Outboard Marine (US)
784		Todd Shipyards (US)
785		GECAMINES (Zaire)*
786		Freeport-McMoran (US)
787		Fort Howard Paper (US)
788		National Cooperative Refinery Assoc. (US)
789		COSPIA (Brazil)*
790		Anchor Hocking (US)
791		BPB Industries (UK)
792		Amdahl (US)
793		Delta Group (UK)
794		Hoover Universal (US)
795		Wheeling-Pittsburgh Steel (US)
796		Eschweiler Bergswerks-Verein (Germany)
797		Kane-Miller (US)
798		Kema Nobel (Sweden)
799		Scottish and Newcastle Breweries (UK)
800		English China Clays (UK)
801		Champion Spark Plug (US)
802		Daicel Chemical Industries (Japan)
803		Dow Corning (US)
804		Capital Cities Communications (US)
805		Inspiration Resources (US)
806		Saora Kopparbergs Bergslags (Sweden)